The

Performance

of

Power

Studies in

Theatre History

and Culture

Edited by

Thomas Postlewait

The Performance of Power

Theatrical Discourse and Politics

Edited by

Sue-Ellen Case

and

Janelle Reinelt

University of Iowa Press

Iowa City

University of Iowa Press, Iowa City 52242

Copyright © 1991 by the University of Iowa

All rights reserved

Printed in the United States of America

First edition, 1991

Design by Richard Hendel

Printed on acid-free paper

Library of Congress Cataloging-in-Publication Data

The Performance of power: theatrical discourse
    and politics/edited by Sue-Ellen Case and Janelle
    Reinelt.—1st ed.

     p. cm.—(Studies in theatre history and culture)
    Includes bibliographical references.
    ISBN 0-87745-317-9 (alk. paper), ISBN 0-87745-318-7 (pbk.)
    1. Theater. 2. Drama—History and criticism.
I. Case, Sue-Ellen. II. Reinelt, Janelle G. III. Series.
PN1631.P47 1991   90-26750
792—dc20   CIP

Contents

Introduction

SUE-ELLEN CASE & JANELLE REINELT

Over the past several years, the field of theater studies has displayed an increasing amount of debate and dissonance regarding the borders of its territory, its methodologies, its subject matter, and its scholars' perspectives. The nature of this debate, one might even say struggle, is political. It concerns the "performance of power"—the struggle over power relations embedded in texts, methodologies, and the academy itself.

The issues at stake include representation (what is represented and who is authorized to represent it), the canon (the deconstruction of it, or the inclusion of previously suppressed voices and cultures), and boundaries (the dissolving of disciplinary distinctions, the separation of high and low cultures, and the blurring of methodological distinctions among theory, history, and criticism). These struggles over representation and invisibility are far from merely "academic": they are based in the economic and social structures of the society, which, in turn, shape the academy. Thus, these scholarly issues are, in every sense, "political."

It might seem strange that, in the face of such efforts to broaden the scope of studies, we have organized this book along lines that retain a focus on drama as a genre. In some ways, this arrangement is out of step with the new political sense that opens out, through notions of discourse and semiotics, to a variety of ways that configure not only what constitutes a discourse but how discourses interrelate. By maintaining this more traditional boundary of genre study, we still resist, to some degree, giving way to the full notion of cultural artifact and thus participate in the old ideas of art and its mystification of class as culture. Yet, in another way, theatrical discourse, as a term, participates fully in the new committed constructs. Clifford Geertz (in "Blurred Genres: The Refiguration of Social Thought") notes, from the point of view of an anthropologist, that "the weight of the [theatrical] analogy is coming to be applied extensively and systematically."[1] Theatricality as metaphor, or analogy, accommodates the materialist perception that there is a "playing out" of power relations, a "masking" of authority, and a "scenario" of events. In other words, power is spectacle. In this collection, Auerbach's article analyzes the way theater as metaphor represented the construction of a certain kind of "self" in the nineteenth century, while the nature of theater's metaphorical status in turn produced its own performance conditions. Likewise, today, that same dynamic allows the critic to negotiate among a variety of strategies and discourses that map the topology of theater studies across its cultural, political, and historical terrain.

For us, the ongoing experience in our professional lives of these cross-currents of politics, academics, and theatrics became especially acute during the past academic year (1989–1990). Perhaps because of our long association as feminists and friends, our recent work for *Theatre Journal*, and our differences of style and rhetoric, and sometimes of affiliation, we found ourselves involved in a gradually developing analysis of the "performance of politics" at the sites of national conferences. Upon three separate occasions, in three different parts of the country, we found ourselves together in conference rooms and hotel lobbies observing and participating in heated discussions. There seemed to be a confluence of papers on politics and political activism at these conferences. This situation became particularly acute at the annual meeting of the American Society for Theatre Research (ASTR) held in Williamsburg, Virginia, in November 1989. At that time, with "theater and politics" as the overt theme of the conference,[2] a number of the issues and debates of the past few years seemed to have reached a watershed—both in the critical strategies employed in the papers and in the state of the profession panel—particularly Gay Gibson Cima's intervention there, which problematized the performance strategies of conferences (see her essay in this volume).

We began to see the need for a book that would bring these concerns together. Upon further reflection, we realized that the Association for Theatre in Higher Education (ATHE) conference in New York (August 1989) actually set up the narrative of conference politicking at Williamsburg, as we perceived it. Thus, we have collected a number of the papers from both New York and Williamsburg, as well as some others, for publication in this collection. In addition, we would like to tie together the two major sections of the book—the thirteen articles and the series of papers on the academic institution and its relationship to the production of knowledge—by illustrating in this introduction how these concerns mesh.

Before moving on to a discussion of the conferences, however, we would like to specify some of the differences that are concealed by this "we." As feminists, we find a crucial difference lodged in our sexual preference (Case is a lesbian, Reinelt a heterosexual) that, in part, determines our two different approaches to political work. While Reinelt works in the interstices, negotiating among political differences, Case is confrontational, retaining an "outsider" position. Yet, in spite of this, we are both operating, in the following narrative, from a perception of ourselves as implied in the privileges and dominant operations that are embedded in our positions as full professors in the academy and as upper-middle-class white professionals, with access to the apparatuses of reading and writing. In other words, the following account is offered as a deconstruction of our own positions, rather than as an indictment of those of others. Moreover, we do not necessarily assume that any of the authors in this collection agree with the following account. Nevertheless, while we may maintain different political positions, we do share the belief that we are seeing a genuine change in the direction of our field—one which requires a clearly situated ideological stance from all participants and one which both of us wish to help promote and ensure.

NEW YORK CITY: THE NEW CONVERGENCE

At the ATHE annual meeting in August 1989, we were both participants in an attempt to perform one of the boundary dissolutions mentioned above. Included in the program, and well-attended by the conference participants, was a two-session panel entitled "History/Theory/Revolution: The New Convergence." The explicit aim of the two sessions, which included four scholars usually associated with "history" and four with "theory,"[3] was to demonstrate that the distinctions between history and theory are no longer tenable and that the dialogue between theorists and historians is not only useful but unavoidable, given the necessity of historicizing theory and theorizing history.

This fruitful dialogue provided an occasion for a mixed constituency to recognize itself in terms of both its sizable number and its shared concerns. Reinelt believes the crucial factor in this change in theater studies has been a crossover phenomenon in which members of various factions have engaged one another in dialogue beyond the boundaries of their traditional discourses. Case stresses the many years of struggle necessary to gain a precarious legitimation within theater studies for the new discourses of feminism and other critical theories.

As one illustration of this struggle for visibility, the ATHE program clearly marks the divisions among the interests of practitioners, theorists, historians, and others (e.g., the Women and Theatre Program and the Black Theatre Network). ATHE as "parent" provides each of its interest groups with organizational strength, internal structure, visibility, and stability. However, it also institutionalizes the existing disciplinary divisions and ideologies by conference scheduling, for example, which frequently precludes "crossing over" because of simultaneous programming.

New York always brings a large number of participants to the conference in the years when it is held there. This city represents the notion of a theater center, and even a cultural center. This construction of centrality brings with it the privileging of urban as cultural and agrarian as folk, as well as notions of central as best, with regional and even more local practices marked as amateur. In a way, New York becomes the vantage point from which one views the profession. Likewise, the stages of New York gain some sort of representational status, exhibiting what Roach, in his article, identifies as the function of the stage as "magnifying lens"—acting, and not only for the profession, as "the illustrator of brave new worlds and the strange creatures in them." New York, as a center, provides the sense that one can see there, or see from there, "what's happening." As Samuel Johnson, a committed urbanite, once put it, "Let observation with extensive view / Survey mankind, from China to Peru." Roach takes up this notion of scopic centrality, a critical tool from ethnography, in order to reveal the base of what he calls a "global empire of the visible" in the Augustan age. By extension, we would like to mark the way in which such critical strategies can also deconstruct our own institutional and locational collusion with strategies of surveillance and colonialism.

Meanwhile, back at the hotel, those of us at the conference walked in from the ethnically mixed, culturally diverse streets of New York—which provided conferees with a variety of potential foods, arts, theaters, life-styles, ghettoes, homeless people, muggings, and rapes—to a lobby with bellhops, access to conference rooms, podiums, and so forth. The conference fees, the hotel and transportation costs (especially for those of us from the western "provinces"), and the credentials required for participation in the discourse ("academic affiliation," it is usually termed) all ensured that whatever knowledge was produced was largely by and for a privileged coterie of those who are fortunately housed in a supporting institution. The sign systems of the site prominently marked privilege. By what right might we think that "The New Convergence" went beyond the self-referential? The panel itself was comprised of four white women and four white men and really bridged only two formal groups, Theory/Criticism and History (and perhaps the Women and Theatre Program since three participants are strongly affiliated members). In other words, on the panel, we both displayed and attempted to deconstruct the structuring of dominant power.

This strategy of deconstructing the sign systems of the mise-en-scène of the conference is shared by most of the articles in this book. Often, in textual operations, the signs are critical terms, or even common nouns that serve to mystify power relations, which they are assumed to describe. For example, in his own self-disclosure, Witham concludes that he had assumed the same "notion of 'communism'" that he was deconstructing. Hall traces the way in which "Englishness" vis-à-vis "blackness" was constructed by the court of James I. Savran notes that the Wooster Group's new performance piece may make "revolution" a "sign without a referent," while Bredbeck traces the Renaissance uses of "sodomy." These articles, as well as our own retrospective analysis of the New York "performance," are specifically deconstructive in settling on the *aporia*, the site in the critical or even descriptive discourse that is both the ruling term of its logic and the place where it is undone. Like Hamlet, the *aporia* is both the motor of the discourse and here, "with his doublet all unbrac'd," undone by the critic, who, unlike Hamlet, can act against the regency, the dominant power that keeps it in its place. Thus, Bredbeck would use this notion of *aporia* to deconstruct the use of sodomy and of Patroclus: "Ulysses' construction of Patroclus leads the Greek world of precept into the mutable world of improvised praxis—the very world that the construction of Patroclus originally sought to efface."

WILLIAMSBURG: OVERTURNING HEGEMONY

While both of us have a long affiliation with ATHE and the former American Theatre Association, neither of us had attended an ASTR conference before going to Williamsburg. ASTR has been the traditional theater history organization of the profession, producing its journal of research on historical topics (*Theatre Survey*) and including in its membership many of those who share the methodologies of positivism and empiricism that have marked the field. As a result of the call for papers on the themes of the conference, and some committed work by the planning committee,[4] over seventy-five submissions were received from a diverse group of scholars representing an array of theoretical and critical as well as historical viewpoints. The resulting mix of participants imbued the Williamsburg meetings with energy and stimulating exchange, especially given the 45-minute discussion periods following each panel.

During the conference, many participants took a walking tour of the original Williamsburg Colony. While informative about the leisure pursuits of the privileged class, the tour avoided the areas in the house where domestic labor occurred, such as the kitchen or the slave quarters in contrast to the gaming room. After a short demonstration of flute playing and the harpsichord, we were entertained by a period scene performed at what was identified as the first theater in America. Local actors performed a scene from George Lillo's *The London Merchant*, a text Roach quotes in his essay here, with the merchant and his assistant as the "corporate vision" that sees mercantilism as evangelical. Roach quotes the merchant Thorowgood:

> Methinks I would not have you only learn the method of merchandise and practice it hereafter merely as a means of getting wealth. 'Twill be well worth your pains to study it as a science, see how it is founded in reason and the nature of things, how it has promoted humanity as it has opened and yet keeps up an intercourse between nations far remote from one another in situation, customs, and religion; promoting arts, industry, peace, and plenty; by mutual benefits diffusing mutual love from pole to pole.

Ironically, this passage is close to the claim made for culture, and even the humanistic base for conferences in general, where ideas are "traded."

Thus, this play on this site seemed particularly apt as the mise-en-scène for the American Society for Theatre Research.

Moreover, the scene performed was not the one to which Roach refers above, but a scene with Millwood and Barnwell, the merchant's apprentice and the tragedy's protagonist/victim. Millwood, for her part, represents the classic misogynist portrait of a woman who is financially and sexually independent. On this site of the first theater in America, we were, as feminists, acutely aware of this dark portrait of a woman who "seduces and abandons" or is forced by the patriarchal structure of society to break (through) the moral code in order to break into the mercantile system from her outsider position—male desire is her only access to the exchange of wealth.

Finally, this site, claiming all the "roots" of culture and class in America, completely mystifies the genocidal appropriation of those lands from the actual "first" culture—the Native American. Mason, in his article on *Metamora*, documents that the play's opening production occurred in the period of vast Indian removal projects, including the removal of 70,000 people, mostly from the region south of Williamsburg, to west of the Mississippi. Mason shows how theater helped to create the reconfiguration of the identity of a people required to enforce and to agree to such acts, concluding that Edwin Forrest's portrait of Metamora "disempowers Native Americans, reserving respect for the Romantic fictions of the past, virtually making the case that they should embrace their own luxuriously melancholy demise, and leaving only contempt for the disappointingly real natives of the present, who, if mere relics, probably deserved to melt away." When theater historians and critics celebrate this colonial site as the first theater in America by watching scenes from *The London Merchant*, we collude in performing that same colonial power process. We partake in the sign systems of the performance and legitimate its reenactment of still-dominant discourses of oppression.

Another disquieting feature of this conference was the perceived disparity on the part of many between the sign system in the hotel for the conference and its topic. The meeting took place in a hotel which displayed the Confederate flag at its entrance—a source of discomfort for many participants, including members of the planning committee, who had successfully created an otherwise hospitable and well-organized event. Of course, the Union flag was there, too, on the opposite wall: the Fort

McGruder Inn marked the site of a battle in the historic conflict over the issue of race. A political analysis of this semiotic site could proceed from a use of Barthes's analysis of a *Paris-Match* cover he saw in his barbershop, upon which a black man in uniform salutes the tricolor. Barthes sets up semiotic categories of signifier, signified, sign, and signification to denote the strategies of the production of meaning that co-create the dominant social myths which support, in the subtext of images, the social practices of racism and colonialism.[5] Likewise, as theater historians and critics performed their entrances to a conference on theater and politics, they came by way of this souvenir of secession and racism.

In this volume, a historical use of such techniques may be found in Hall's study of the masque, in which she unpacks such souvenirs. However, unlike Barthes, Hall adds a gender critique to her reading of the sign. Bryant-Bertail employs a variety of semiotic strategies to a materialist end, from tracing the dynamism of the sign, its ability to change its connotative and even denotative signifieds,[6] in her treatment of the rifle in *Schwejk* to a semiotic consideration of the characterization of Schwejk himself in "his physical aspect, the manner, speed, and direction of his movement, and his spatial relationship to his own narratives."

SAN DIEGO: BIPOLAR OPPOSITION

Winter 1990: San Diego this time—a special conference on "The Classics in the Contemporary Theatre," sponsored by the Theater Department, University of California, San Diego, and La Jolla Playhouse. This conference represented another convergence, this time among regional theater practitioners and theater scholars. It was beginning to seem like there was redefinition and reassessment everywhere we looked, this time of audience demographics, venues, and season development as well as of the analysis of performances and texts.

This conference was different from the others: for two days a real struggle took place on the meeting hall floor. On one side (for there really were two identifiable sides) were those in the academy and in theaters who did not want to talk about gender, race, or class but rather wanted to talk about interesting new productions of such enduring classics as Shakespeare and Molière. On the other were those who wanted the whole notion of the classic canon put under scrutiny and reshaped or abolished. The keynote speaker was the British director Jonathan Miller, currently producing at the Old Vic, whose reputation for doing the "classics" has varied as his approach has changed. Now, it seems, he no longer tries to find the connections between history and the present contemporary moment: he thinks that history is "interesting" in and for itself, that it can be directly represented, and that any feminist nonsense about *The Taming of the Shrew* is simply "a bore." Case walked out, not wanting to add her presence to such a gathering; Reinelt stayed, hoping to intervene in the following discussion.

Miller played out, above the large crowd, another strategy of surveillance. In describing California culture as that of shopping malls and London as a place where Shakespeare was "bred in the bone," Miller revealed the way in which, as Janice Carlisle has put it, culture can be employed as a means of class control. Carlisle takes up Foucault's notion of the gaze as panopticon, particularly, in this essay, the bourgeois surveillance mechanisms of the working class which are structured into a night of theater in 1860. What Carlisle reveals that is useful in understanding the way Miller's keynote address worked is the way in which, through the construction of sight-lines and other factors, "the person on the stage is not the object of the audience's gaze, but the overseer of the audience as spectacle." From Carlisle, one can see how that privileged speaking site is a place from which one sees the audience—policing its behavior and constructing the exact nature of its Otherness. How the audience responds illustrates what it must do in order to pass the requirements of culture control. In Miller's case, he combined this strategy of surveillance with the imperial one described by Roach. Together, these two strategies created the audience as Other, in class and colonial status, authorizing his discourse on the "classic" as Shakespeare performed in London while anything else (from popular culture to Chicano theater) was deemed amateur.

Happily, however, within such models, resistance may still be registered. In San Diego, Paul Carter Harrison broke through appropriative techniques on the part of the dominant ethos to note the limited effectiveness of color-blind casting for building a multiethnic audience. On the last morning, some of the people of color in the audience, including two professors from UC San Diego, spoke up about their disinterest in the classics in light of the pressing need to foster and produce new writing based in the lived experiences of ethnic communities. Jorge Huerta described the conference UC San Diego was planning on ethnic theater—of comparatively higher priority for his students and colleagues than this one.

In a similar way, the political strategies found in this book owe their strength and precision to the social activist movements behind them. Kim Hall's study of "blackness" reflects the success of those civil rights activists in the 1960s who performed the uses of the masks of "whiteness" and "blackness" when they desegregated schools, rode in the front of buses, and so forth. Hall's critique of "beauty" in the court of James I rests upon the distinctions made by feminist activists who disrupted beauty contests as both sexist and racist. Bredbeck's study of the discourse of sodomy rests upon the breakthroughs achieved by the Gay Rights Movement and AIDS activists that have constructed a new sense of gay male subjectivity—the foil for its negative construction by the dominants. The committed strategies in these articles, then, are impelled by the conditions in the world. They can go no further than social history has gone. Thus, these strategies are specific to those they represent—they cannot be whimsically exchanged.

While we have organized much of this material around specific academic events of the past year, we are aware of at least one significant historical change that will undoubtedly transform the critical discourse about European theater productions and texts. The complex process of reconfiguring what used to be called the East bloc, in combination with the new passport status of the European Community and the European Parliament in 1992, is already prompting the redefinition of national borders and ethnic identities there. What will constitute "German" theater, for example? How will "communism" and "capitalism" mean? Here Golub's essay sketches a kind of transmission/reception between these cultures. While the period Golub studies is rife with agonistic models and hegemonic signs, it provides historical data about the formation of notions of subjectivity and identity in those cultures which, through the operations of anticommunist discourse, have fallen out of the canon. The complex negotiations begun in these articles will exponentially increase as these complex new identities are constructed, along with the dynamic changes in Latin America, Africa, and Southeast Asia.

We feel that this is a kind of entry-level text—a how-to for beginning to apply such considerations to theatrical texts and practices. Therefore, we have arranged these articles according to their political strategies or projects. Although semiotics, deconstruction, and theories of the gaze are generally bound up with one another, we have created them here as discrete categories, in order to foreground different kinds of approach. The last section represents six views of the current institutional situations in which we live and work. In his introduction to these papers, Postlewait points out the complexity and diversity of the problems confronting theater studies. The production of knowledge is shaped by these current crises as much as by the ideas in the scholarly essays which precede this section.

This book is dedicated to our friend and mentor, Ruby Cohn, whose scholarship and professional ethics have provided inspiration and support for a generation of theater scholars.

NOTES

1. Clifford Geertz, "Blurred Genres: The Refiguration of Social Thought," in *Local Knowledge: Further Essays in Interpretive Anthropology* (New York: Basic Books, 1983), 26.

2. Colonial theater was also an authorized topic of the conference and had an application beyond American colonial theater, as is obvious in the essays.

3. These panels also included Rosemarie Bank, Marvin Carlson, Elin Diamond, Timothy Murray, Thomas Postlewait, and Joseph Roach.

4. Gay Gibson Cima, Alicia Kay Koger, Tom Postlewait, Joseph Roach, Gary Williams, Simon Williams, and Bruce McConachie (local arrangements).

5. See Roland Barthes, "Myth Today," in *Mythologies*, trans. Annette Lavers (New York: Hill and Wang, 1972), 109–159.

6. For a general discussion of these principles, see Keir Elam, *The Semiotics of Theatre and Drama* (London: Methuen, 1980), specifically for the Prague notion of dynamism, 12.

Materialist
Semiotics

Sexual Politics and Cultural Identity in *The Masque of Blackness*

KIM F. HALL

When she commissioned Ben Jonson to write her first court masque, Queen Anne specifically asked for a performance in which she and her ladies would appear disguised as "Blackamoors." The result, *The Masque of Blackness* (1605), inaugurated a new era in the English court which demonstrated a renewed fascination with racial and cultural differences and their entanglements with the evolving ideology of the state. The Jacobean court was a crucial site for England's development of its sense of national empire: the country earnestly stretched its imperial grasp and England's poets began identifying it as "Great Britain" when James became king of Scotland, England, and Wales. *The Masque of Blackness* and its later counterpart, *The Masque of Beauty* (1608), became the catalyzing agents for a discursive network of "blackness" which participated in this process of identity and empire formation by dramatically reconfiguring issues of racial/cultural identity and gender difference.

Many critics who study *The Masque of Blackness* hasten to note that the conceit of blackness in a court masque was by no means a new invention. Enid Welsford argues that Jonson was influenced by the Florentine tournament which commemorated the marriage of Francesco de' Medici and Bianca Cappello.[1] Stephen Orgel minimizes both the significance of the disguise and the possibility of Anne's influence on the performance in noting that "Queen Anne's bright idea for a 'masque of blackness' was by 1605 a very old one."[2] More recently, Anthony Barthelemy has suggested that the request for blackness in the masque was "nothing extraordinary," given the history of Black characters in court masques, although he does concede that the masque itself had a recognizable impact on its audience.[3] Although it is very true that blackness was long a part of court tradition in Europe, critical attempts to discount the issue of actual racial blackness in the interests of historical continuity or misogyny ignore the persistent presence of a discourse of blackness in James's court.

In focusing merely on the chronological, such criticism works to preclude investigation of the issues of imperialism, race, and gender difference raised by the masque. The reactions of the audience to the masque and growth of actual contact with Africans, Native Americans, and other racially different foreigners (which went much beyond anything seen previously in England) indicate that a more disruptive reading of both the text and the performance may be useful. The political import of Anne's request for a racial disguise is often effaced by this insistence on locating the masque solely within a dramatic tradition. Interest in the importance of this first collaboration of Ben Jonson and Inigo Jones ignores the very central political question of why such a landmark production involves bringing "Africa" (albeit a European version) to the English court. By examining these masques in conjunction with other dramatic modes of court presentation and within a more overtly political context of empire formation, this essay insists on the centrality of racial difference in the Jacobean court as well as in the masques themselves. I further suggest that the "aesthetic" values of the audience, the playwright, and subsequent critics of the masque are actually political concerns which address crucial anxieties over gender and racial difference.

Representations of Blacks, as well as actual Blacks, were an integral part of Scottish court entertainment during James VI's reign. At his wedding to Anne, princess of Denmark, James arranged an entertainment for his Oslo hosts: "By his orders four young Negroes danced naked in the snow in front of the royal carriage, but the cold was so intense that they died a little later of pneumonia."[4] This spectacle, the first entertainment by the royal couple, was followed by a wedding pageant featuring forty-two men dressed in white and silver and wearing gold chains and visors over blackened faces. Such engagement with "outsiders" followed from the very inception of James I's reign in England and contrasted sharply with Elizabethan insularity. The cult of Elizabeth fostered an identification of the queen's bodily integrity as a virgin with the integrity of the English nation.[5] However, James's ascension brought to the surface acute and pervasive threats to that identity. His joint rule of England and Scotland and his pet project of creating a "Great Britain" gave rise to a more complex figure of English nationalism. James was himself a foreign king bringing a broad Scots accent and his Scottish cronies to court. The policies of a king whose motto was *rex Pacificus* (the royal peacemaker) and whose foreign policy involved the forging of political alliances with foreigners, including traditional enemies like Spain, contrasted strongly with Elizabeth's motto, *semper edem* (always one—and always English). The Jacobean royal engagement with blackness and foreign difference created strategies in representation for articulating and thereby solving the problem of difference in this court through the manipulation of blackness and of gender.

One example of the primacy of blackness and gender is found in the objection of an observer who, in writing "to discerne the humor of the time," describes *The Masque of Blackness*: "At night there was a sumptuous shew represented by the Queen and some dozen Ladies all paynted like Blackamores face and neck bare and for the rest strangely attired in Barbaresque mantells to the halfe legge."[6] While this "humor of the time" was very likely the much-noted conspicuous consumption of the Jacobean court, it is equally likely that the reference is to the Blackamoor disguise itself and the entire aura of strangeness and novelty that the masque strives to attain. Fascination with the culturally different and ongoing anxieties over gender coalesce in the unsettling vision of these English ladies posing as African nymphs.

The twin concerns of patriarchy and imperialism meet as Jonson's masque dramatizes the collision of the "dark lady" sonnet tradition with the actual blackness encountered in the quest for empire. This collision was not necessarily to the popular taste, as Sir Dudley Carleton's now famous criticism of the masque illustrates:

> Their Apparel was rich, but too light and Curtizen-light for such great ones. Instead of Vizards, their faces, and arms up to the Elbowes, were painted black, which was Disguise sufficient, for they were hard to be known; *but it became them nothing so well as*

their red and white, and you cannot imagine a more ugly Sight,
than a troop of lean-cheek'd Moors. [The Spanish ambassador
danced with] the Queen, and forgot not to kiss her Hand, though
there was Danger it would have left a Mark on his Lips. (emphasis
added)[7]

Carleton's description hints at the compelling "difference" of this masque.[8]
Rather than using the vizards courtiers usually wore to impersonate
Black characters, Anne and her ladies painted themselves, making this
the first recorded use of blackface pageantry in a court masque. This is a
crucial change which Carleton notes again in a later letter: "Theyr black
faces and hands which were painted and bare up to the elbowes, was a
very lothsome sight, and I am sory that strangers should see our court so
strangely disguised."[9] The connection of their face-painting with their
"Curtizen-like" apparel points to a time-honored association of blackness with lechery as well as supporting the greater concern that the
masque projects the wrong, "strange," image to outsiders, themselves
strangers.

Carleton's first letter is telling in its comparison of the theatrical paint
disguising the maskers with more traditional cosmetics, "their red and
white." In borrowing from the sonnet tradition's praise to evaluate this
"racial" disguise, Carleton touches on a link among poetic discussions of
blackness, racial difference, and beauty practices which recurs throughout Renaissance texts and reveals one way in which the discourse of racial blackness is continually gendered. Praising blackness by denigrating
face-painting is fairly ubiquitous. For example, in *Love's Labour's Lost*
Berowne claims that his "black" beauty, Rosalind, is pure and needs no
"painted rhetoric" (V.i.253):

> Devils soonest tempt, resembling spirits of light
> O, if in black my lady's be deck'd
> It mourns that painting [and] usurping hair
> Should ravish doters with a false aspect:
> And therefore is she born to make black fair.
> Her favor turns the fashion of the days,
> For native blood is counted painting now;
> And therefore red, that would avoid dispraise,
> Paints itself black, to imitate her brow.[10]

Berowne's description of Rosalind encapsulates much of the paradox of praise of blackness. The use of cosmetics is so pervasive that it literally taints all "native" beauties with the suspicion that they are painting. However, Berowne's "praise" paints women into a box, as it were, by suggesting that these women are painting themselves black to avoid the imputation of cosmetic use. This circular reasoning makes all women dissemblers because we cannot tell which women are truly "white" and which are not.[11] Jonson evokes this paradox in *Blackness*, when Niger speaks of how his daughters compare themselves to "the painted beauties other empires sprung" (133). Similarly, Jonson corners the royal maskers who are "painted" both in their roles as African nymphs and in terms of the "native blood" suspected of "red and white" painting.[12] This uncertainty is only broken by a powerful male, usually a poet (or a poet-king), who confers whiteness and "pure" beauty. Berowne's use of the proverbial "devils soonest tempt," also dramatized in Webster's *The White Devil* and *The Devil's Law-Case*, draws upon this misogynistic tradition: devils appear disguised as white and beautiful women, thereby throwing all women's virtue into doubt.

At court, Jonson reenacts and complicates the manipulation of blackness and gender inherent in the Elizabethan sonnet sequence, a process itself complicated by the conditions of performance. Although a troop of "lean-cheek'd Moors," the maskers are still aristocratic ladies who are part of the "golden world" of the court; this poses the problem for Jonson of presenting a spectacle of cultural difference without slighting the royalty and beauty of the participants. The conceit of *Blackness* is that twelve African nymphs, the daughters of the river Niger, discover that they are not beautiful, but Black, and are promised in a dream that if they find a country "whose termination . . . sounds -tania" (53) they will be turned white. In Niger's opening plea to the court, he laments his daughters' sense of inferiority. Alluding to the popular myth that the sun caused blackness, Niger claims that his daughters are beautiful as well as Black:

> Of these my daughters, my most loved birth:
> Who, though they were the first formed dames of the earth,
> And in whose sparkling and refulgent eyes
> The glorious sun did still delight to rise;
> Though he—the best judge and most formal cause

> Of all dames' beauties—in their firm hues draws
> Signs of his fervent'st love, and thereby shows
> That in their black the perfec'st beauty grows,
>
> .   .   .   .
>
> All which are arguments to prove how far
> Their beauties conquer in great beauty's war.[13]

However, Jonson opens *Blackness* with a hymn of praise to Niger's daughters, which, in reminding us that the African nymphs are to be seen as beautiful in everything except their color, directly contradicts Niger's praise of blackness.[14] Here Jonson draws upon the "Black, but comely" formulation of the Song of Songs; like Solomon's Bride, Niger's daughters become the meeting ground between East and West, as the opening song announces:

> Sound, sound aloud
> The welcome of the orient flood
> Into the west
> With all his beauteous race,
>
> .   .   .   .   .   .
>
> Who, though black in face,
> Yet they are bright,
> And full of life and light,
> To prove that beauty best
> Which not the color but the feature
> Assures unto the creature. (50–51)

The masque specifically warns the audience not to imagine these women as actual Africans ("not the color, but the feature") by pointing out that these disguised nymphs still have the features of European women, a paradox which ironically occasions Carleton's disparaging, "you cannot imagine a more ugly Sight, than a troop of lean-cheek'd Moors."

The masque reveals that these nymphs' dissatisfaction with their color springs from their contact with Western poets. The English poetry which celebrates bright/white beauty also represents them as inferior:

> Yet since the fabulous voices of some few
> Poor brainsick men, styled poets here with you,
> Have with such envy of their graces sung

> The painted beauties other empires sprung,
> Letting their loose and winged fictions fly
> To infect all climates, yea our purity. (50–52)

Jonson here reveals the cultural imperialism rampant in European discussions of beauty. The assertion that poets, with "their loose and winged fictions," were the promoters of eurocentric notions of beauty suggests that early cultural mavens such as Jonson well understood the damaging imposition of white standards of beauty, which author Toni Morrison has called one of "the most destructive ideas in the history of human thought." [15]

Empire works with the same efficacy in delimiting an Other. It is no accident that this first court masque is both an elucidation of the nature of blackness and a celebration of empire. *Blackness* was performed shortly after the coining of the term "Great Britain." Although the term was not legally adopted until 1707, James I spent much of his energies trying to make the term official; consequently, it was the site of much discussion and debate over England's imperial growth and identity. *Blackness* is filled with references to the new status of England as the seat of a growing empire and the significance of its identity as Britannia:

> With that name Britannia, this blessed isle
> Hath won her ancient dignity and style,
> *A World divided from the world,* and tried
> The abstract of it in his general pride.
>
> .   .   .   .
>
> Britannia, whose new name makes all his wealth a ring,
> Might be a diamond worthy to encase it. (55–56)

This pride in the revival of ancient Britain is continually yoked to the glorification of whiteness. In guiding his daughters to the promised land, Niger circles the globe, finding "Black Mauretania first, and secondly / Swarth Lusitania; next we did descry / Rich Aquitania" (54). Visiting these countries in an ascending (lightening) order of color, Niger at last happens upon England, which is throughout associated with whiteness. England is identifiable by its white cliffs: "This land that lifts into the temperate air / His snowy cliff is Albion the fair / So called of Neptune's son, who ruleth here" (54). This primary name of England—Albion (white land)—assumes great importance as its repetition throughout the masque stresses England's titular link with whiteness.

While *The Masque of Blackness* does deal with the fact of "blackness" itself, it cannot be made too obvious that such discussions of blackness are almost inevitably yoked to problems of gender difference. The cultural imperative of both masques is turning females white: none of the male "Blackamoors" seems to feel any such need. In general, little critical attention has been paid to the place of gender either in the masques or at court. Anne's role as Jonson's patron is not much discussed, perhaps because of the widespread opinion that Anne was an empty-headed spendthrift in endless pursuit of the unusual or the bizarre.[16] Although Jonson's claim that Anne specifically asked for "some Daunce, or shew, that might precede hers, and have the place of foyle, or false masque" (*Masque of Queenes*, 14) does not suggest that her creation of the antimasque is anything more than a continuing quest for novelty, it is also possible that her request reflects some awareness on the queen's part of her own female estrangement from James's court. Further, it plays up the transgressive nature of female "painting" or the use of cosmetics, long a basis for attacks on women. The patriarchal structures which underlie many discussions of female beauty often create unstable subject positions for women. As women come to be judged solely by their adherence to male standards of desirability and decorum, they are often put into the position of competing for patriarchal approval.

Blackness, a culturally authorized trope for distinguishing between women, is rooted in such competition between women. Blackness is often a mutable and relative quality; in early modern England, it is less a sign of complexion than of status. Women are only "Black" or fair in competition with, or in relation to, each other. In this special sense of inequality, all women were "Black" in King James's court. Female beauty was fairly powerless next to the "fair" men who enjoyed James's acutest attention. If, in the play world, James beneficently integrates these "dark" ladies into court, in the real world, James's attentions to his favorites denied women the status that accrues from being sought-after prizes in erotic competition. Stephen Orgel suggests that *Blackness* and *Beauty* may work together as an antimasque and masque.[17] Jonson tells us that the idea of the "foyle or false masque" was also Anne's and it may be that her masque allowed her the creation of a strange Other which worked to place her closer to the center of court, much in the way that *Blackness* prepares for and privileges *Beauty*.

The promise of *Blackness*—turning the nymphs white—is fulfilled two years later in *The Masque of Beauty*. The denigration of Anne's part in the creation of the masques may be sparked by the dynamic of the masques themselves. The blackness which originally marks her as different also marks her as inferior. For, in the execution of Anne's royal will, the masques concede power to the court males. Although Anne was the impetus for the performance of the masques, the actual power to do the impossible, proverbially described as "washing the Ethiope white," is credited to Britain's chief poet and sun, James, "Whose beams shine day and night and are of force / To blanch an Ethiope, and revive a corse" (56); the force behind the masque becomes the royal James, who watches a spectacle brought about by his kingly powers, "Which now expect to see, great Neptune's son, / And love the miracle which thyself hast done" (66). James's authority is called upon to break the deadlock of feminine beauty, to make the maskers, neither painted Black nor painted white, but simply "beautiful." The whitening of the nymphs is presented in terms of conquest as the language of blackness surrenders to a more powerful heliocentric language:

> Yield, night, then, to the light,
> As blackness hath to beauty,
> Which is but the same duty
> It is for beauty that the world was made,
> And where she reigns Love's light admits no shade. (71)

Such a "surrender," even more than beautifying the nymphs, glorifies the king and his country: "And now by virtue of their light and grace, / The glorious isle wherein they rest takes place / Of all the earth for beauty" (65).[18]

The completion of *The Masque of Beauty* proclaims the triumph of Albion and the return of proper Platonic order to the world:[19]

> Now use your seat—that seat which was before
> Thought straying, uncertain, floating to each shore,

And to whose having, every clime laid claim;
Each land and nation urge[']d as the aim
Of their ambition beauty's perfect throne,
Now made peculiar to this place alone,
And that by impulsion of your destinies,
And his attractive beams that lights these skies . . . (74)

As the verse suggests, James's England was beset by subterranean anxieties of cultural impotence which are offset by the cultural imperative, mandated by the demands of patriarchy and colonialism, of establishing the primacy of white/beauty. In asserting the power of Albion and of James to convert cultural difference into European whiteness through the return of the now-white nymphs to court, Jonson dramatizes a "positive" model for the confrontation of cultures. This model explicitly reveals the ways in which imperial contact is shaped by an organization of cultural and racial values rooted in the control of gender mandated by patriarchy.

The Masque of Beauty presents an idealized world in which normally intransigent blackness is subdued by a European order predicated on white, male privilege and power. In actuality, female unruliness was not so easily contained: the performance itself featured many women who resisted patriarchal standards of female decorum. Along with Philip Sidney's "dark lady," Penelope Rich, who was the mistress of Edward Blount and the mother of four illegitimate children, the play cast Lady Arabella Stuart, who would later be sent to the Tower (again) for her secret marriage to Lord Seymour; Frances Howard, who later became notorious for poisoning her husband in the Overbury affair; and Lady Mary Wroth, who had two illegitimate children by her first cousin and was sent down from court after the publication of her prose romance (the first by a woman), *The Countess of Montgomerie's Urania* (1621). From the first entrance of James into England, the ladies at court are associated with lawless, transgressive behavior. In her diary, Lady Anne Clifford comments on the reputation of the queen's ladies, connecting their scandalous behavior with the performance of masques: "Now there was much talk of a masque which the Queen had at *Winchester* and how all the ladies about the Court had gotten such ill names that it was grown a scandalous place, and the Queen herself was much fallen from her former greatness and reputation she had in the world."[20] If the imaginative control of women in the masque did not transfer into the daily life of the court, the uniting of English and Scottish differences under the glorification of whiteness proved equally problematic.

The Masque of Blackness was not an isolated incident of "strangeness," but the best-known (and most visual) sign of a discourse of blackness emanating from the court. While the implication of blackness in the masque depends on the actual painting of these court beauties, Jonson provides many verbal "signs" of Otherness in his printed text. The sight of blackness is invariably accompanied by a vocabulary similar to what Edward Said terms the representative figures or tropes of Orientalist discourse.[21] As Jonson himself notes in claiming that he chose hieroglyphics to signify the nymph's names, "as well as for strangeness as relishing of antiquitie" (239–240), these signs carry the religious and cultural associations of and assumptions about blackness. Jonson's textual emendations and stage descriptions contribute to the illusion of cultural difference even as they display his erudition; for example, he describes the nymphs as having ornaments of "the most choice and orient pearl" (60) and hair "thick and curled upright in tresses, like pyramids" (50).

By such specificity we see that, as early as *The Masque of Blackness*, blackness had become part of the linguistic currency of James's rule. Not only did James keep Africans at court as part of his passion for oddities: the actual excesses of the court seem to have been perceived as "Oriental." Racial difference, particularly in descriptions of the perceived decadence of the court, was a privileged idiom for self-description and critique. Orientalism, another trope of difference with a broad arsenal of effects, opens up religion as a category of difference. Sir John Harrington's description of the entertainments for King Christian of Denmark in 1606 links James's court with the alleged idolatry and licentiousness of Islam: "The sports began each day in such manner and such sort, as well nigh persuaded me of Mahomet's paradise. We had women, and indeed wine, too, of such plenty, as would have astonished each sober beholder. Our feasts were magnificent and the two royal guests did most lovingly embrace each other at table."[22] From the Middle Ages on, Mohammed and "Mohammedism" had been a sign for sexual and moral depravity.[23] Harrington's description of the court as Mohammed's paradise would seem to be less a way of bringing the East closer to the West than of distancing the "private" indecorous behavior of these Western rulers from their royal function. Indeed, the entertainments Harrington describes sound much like the representations of James's public kingly persona. For example, a masque designed for the same occasion used the common motif of James as Solomon:

> One day, a great feast was held, and after dinner, the representation of Solomon, his temple and the coming of the Queen of Sheba was made, or (as I may better say) was meant to have been made, before their Majesties, by device of the Earl of Salisbury and others. . . . The lady who did play the Queen's part, did carry most precious gifts to both their Majesties; but forgetting the steps arising to the canopy, overset her caskets into his Danish Majesty's lap, and fell at his feet, though I rather think it was in his face. . . . His majestie then got up and would dance with the Queen of Sheba; but he fell down and humbled himself before her, and was carried to an inner chamber and laid on a bed of state; which was not a little defiled with the presents of the Queen, which had been bestowed on his garments, such as wine, cream, jelly, beverage, ales, spices and other good manners.[24]

Harrington's rhetoric, which sounds much like the official descriptions of court entertainments, only throws into relief the strangely burlesque nature of the occasion. The fascination with alien difference Scottish James brought to court becomes speakable as Orientalism in Harrington's discourse.

Such a description of court debauchery takes on an added resonance when one remembers the popular representation of James as an English Solomon. The lengths to which the proponents of this analogy went can best be shown by Bishop Williams's funeral oration on James: "Solomon was of a complexion white and ruddy. . . . Solomon was a great maintainer of shipping and Navigation . . . a most proper Attribute to King James. . . . Every man lived in Peace under his Vine and his Fig-tree in the days of Solomon. And so they did in the blessed days of King James. And yet, towards his end, King Solomon had secret Enemies, Razan, Hadad, and Jeroboam, and prepared for a war upon his going to his grave."[25] For Renaissance England, the biblical Solomon provided two models for relations between Western males and "Other" females. In one, the Song of Songs, we see the white male refashion and whiten the dark foreign fe-

male into an object of a transcendent wedded love; this "positive" aesthetic model reverberates through sonnet cycles and *Beauty* and *Blackness*. In the other, we have a Solomon too much given to pleasures of the
flesh, which are associated with the allures of a foreign female.

Thus, in the entertainments for King Christian, we see how easily the
control exercised in the one model slips into the degeneration and excess
warned of by the second. The domination over (and eradication of) foreign difference seen in *The Masque of Beauty* is inverted into a carnivalesque spectacle which shows the threatening nether side of cultural interaction when the powerful Western ruler is seen to succumb to Eastern
disorder and riot. The king's drunken departure echoes the problematic
side of Solomon's womanizing, described as "defiling" the bed of state
(albeit with food and drink). Harrington also reads the scene as a subversion of gender roles and cultural imperatives: the aptly named King
Christian is described as "humbling himself" before Sheba.

Traditional notions of "Englishness" and concomitant problems of social disorder were being interrogated and threatened on all sides by the
growing pains of imperialism. For, in addition to internal court tensions,
James's subjects were going abroad in increasing numbers, implementing
his plantation policies, exploring "undiscovered" lands, and seeking new
economic opportunities. These displaced subjects were forced to grapple
with the problem of maintaining their sense of an "English" self in a
strange land. While it is difficult to estimate precisely how questions of
birthright, religious toleration, economic viability, and gender organization affected the English sense of self and country, one measure may be
the predominance of the trope of blackness in the drama of the period. As
Sander Gilman has noted, such an evocation of an Other is not unusual in
times of stress: "A rich web of signs and references for the idea of difference arises out of a society's communal sense of control over its world. No
matter how this sense of control is articulated, whether as political power,
social status, religious mission, or geographic or economic domination, it
provides an appropriate vocabulary for the sense of difference."[26] With
the loss of this "communal sense of control" at a moment of real historical change, Black figures—both "actual" and disguised—become the
focal points for an extraordinarily dense system of signification, which,
unpacked, reveals layered and interconnected anxieties over difference. In
court entertainments, tropes of racial and cultural difference are used to

present this seat of political authority as the center of a stable, ordered, and ultimately English world. However, such manipulations reveal that race is indeed "a dangerous trope,"[27] which highlighted the problematic differences of the Jacobean court even as it helped create the illusion of power.

NOTES

1. Enid Welsford, *The Court Masque* (Cambridge: Cambridge University Press, 1927), 170.

2. *The Jonsonian Masque* (Cambridge, Mass.: Harvard University Press, 1965), 65.

3. Anthony Gerard Barthelemy, *Black Face, Maligned Race: The Representations of Blacks in English Drama from Shakespeare to Southerne* (Baton Rouge and London: Louisiana State University Press, 1987), 20.

4. Ethel Carleton Williams, *Anne of Denmark* (London: W. and J. Mackay, 1970), 21.

5. Roy Strong, *Gloriana: The Portraits of Queen Elizabeth I* (London: Thames and Hudson, 1987), 96–99.

6. Charles Harold Hereford and Percy Simpson (eds.), *Ben Jonson* (Oxford: Clarendon Press, 1925), 449. All texts from this edition have been normalized.

7. Hereford and Simpson, 448.

8. Although Carleton at times displays a Bottom-like need for verisimilitude in his criticisms of the masque (for example, when he describes "images of Sea-Horses with other terrible fishes," he complains that "the indecorum was, that there was all Fish and no water"), his commentary in other respects is not very different from that of other court observers.

9. Hereford and Simpson, 449. For more on the costumes worn by "Black" characters, see Barthelemy, 18–21.

10. *The Riverside Shakespeare* (Boston: Houghton Mifflin, 1972), IV.iii.254–261. All references to Shakespeare's plays are to this edition, hereafter cited in the text.

11. For more on the traditional criticism of face-painting, see Annette Drew-Bear, "Face Painting in Renaissance Tragedy," *Renaissance Drama* 12: 71–76; and Lisa Jardine, *Still Harping on Daughters* (Totowa, N.J.: Barnes and Noble, 1983), 93–95.

12. Anne Cline Kelly ("The Challenge of the Impossible: Ben Jonson's *Masque of Blackness*," *College Language Association Journal* 2 [1977]: 341–355) glosses "painted" in this line as "superficial" or "inconstant." However, I think at this moment the masque literally refers to the paint of the participants.

13. Stephen Orgel (ed.), *Ben Jonson: The Complete Masques* (New Haven and London: Yale University Press, 1969), 47–60. All references to Jonson's masques are to this edition, hereafter cited in the text.

14. Barthelemy, 21.

15. Toni Morrison, *The Bluest Eye* (New York: Washington Square Press, 1970), 97. For more discussion on the lasting effects of the imposition of euro-centric beauty standards on Black cultures, see Toni Cade, *The Black Woman* (New York: New American Library, 1970), especially 80–89, 90–100; Audre Lorde, "Eye to Eye: Black Women; Hatred and Anger," in *Sister Outsider: Essays and Speeches by Audre Lorde* (Trumansburg, N.Y.: Crossing Press, 1986), 145–175; Jeanne Noble, "Bitches Brew," in *Beautiful, Also, Are the Souls of My Black Sisters: A History of Black Women in America* (Englewood Cliffs, N.J.: Prentice-Hall, 1978), 313–344; and Alice Walker, "If the Present Looks Like the Past, What Does the Future Look Like?" in *In Search of Our Mother's Gardens* (New York and London: Harcourt, Brace and World, 1983), 290–312.

16. When she is even mentioned, Anne is roundly condemned by James's biographers and other students of the Jacobean court. Antonia Fraser (*King James* [New York: Alfred A. Knopf, 1975], 53–55) comments on the way this phenomenon overlooks Anne's significance as a patron. William McElwee (*The Wisest Fool in Christendom: The Reign of King James I & VI* [London: Faber and Faber, 1958], 122) faults Anne's spending and her "placid stupidity." Stephen Orgel (*The Jonsonian Masque* [Cambridge, Mass.: Harvard University Press, 1965], 65), although somewhat less scathing, notes Jonson's "sensitivity to his audience" and proceeds to ignore or belittle Anne's place as patron, most obviously in his comment on Anne's "bright idea" for *Blackness*.

17. Orgel, 119.

18. Richard Peterson ("Icon and Mystery in Jonson's *Masque of Beautie*," *John Donne Journal* 5 [1986]: 169–199) sees this as "the almost imperialistic conquest of night by day," but insists that it does not overcome "the genuine strain of seductiveness in the masque" (190).

19. For a thorough discussion on the basis of the masque's symbolism in Renaissance Platonism, see D. J. Gordon's "The Imagery of Ben Jonson's *The Masque of Blackness* and *The Masque of Beautie*," *Journal of the Warburg and Courtauld Institutes* 6 (1942): 122–141, and his expansion of those ideas in *The Renaissance Imagination: Essays and Lectures by D. J. Gordon*, ed. Stephen Orgel (Berkeley and London: University of California Press, 1976).

20. *The Diary of Lady Anne Clifford*, ed. Vita Sackville-West (London: William Heinemann, 1923), 17.

21. Edward Said, *Orientalism* (New York: Random House, 1979), 71.

22. John Nichols, *Progresses of James I*, 4 vols. (New York: AMS Press, 1972), 2:72. Samuel C. Chew gives further examples of English allegations of carnality in "Mohamet's Paradise," in *The Crescent and the Rose: Islam and England during the Renaissance* (New York: Oxford University Press, 1937).

23. Said, 62.

24. Nichols, 72.

25. Quoted in Robert Ashton (ed.), *James I by His Contemporaries: An Account of His Career and Character as Seen by Some of His Contemporaries* (London: Hutchinson, 1969), 19–20.

26. Sander Gilman, *Difference and Pathology: Stereotypes of Sexuality, Race and Madness* (Ithaca and New York: Cornell University Press, 1985), 21.

27. Henry Louis Gates, Jr. (ed.), *"Race," Writing and Difference* (Chicago: University of Chicago Press, 1986), 5.

The Good

Soldier Schwejk

as Dialectical

Theater

SARAH BRYANT-BERTAIL

My calculation of time begins on August 4, 1914.
  From that point the barometer registered:
    13 million dead
    11 million crippled
    50 million soldiers in combat
    6 billion shells fired
    50 billion cubic meters of poison gas used
Where is "personal development" in all this? No one develops in a
personal way. Something else develops him.

These were the opening words of director Erwin Piscator's
1929 book *Das politische Theater.*[1] As the founders of epic theater,
Piscator and Bertolt Brecht wanted to stage not only the "person," but
that "something else": the political, social, economic, and ideological ac-
tants that determine the "personal." For their generation of radicalized
artists, the idealistic belief in the autonomy of the individual and of art
had been exploded by several events: the massive death and destruction
of World War I, the involvement of German religious and cultural institutions in promoting and prolonging the war, the Bolshevik Revolution,

and the German rightists' crushing of the Spartakus Revolt. Significantly, Piscator's time did not begin with his own birth, but was calculated impersonally, registered in mass statistics by a "barometer." In other words, human experience was being "written" in vastly expansive ideological discourses and through modern technology. In no production was that "writing" more powerfully and concretely staged than in *Die Abenteuer des braven Soldaten Schwejk* of 1928. This essay shows how, in *Schwejk*, the war itself took center stage, its time and space no longer smoothly contained within the dramatic form, but openly and materially constructed before the spectators by the machine-age theater—visibly and audibly written in the discourses of the twentieth century.

Yet Piscator and Brecht tried to show that these discourses were still within the power of human beings to change, even if beyond that of the individual. To this end, the epic theater should not only naïvely reflect our images of historical change, causality, and agency, but expose these images as ideological discourse, to catch them in the act of mechanical self-reproduction, so to speak. The "dialectical" theater would demonstrate human existence as a work-in-progress by openly pointing to itself as an operating model of that work. Stage events were explicitly related to the sociopolitical and economic situation of the characters and spectators, but not in the manner of naturalism, which presented these situations as impenetrable, inevitable "milieux." Instead, the epic theater functioned as a kind of narrating podium, using both the old, aristocratic-based media of actors and pictorial set and the new media of the conveyor-belt stage, films, slides, radio, phonograph, telegraph, electric signs, and loudspeakers. The ideological basis of this practice was Marx's historical materialism.

Piscator and Brecht also followed Marx in showing that political reality was often produced by outrageously theatrical means. If theatrical means were appropriated in gaining real political power, then the epic theater could at least reveal the working of its own machinery of illusion. There was a great potential for humor of a liberating and even revolutionary kind in Marx's own writing. *The Communist Manifesto*, for instance, makes a caricature of German idealism, and *The Eighteenth Brumaire* documents step by step the French bourgeois state's setting up and legitimizing of itself, exposing the whole process as a splendid *coup de théâtre*.[2]

Long before the production of *The Good Soldier Schwejk*, Piscator had begun exploring the dialectical comic potential of the stage. German dadaism of 1918–1920, in which Piscator actively participated, had already formulated the aesthetic and ideological principles that would be central to epic theater. The photomontage, invented by John Heartfield and George Grosz, visually condensed the experience of the twentieth-century metropolis: the perspective of the individual was shattered and multiplied through technology and thus turned into the perspective of the masses. The dadaist montages offered a simultaneous collective view of such surfaces as the battlefield and the city, where poster reproductions of great art might share a wall with graffiti. As Walter Benjamin notes, through photography and above all film, these simultaneous multiple surfaces could be captured and the masses could view themselves as such.[3] Anticipating the effect of film, dada's juxtaposition of art with material reality "hit the spectator like a bullet."[4] In contrast to the expressionists, dada treated the machine comically, as would *Schwejk*. One dada happening of 1918, for instance, featured a contest between a sewing machine and a typewriter, with George Grosz acting as master of ceremonies. The two machines displaced the theater's traditional protagonist and antagonist and parodied their conflict. The defeat of the typewriter also ironically materialized the fall of language from a transcendental medium to a clattering stream of type.[5] But even before dada, such juxtaposition had become fundamental to Piscator's thinking. As a draftee in World War I, he volunteered to become an actor in the German Front Theater, which featured folk comedy and operettas. The bizarre irony of acting in plays like *Charley's Aunt* amid the bombed ruins of Flanders had an impact clearly discernible in all his later work.[6] This was a real-life instance of dadaist juxtaposition and of the dialectical montage.

For his own theater productions, Piscator at first used film and stage machinery primarily to lend the proletariat mechanical, architectural, or geographical strength, as in *Flags* of 1924, which shares many effects with Sergey Eisenstein's *Battleship Potemkin*. The protagonist was set down upon various powerful, high-speed "people movers," so to speak, and the old temporality defined by the rhythm of human speech and bodily movement was expanded and carried along by new nonhuman rhythms. The self-containedness of dramatic space and time was thus

Max Pallenberg as Schwejk.
Akademie der Künste, Erwin-Piscator-Center, Berlin.

broken, and with it the "enchanted circle" of illusion that the theater of Richard Wagner and Max Reinhardt had tried to create. By 1929, a year after the *Schwejk* production, Piscator could evaluate the significance of his innovations:

> The two most important results of our theater, stage design and dramaturgy, came about through its *lack of architecture* and *lack of new drama*.
>
> Four of my productions, *Hoppla, Rasputin, Schwejk,* and *Konjunktur,* each had a different type of stage design. This was not the result of a restless technical fantasy constantly looking for new sensations, but was based, strange as it may sound, on Karl Marx's historical materialism. . . . [We needed] to relate each individual scene to political events of world importance, and thus to raise it to a level of historical significance. . . . In the stage construction a dynamic principle was developed: [in *Schwejk*] the *rolling* stage or conveyor belt and the dramatic-dynamic construction of the play . . . represented a comic moment in revolutionary theater architectonics . . . it became an integral part of the play's action and thus represents a true *dialectic,* that is, an oscillating interplay between dramatic and technical events.
>
> Similarly, the use of film should be understood . . . as a means to demonstrate the drama's great historical significance, as well as to place the play itself into a historical process. The same ideas apply to our new *dramaturgy.* . . . A private fate or individual . . . is no longer the center of the action. *The function of the human being has been changed.* The social aspect of existence is now in the foreground. . . . [If this produces] a caricature human being, . . . it is [due to] the disharmony under which human beings live today, which makes every aspect of life political.[7]

The political comic potential of dialectical montage and of the juxtaposition of media, stage, actors, and machine was realized in the production of *The Good Soldier Schwejk.* George Grosz and John Heartfield themselves, along with Brecht, became collaborators. Of all Piscator's productions, *Schwejk* most strikingly demonstrates why epic theater effected such a revolution in representation. In *Das politische Theater* he explains that he wanted to translate into theatrical terms the biting social criticism of Jaroslav Hašek's epic novel, to "expose the whole complex of the war under the spotlight of satire, and to illustrate the revolutionary power of humor."[8]

Max Brod, champion of Kafka and other Eastern European writers, discovered the novel of the obscure Bohemian writer, who had died before its completion. Brod and Hans Reimann wrote the first stage adaptation, which disappointed the Piscator collective because it turned the episodic narrative into a three-act drama, destroying the sense of restless flux and imposing the formal symmetry of a classical comedy. The axis of Brod and Reimann's plot was a triangle involving Schwejk's aristocratic young lieutenant, the lieutenant's true love, and the villain to whom she was engaged. Like the age-old comic servant, Schwejk, through the cliché of the misplaced confessional letter, accidentally foiled the villain, brought the lovers together, and ended the play by asking to be the godfather of their children.[9] Felix Gasbarra, also a collaborator, explained the group's objections to this adaptation:

> . . . the flow of a dramatic plot narrowed and shrank every-
> thing. . . . No longer were the environment and its representatives
> the decisive factors, but rather the insignificant individual charac-
> ters brought in to fulfill the scenic requirements of the comedy.
> Hašek's thrusts at the monarchy, the bureaucracy, the military, and
> the church thereby lost all their power. Instead of the Schwejk who
> takes everything so seriously that it becomes ridiculous, who obeys
> every order to the point that it becomes sabotage, who affirms
> everything, but in a manner that negates it, there was now an idi-
> otic orderly who unknowingly turns the fate of his lieutenant to the
> good![10]

Placing the episodes of the novel into a three-act format had forced them to be isolated spatially and temporally from each other. Schwejk would thus be trapped *inside* each institutional situation, which meant that the church, army, court, and police systems remained self-contained worlds undisturbed by the other domains. But Piscator aimed to find a way to present Schwejk's environment as the main actant and Schwejk as the figure who is carried along. He explained that he was attracted to the novel because "other writers consciously 'make a stand' and attempt to formulate an attitude to the war, but the war in Hašek's novel cancels itself out."[11] It was thus necessary to go beyond the single-room space of naturalism, so that the overall process of war could become the focus. The stage design was simple and economical:

> Two pairs of white flats joined by borders stood 10 and 20 feet behind the proscenium arch, masking the flies and side stage. . . . [Two conveyor belts 9 feet wide ran parallel with each other across the length of the stage.] At the back was a huge white backdrop. The electric conveyor belts . . . were controlled independently. They served as a treadmill on which Schwejk marched, and brought in props like the . . . latrine or the bar. . . . Large pieces . . . came . . . [on the back conveyor belt]. The [white side flats] and backdrop were used for projections (the contents of letters or orders written onstage) and filmed scenery (the streets of Prague) or commentary (George Grosz's cartoons). The play opened with a Czech folk song accompanied by a hurdygurdy, then an erratic black line traveled across the screen, eventually forming the figure of a bloated Austrian general, quickly joined by a scowling, be-medaled Prussian general, then between the two a judge with a death's head and a whip, and finally an obese, unshaven clergyman balancing a crucifix on his nose.[12]

The dynamic new principle upon which the plot moved was Schwejk's picaresque march, first to Belgrade and then to Budweis. Along this long walk the protagonist literally met the various scenes. When Schwejk walked, always staying on the same spot, from one institution to another across the neutral space, the spectators saw the church, the military, and the war as something more akin to actors than to inert backdrops or in-teriors. These set pieces—an officer's quarters, a courtroom, a pulpit, an army prison, a military train, and so forth—were cartoon cutouts designed by Grosz, and rolled in and out via the conveyor belts. The in-stitutions thus took on the aspect of obstacles in a steeplechase terrain, absurdly arbitrary but still dangerous. That terrain now became apparent as a *system*. The smaller properties, too, often attained the status of hu-man actors: in one scene, for instance, all dialogue stopped as a chair rolled in by itself and stopped just behind the person who had expressed a need to sit down. A sense of the play's reception can be gained from an opening-night review by the critic of *Die Vossische Zeitung*, a liberal bourgeois newspaper in Berlin:

> Piscator has obviously conquered the standstill of the narrative by banishing all standing still from his scene. . . . He has replaced the floor with two conveyor belts . . . separated from each other only by a narrow strip of solid land. When the stage manager pushes a button, the earth marches forth. Sets, people, and clouds wander by, quickly or slowly, whisking past or staying. . . . Everything is still in flux. . . . Nothing was more effective last night than the mute wandering of Schwejk through the countryside, in search of his battalion. The conveyor belt, precipitating the body in one direction, proportionately slows its march in the other direction. The actor walks on and on, and a distance that can be traversed in ten steps becomes the path of a whole life. On the second conveyor belt the world rolls by with its phenomena, the snow falls from the sky, and it seems as if the stage has conquered time and space. . . .[13]

This was not the first production to use the treadmill stage; it had been introduced by the Königliche Oper in 1900. But unlike the Wagnerians or Reinhardt, Piscator was not using this machine to promote the illusion of a world complete unto itself. Nevertheless, it took the collective some time to realize its full significance for *Schwejk*:

> When we heard the belts in action for the first time . . . they sounded like a traction engine under full steam. They rattled and snorted and pounded so that the whole house quaked. Even at the top of your voice you could hardly make yourself heard. The idea of dialogue on these raging monsters was quite unthinkable. I seem to remember we just sank into the orchestra seats and laughed hysterically. There were twelve days to opening night. The technicians assured us that they could cut down the noise, but there was no longer any mention of silent operation. . . . [Max] Pallenberg [was] an actor of unheard-of good will who would make any sacrifice to cooperate, but he was [also] a very temperamental artist, and natu-

rally apprehensive about the unusual apparatus, especially if it was not even going to work. . . .

It seemed to me that this apparatus had a quality of its own; it was inherently comic. Every application of the machinery somehow made you want to laugh. There seemed to be absolute harmony between subject and machinery. And for the whole thing I had in mind a sort of knockabout style, reminiscent of Chaplin or vaudeville.[14]

The treadmills became a humanized materialization of our ancient concepts of life as a road and of time as a river—no quietly flowing natural river, but a visible, loudly audible mechanism. It is one thing to say that our lives are being taken over by the machine, that war is sweeping us along, or that we are forced along a certain track by unseen forces. But it is another to see these familiar narratives as actual machinery in operation. The Piscator-Bühne had accidentally come to realize the potential for subversive humor inherent in the modern stage apparatus itself. In one stroke, not only was the arbitrariness of ideological narrative made concretely apparent, but the mystical *aura* of the machine evaporated. No one spatial or temporal dimension was ever allowed to fill the stage physically, and thus no integrated, continuous world was presented: neither the institutions nor the filmed landscapes and city streets could dominate, not even the open road: the emptiness and neutrality of the stage remained visible and audible.

Besides human actors, there were cutout puppet figures designed by Grosz that ranged from life-sized to ten or twelve feet tall. There were also varying degrees of artificiality from actors with masks and stylized costumes to actual marionettes; the aim was to create a hierarchy of familiar bureaucratic and military types. Sometimes the human figures projected on the screens were large threatening shadows looming over or following Schwejk, while at other moments they became a line of weary soldiers marching silently over the horizon. Like the sets, the films and human figures were a mixture of the naturalistic with the mechanistic and the cartoonlike. Again, instead of a seamless fictional world, an *ideological apparatus* was shown, a representation of the social, military, and bureaucratic system.

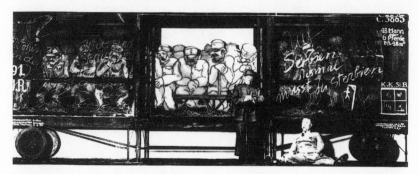

The Adventures of the Good Soldier Schwejk, *part 2, scene iii(e). Schwejk, rifle innocently in hand, talks the Sergeant to the ground. The boxcar is filled with cutout soldiers designed by George Grosz. From Erwin Piscator,* Das politische Theater, *1929.*

As a character, Schwejk had to "affirm everything," that is, to perform the discourses of nationalism, tyrannical politics, the military, the church, and so forth, with gusto unbefitting their pawn and victim. The discourses thus became conspicuous in their artifice. Schwejk's language was full of military slogans, patriotic homilies, and propaganda, but, in the context of this character and his experiences, they became a satiric weapon against the war rhetoric: coming from the cheerful, peaceable Schwejk, such graffitilike slogans as "Jeder Schuß ein Ruß" and "Jeder Stoß ein Franzos" (every shot a Russian, every thrust a Frenchman) attained a comic horror. But the discourses were also quite literally "objectified": they entered the scene through objects met on Schwejk's way, rolling out from the wings and across the spectators' view as stage materializations. Because they could be seen to take up space and time, they were deprived of their aura of transcendence.

In one scene, Schwejk zealously adopts the same discourse of numbers that was used to dehumanize the war casualties by rhetorically representing them as statistics. The sequence takes place on an army transport train of the type that moved millions of soldiers—an inexhaustible flow of human statistics—to the front. After a long walk in search of his battalion, Schwejk is glad finally to be riding a train, not realizing he is being sent into the battle zone by the military leaders, who hope to get rid of him. His enthusiastic obedience and praise of the war have only convinced them that he is not only a deserter but perhaps even a master spy for the Allies cleverly disguising himself behind a stupid appearance. Schwejk's virtuoso command of the discourse of numbers allows him temporarily to conquer his oppressors: he has aroused the suspicions of the officers by going through a routine of military exercises so as "not to waste the precious time" on his hands. The bullying Sergeant Nasakla has subsequently been assigned to fill Schwejk's time by drilling him in rifle maneuvers to the point of exhaustion. However, as the Sergeant finishes and lights a cigarette, Schwejk examines the number on this rifle and launches into a numerical dissertation, which will bring his opponent to the floor:

> SCHWEJK: 4268! A locomotive in Petschek on track 16 had that number. It was to be towed away, to Lissa on the Elbe, to the repair shop, but that wasn't so easily done, Sergeant, because the engineer that was supposed to drag it away had a very bad memory for numbers. So the Station Master called him into his office and said to him: "On track 16 is number 4268. I know you got a very bad memory for numbers and if somebody writes it down for you . . . you only lose the paper. Now pay close attention to me. . . . The first number is a 4, the second a 2. So alright, you can already memorize 42, that's 2 times 2, starting at the beginning with the first number, is 4 divided by 2 is 2, and what have you got, 4 and 2. Now, don't be frightened, how much is 2 times 4—8, ain't it? . . . Now [it] will never be lost out of your memory . . . or can you think of a simpler way of getting the same result?"
>
> NASAKLA: Cap off!
>
> SCHWEJK: So then he began to explain to him in a simpler way. . . . "Remember," the Station Master said, "that 2 times 42 is 84. The year has 12 months. . . . With division . . . it's just as easy. You figure the lowest common denominator out by taking the tariff duties." Ain't you feeling well, Sergeant? If you want, I'll begin all over again with the rifle discharge. . . . For heaven's sake . . . I got to get a stretcher.
>
> (People arrive . . . with a stretcher. . . . Nasakla is quite ill.) [He has collapsed and is being carried away as Schwejk bends over him, continuing to speak]

But I don't want you to miss the end of this story, Sergeant. You
think maybe the engineer remembered it, don't you? He got all
mixed up and multiplied everything by three—because all he
could remember was the Holy Trinity, . . . and he never even
found the locomotive and it's still standing there on track 16.[15]

Is Schwejk actually talking to the "real" Sergeant when he says, "Now
pay close attention"? If this could be proved, then he might be accused of
insubordination, but instead he has removed himself from his story to the
safe distance of the fictional stage present and is only quoting another
storyteller's words, impersonating the narrator within the narration. Not
accidentally, the latter is the Station Master, who has an overview of the
comings and goings of the trains, the schedules, the numbers of the cars,
and, of course, the human miscalculations—in short, of the entire network of operations. Schwejk plays the role of the Station Master down to
the last exhausting detail and thrusts the Sergeant into the role of hapless
listener: this is a turnaround of their normal power relationship and is
also signaled by a shift in spatial relationships. In the fictional stage
present, Schwejk is a statistic, a military prisoner being railroaded to his
trial, at the mercy of his *Vorgesetzte*, conventionally translated as "supe-
riors," but literally "those who have been set in front of him"—in other
words, obstacles. The narrative he is enacting places the Station Master,
and thus Schwejk himself, in control of all the movements of the lis-
tener(s). Although the two actors are physically on a treadmill representing a piece of land in front of a stopped railroad car, Schwejk's narrative
has trapped the listening Sergeant as another "Locomotive Driver" in the
office of the Station Master.

Like other objects, both visible and invisible, the rifle can be appropriated by more than one discourse and is therefore treacherous. Discursively, it can and does backfire: in the first instance, the Sergeant has
forced Schwejk to perform ritual military movements with the rifle, load-
ing, shouldering, and firing in time with his commands. In the second, the
rifle remains innocent and passive in Schwejk's hands during his whole
narrative. But by using its serial number alone, Schwejk succeeds in killing time, especially the time of his adversary. Thus, the rifle remains a
weapon even twice removed from the battlefield, because it did, after all,
set off the first and second rounds of discourse, the latter numerical nar-

rative in effect drowning the previous military ritual. The number on the rifle has been taken on a dizzy trip through Schwejk's subversive narrative. He never has to fire the gun, because the complex—indeed almost mystical—numerical connections in the story among guns, railroad cars, the calendar, and the tariff duties have felled the Sergeant. As a figure of authority, the Sergeant has at his command only the limited ritual of the military. He is no match for the rhetorical figure of *enumeratio* that Schwejk marshals against him—that is, the endless proliferation of numbers by which any claim whatsoever can be "proved." *Enumeratio* is the principle of endless semiosis itself, the proliferation of chains of signifiers and signifieds that are never arrested anywhere as meaning and so can be channeled toward any meaning at all. Schwejk functions here as a kind of switchboard vandal who heads the discourse of numbers off into all sorts of directions and systems, thereby rendering unintelligible the central "intelligence" of the military, who thought to maintain control of the whole semiotic process.

As the Sergeant lies on the ground, Schwejk, good sport that he is, asks if he should "begin the rifle charge" again; this would allow the other to have a head start in one last defense of himself and his authority. But the Sergeant has now been rendered incapable of replying at all. As a climactic finale, Schwejk, still impersonating and borrowing the discourse of the Station Master, performs the last rites for the Sergeant by letting his numbers dramatically stop at the Trinity. Thus, Schwejk manages to derail and reroute the system by which railroad cars and common soldiers are hauled away to the front.

In an interrogation at another Gendarmerie, it is not a real object but a hypothetical one that generates a whole discourse—which again becomes entangled with a train station. This time the object in question is a camera and can represent other objects. Even though it is a camera that does not exist, the secret policeman uses it to fabricate an incriminating narrative of Schwejk as master spy:

GENDARME: . . . Do you know how to take pictures?
SCHWEJK: Yes.
GENDARME: And why haven't you a camera with you?
SCHWEJK: Because I ain't got one.
GENDARME: But if you had one, you'd take pictures, wouldn't

you? Do you find it difficult, for example, to photograph a
railroad station?

SCHWEJK: That's easier than some other things, because it don't
move and you don't have to say: hold it, now smile.

GENDARME: (writes) "During my cross-examination, he admitted,
among other things, that he was not only able to take pictures
but that he likes to photograph railroad stations most of all.
Beyond a doubt, only the fact that he had no camera in his
possession prevented him from making photographs of the
station structure. The fact that he did not have a camera at hand
is directly responsible for the fact that [it was] impossible to find
any photographs on his person." [16]

As the Gendarme's report is being written in a notebook, it is also
projected upon the screen—mechanically reproduced at the same moment that the Gendarme is accusing Schwejk of photographing (i.e.,
mechanically reproducing) the railroad stations. While Schwejk has no
camera, the Gendarme is not wrong to suspect the presence of one. It is
the whole production that is the "camera"—both the projected image
and the apparatus that produces it. The stage is at once the dark room,
the interior of the camera, the moving film, and the picture. It produces
the slides, films, and animated cartoons that lay out before the spectator
Schwejk's journey over the terrain of the war.

It is not only Schwejk's language, but also his physical aspect, the manner, speed, and direction of his movement, and his spatial relationship to
his own narratives and to the objects and persons of the "outside world"
that become an "antidiscourse": he walks against the forces rushing toward or towering over him. Yet he is already crippled for—and perhaps
from—this march before we see him: he has rheumatism in his legs and
feet. In the third scene, he receives a draft notice and immediately wants
to join the fighting, calls for crutches and a wheelchair, and sets off into
the streets of Prague. The path of his journey is shown by traveling film
footage of the city, which actually proceeds in the same direction as the
treadmill, with Schwejk staying in the same spot. Amid all this fruitless
effort, he cheerfully points his crutch forward like a saber and rolls off to
find his company.

SCHWEJK: Fight! . . . Except for my feet, I'm a good healthy piece of cannon fodder and in times like this . . . every cripple has got to be in his place. Mrs. Müller, I need a pair of crutches! Ain't the confectioner across the street got some? He has? Get them! He's got a little go-cart too, ain't he? Get it! And a flower for my buttonhole.

MRS. MÜLLER: (crying) I'll buy it.

SCHWEJK: And my Army cap!

MRS. MÜLLER: I'll get that too. (Begins to sob loudly)

(Scene: Street in Prague . . .)

SCHWEJK: (in a wheelchair . . . he is waving his crutches . . .) On to Belgrade! On to Belgrade![17]

It ultimately can never be proved whether Schwejk was a fool who un-wittingly subverted the discourses of the war or whether he was only playing the fool. The spectators were divided in their reactions: some re-ported that Max Pallenberg's naïveté showed "something of the good, in-nocent, long-suffering animal who does not know," while others, like Piscator and Brecht themselves, saw an edge of "vicious irony" beneath the innocent manner. Piscator realized that Schwejk's power of negation went beyond any political agenda: "This was Schwejk's significance: he was not just a clown whose antics ultimately affirm the state of things, but a grand skeptic whose rigid, untiring affirmation of reality reduces reality to nullity. Schwejk, we argued, is a deeply asocial element: not a revolu-tionary who wants a new order, but a type without any social links who would be destructive even in a Communist society."[18]

The crucial point is that Schwejk's character acted as a sounding board upon which the discourses bounced back to reverberate in his quotation of militaristic slogans and that his mobile face all too faithfully reflected the enthusiasm of patriotic propaganda. He was the epic character par excellence, able in effect mechanically to "play back" the discourses, thus submitting them to the *Verfremdungseffekt*. But to do so he had to be suspended between multiple space and time dimensions, and between the human and the machine.[19]

In Schwejk's last march, which he believed was still in the direction of

Budweis and his company, the filmed landscape gradually changed. The progression in the filmed landscape from railroad track to highway to woods was a moving away from the temporalities and spaces of the war. Schwejk's erratic journey to the front was "followed" by a dotted line on a map projected onto the screen:

THE ANABASIS—THE MARCH TO BUDWEIS:

Scene 5	Film
Railroad tracks, then a Highway, then a Forest	(Railroad tracks, signal lamps, signal posts, a watchman's shack, gates at a crossing and then the highway, from which the lights of Tabor can be seen. . . . The lights travel along for a stretch, keeping pace and shifting toward the middle, slip back into the distance and disappear entirely, as if behind a hill. In the background, the night sky, against which a hilly landscape with woods is dimly silhouetted. Fade into a map showing Budweis. The arrows point out Schwejk's direction. The following appears in white print on the screen:)
Schwejk marches	"Xenophon, a general of ancient times, hastened through entire Asia Minor, and ended up, without maps, God knows where. Continuous marching in a straight line is called Anabasis. Far off, somewhere . . . on the Gallic Sea, Caesar's legions, which had also arrived there without the aid of maps, decided to return to Rome by a different route and were successful. Since then . . . it has been said that all roads lead to Rome. It might just as easily be said that all roads lead to Budweis, a statement which Schwejk fully believed. And the devil

> knows how it happened that he, instead of
> going south to Budweis, marched straight
> toward the west."

Schwejk: (sings . . . a melancholy air . . . stops and lights his pipe)

(The shots of the distant landscape have continued to travel past throughout the titles. The landscape in the distance begins to move faster and faster, while the scene in the immediate proximity retains Schwejk's marching tempo. . . .
Fadeout. Cut into shot of snowy wood) [20]

The war machine had appropriated railroads primarily and highways secondarily, transforming them into the "arteries" of its own abstract organism, which was imposed upon the natural terrain. Soldiers and ammunition were conveyed via these now fatal arteries, and thus the spaces of war were created. The lines of the railroad and highways were used in the redrawing of the terrain as a military map. The temporality of official history was literally written on the screen by a projector, and the space of the stage was traversed by historical discourse moving in a certain tempo: the narratives of Xenophon, Caesar, and Schwejk marched by in white printed letters, a mechanized realization of the proverbial writing on the wall. This "march of living history" was time as represented by the twentieth-century newsreel—which had appropriated and was now mechanically animating the history book's time line. Schwejk's journey was also transcribed into the military's writing of space and time: his maneuvers were reduced to dotted lines, maps and arrows, geometrical designs projected upon the screen. The stage conveyed the sad irony of this map being superimposed upon the slowly moving landscape. Schwejk's song— the voicing of human temporality—was sad. In the same slow rhythm as the song, the films of a starry night sky and of snow falling in a forest presented time as the cycle of seasons. These temporalities were sharply juxtaposed with both the newsreel's reduction of time to links in a chain of incongruous events forced into contiguity and the military's image of time as a moving line.

Because Hašek died before he could end the book, the Piscator-Bühne collective had to invent an ending. Several different endings were consid-

*Cartoon on the Piscator-Bühne. The tyranny of the machine-age director
Piscator is satirized. The wagon of Thespis is motorized and outfitted with the
latest technological devices, with the actors held hostage. Max Pallenberg as
Schwejk walks at center. From* Simplicissimus 43 *(Munich, 1928): 589.*

ered, none of them satisfactory to everyone. Their struggle illuminates
how difficult it was—and is—to confront the ideological meanings entrenched in our theatrical conventions. Reimann and Brod's ending was
clearly unacceptable, since it forced the events into a static circle, with an
archetypally happy ending: marriage and the birth of a child "rounding
off" everything, a ritual reinstating stable values and continuity. Grosz's
idea was "a slapstick scene: 'everything in ruins.' Or: The characters sit
around as skeletons with death's head masks. They drink each other's
health."[21]

Piscator finally decided to end the play with a scene called "Schwejk in
Heaven," wherein the protagonist faced God, a projected cartoon figure
who resembled another mustachioed Austro-Hungarian authority: the
figure was initially huge, filling the whole screen, but as Schwejk's dis-

course continued it gradually shrank to nothing. As a part of this final scene there was also a "parade of cripples before God" in which a line of wounded, disemboweled, and disfigured soldiers and civilians, children, and marionettes rode across the stage on the conveyor belt. The audience was so shocked by the scene that it was only played once at a preview.[22]

Piscator does not clearly say what was substituted afterward for this ending, but a typescript preserved by Brecht shows Schwejk crouching with another soldier behind two mounds on the battlefield. Schwejk says he wants to stick it out so that his bones can be turned into ashes for the sugar refinery to "sweeten his children's coffee." The other soldier leaves, preferring the hospital instead. A cartoon shows a Russian soldier swimming in a pond; a bush with the Russian's clothes hanging on it glides onto the stage, after which he runs away. Schwejk tries on the Russian's uniform and is arrested by a Hungarian who does not understand that the former is on his side. A shell explodes and Schwejk falls. Then a film of a line of crosses is projected onto the back screen, which makes them seem to march from the horizon toward the spectators: they first appear at the top of the screen, then grow larger in perspective as they reach the bottom of it, after which the film is picked up by gauze lowered downstage near the spectators, causing the crosses suddenly to loom up just in front of them.[23]

The violence of this ending is no longer naturalistic but is effected by an abrupt shift in the spatiotemporal orientation. The dominant movement of the play has been from side to side across the stage, like the eye traveling over lines of type. But without warning the "page" explodes in the middle of Schwejk's speech. The war has killed Schwejk's time and space. The treadmills representing time as a river come to a standstill, and the landscape, which has always followed parallel to the path of Schwejk in the far distance, suddenly seems to wheel around toward the audience, advancing from the back of the stage. It "steps over" the tracks of Schwejk's picaresque journey at a perpendicular angle, pours over the edge of the stage, and invades the space of the spectator.

In this ultimate moment the spectators achieved a "Station Master's view" of the whole topographical narrative, written by technology. In summary, it was significant that in *Schwejk* the various spatial and temporal dimensions were not dictated only by the traditional media of human voices and bodies, scenery, and music, but by the twentieth-century machines of mass media and mass production: electric conveyor belts, film footage, slides, graffiti, cartoons, films, typewriting, and disembodied voices over a loudspeaker. As a materialized image of the "passage" of Schwejk's time, the conveyor belt referred to the old metaphors of time as a river and a road, but here the road/river was mechanical, clattering over the empty stage floor. This was the new *writing of history*, which the epic theater staged in order to say that real politics and wars are theatrical productions as well and that it is within the spectators' power to dismantle the entire machine.

In *The Good Soldier Schwejk* the picaresque travels of its hero over the World War I landscape brought together the European continent as a topography, under the temporary control of an anarchic humor and a political imagination that transgressed the lines set up by nationalistic and military zoning. Indeed, the humor of *Schwejk* was powerful enough momentarily to halt the flow of ideological discourse and to erase the borders dividing the original Weimar audience: spectators from the left, right, and center of the increasingly polarized political spectrum laughed at Schwejk's adventures. But, as we know from the newspaper reviews, they could not appropriate them for or against any single political ideology.

NOTES

1. Erwin Piscator, *Das politische Theater* (Berlin: Adelbert Schultz Verlag, 1929), 1. After fifty years, this important book has finally become available in English: Erwin Piscator, *The Political Theatre*, trans. Hugh Rorrison (London: Avon, 1978). Rorrison's commentary is useful in supplying more information about the productions than Piscator had originally included. Wherever I have supplied my own translation, as here, the note lists the German version first. Where Rorrison's translation is used, the English version is listed first.

2. This insight is indebted to Wlad Godzich's analysis of Marx's *The Eighteenth Brumaire* (New York: International Publication, 1935), seminar: "Writing Literary History," University of Minnesota, Minneapolis, 1979.

3. Walter Benjamin, "The Work of Art in the Age of Mechanical Reproduction," in *Illuminations*, trans. Harry Zohn, ed. Hannah Arendt (New York: Schocken Books, 1969), 251. The last line of this essay is relevant to the *Schwejk* production: "mass movements, including war, constitute a form of human behavior which particularly favors mechanical equipment."

4. Benjamin, 238. Benjamin explains why dada acquired this "ballistic qual-

ity": "The distracting element [of dada] . . . is . . . primarily tactile, being based on changes of place and focus which periodically assail the spectator."

5. Wieland Herzfelde, "Dada-Show," summer 1918, in Franz Jung, *Der Weg nach Unten* (Berlin: Neuwied, 1977), 1242, Akademie der Künste, Erwin-Piscator-Center, Berlin, FRG.

6. Piscator, *The Political Theatre*, 14–15 (*Das politische Theater*, 16–17).

7. Erwin Piscator, "Rechenschaft (1)," an account of the work of the Piscator-Bühne in Berlin, lecture at the former "Herrenhaus" in Berlin, 25 March 1929, in *Erwin Piscator: Schriften 2: Aufsätze, Reden, Gespräche* (Berlin: Henschelverlag Kunst und Gesellschaft, 1968), 51–52. In English under the title "An Account of Our Work 1929," in *Erwin Piscator: Political Theatre, 1920–1966* (London: London Arts Council, 1971).

8. Piscator, *Das politische Theater*, 188 (*The Political Theatre*, 254).

9. *Materialien zu Bertolt Brechts "Schweyk im zweiten Weltkrieg,"* ed. Herbert Knust (Frankfurt: Suhrkamp Verlag, 1974), 17–18. In 1967, Brod published a "revision" of the 1928 Brod-Reimann adaptation, for which, Knust claims, he incorporated almost all of the Piscator-Bühne's changes and left little of his own text.

Knust's work includes a summary of the Brod-Reimann script, the full original version *Die Abenteuer des braven Soldaten Schwejk* by the Piscator collective from 1928, photos, an essay, and a few surviving drawings by George Grosz, as well as Brecht's 1943 script *Schweyk im zweiten Weltkrieg* and editorial markings in Brecht's personal copy of Hašek's novel.

10. Felix Gasbarra, *Die Welt am Abend*, January 1928, quoted by Piscator, *Das politische Theater*, 190–191 (*The Political Theatre*, 259–260).

11. Piscator, *Das politische Theater*, 187 (*The Political Theatre*, 256).

12. Hugh Rorrison, "Introduction" to chapter 19, "Epic Satire: The Adventures of the Good Soldier Schwejk," in *The Political Theatre*, 250–251 (*Das politische Theater*, 258).

13. Monty Jacobs, "Pallenberg auf Rollen: 'Schwejk' auf der Piscator-Bühne," *Vossische Zeitung*, 24 January 1928 (found in the Erwin-Piscator-Center, Akademie der Künste, Berlin, FRG). Also included, along with excerpts from other press reviews of this production, in *Theater für die Republik 1917–1933: Im Spiegel der Kritik*, ed. Günther Rühle (Frankfurt: S. Fischer Verlag, 1967), 840–848.

14. Piscator, *The Political Theatre*, 260–261 (*Das politische Theater*, 182).

15. *Schwejk—The Good Soldier*, "Dramatized from the novel by Jaroslav Hašek, as revised and staged by Erwin Piscator," manuscript in the Akademie der Künste, Erwin-Piscator-Center, scene iii (e). All quotations of the play in English are taken from this translation, unless otherwise indicated. Minor changes have been made to conform more closely to the original German.

16. *Schwejk—The Good Soldier*, act II, scene ii (*Die Abenteuer des braven Soldaten Schwejk*, in Knust, 89).

17. *Schwejk—The Good Soldier*, act I, scenes iii and iv (*Die Abenteuer*, 40).

18. Piscator, *The Political Theatre*, 268 (*Das politische Theater*, 202).

19. Walter Benjamin and Roland Barthes offer profound insights into the aesthetic and cultural significance of the epic theater. See, in particular, Walter Benjamin, "What Is Epic Theater?" in *Illuminations*, 147–154, and "The Author as Producer," in *Reflections*, trans. Edmund Jephcott, ed. Peter Demetz (New York: Harcourt Brace Jovanovich, 1978), 220–238; and Roland Barthes, "Diderot, Brecht, Eisenstein," in *Image, Music, Text*, trans. Stephen Heath (New York: Hill and Wang, 1977), 69–78.

20. *Schwejk—The Good Soldier*, act II, scene v (*Die Abenteuer*, 77–78).

21. Piscator, *The Political Theatre*, 261–262 (*Das politische Theater*, 195).

22. Piscator, *The Political Theatre*, 252–253. Rorrison takes this version of the new ending from Brecht's typescript in the Bertolt-Brecht-Archiv, Berlin, GDR. See also *Das politische Theater*, 194–196.

23. Piscator, *The Political Theatre*, 253 (*Das politische Theater*, 201).

Revolution . . . History . . . Theater

The Politics of the Wooster Group's Second Trilogy

DAVID SAVRAN

If you came to us and said, "I want to create a political polemic,"
we would not fund that. If you on the other hand said, "I want to
paint a 'Guernica,'" we would fund that. And the difference is we
make our decision on the artistic content.
—*John E. Frohnmayer, chair of the National Endowment for the*
   Arts, 1989

What strikes me as beautiful, what I would like to do, is a book
about nothing, a book with no external tie, which would support
itself by its internal force of style, a book which would have hardly
any subject or at least where the subject would be almost invisible,
if that can be so. The most beautiful works are those where there is
least matter; the nearer expression draws to thought, the more each
word sticks to it and disappears, the greater the beauty. . . .
—*Gustave Flaubert, letter to Louise Colet, 1852, quoted in the*
   program for Frank Dell's The Temptation of Saint Antony

After generating a storm of protest over the use of blackface
in *Route 1 & 9 (The Last Act)* (1981) and barely evading a lawsuit over
borrowings from *The Crucible* for *L.S.D. (. . . Just the High Points . . .)*
(1985), the Wooster Group has recently completed the least controversial

part of its second trilogy, *The Road to Immortality*. No protests in the *Village Voice*, no funding cuts, no threats of litigation have dogged *Frank Dell's The Temptation of Saint Antony*. And while the Group avoided opening the piece to the usually hostile New York press, it still managed, in the fall of 1989, to fill the Performing Garage for almost two months of performances. After four turbulent years of work on what director Elizabeth LeCompte has identified as the most difficult and elusive of projects, the Group has skillfully evaded its antagonists and completed its most beautiful, richly allusive, and demonstrably apolitical work.

Having written about a nascent *Saint Antony* (1986),[1] and having observed its many stages of development in the interim, I am compelled, after seeing two October performances, to try to understand why this most aggressively political of theater companies has taken refuge in what appears to be a kind of pure aestheticism. To explore this circumstance, I want to examine *Saint Antony* in light of *The Road to Immortality* as a whole, Flaubert's artistic and political practice, and the recent controversies over funding by the National Endowment for the Arts for work it deems obscene or propagandistic.

I begin with a working hypothesis: that *The Road to Immortality* is less an individual subject's passageway to renown or beatitude than the path of revolutionary history, as described by Walter Benjamin—that temporal continuum whose "every second" is "the strait gate through which the Messiah might enter." For Benjamin, every step, every historical moment, comprises "a configuration pregnant with tensions," which encodes the possibility of revolution—that sudden "shock" or precipitous "leap" out of linear time. It is my belief that *The Road to Immortality* articulates a series of these tension-filled moments, a procession of texts and social practices exploded out of calcified traditions that both stages and reflects upon revolution. The trilogy begins with *Route 1 & 9*, the most violently confrontational of the Group's pieces and the one that most clearly enacts Benjamin's sense of revolution as the will to "blast open the continuum of history."[2] It proceeds to *L.S.D.* and the textualization of history and revolution and then to *Saint Antony*, whose deeply ambiguous attitude toward the possibility of revolution I now examine.

In reviewing my original article, I am struck most by how radically both the structure and the texture of *Saint Antony* have changed and yet how apropos my enumeration of its "themes" remains. The plot of the piece is

still based on Ingmar Bergman's film *The Magician* and concerns a theater troupe on the run. Led by one Frank Dell (an alter ego adopted by
Lenny Bruce) and walled up in their hotel room, they rehearse their act
and convince the hotel maid and her boyfriend to join in. Then they perform their phony magic show and prepare to skulk off, only to be saved,
at the last minute, by a call from the king of Sweden, who summons them
to his palace. Onto this narrative is superimposed the story of Flaubert's
Saint Antony during his long night of temptation, visited by a succession
of heresies incarnate, each more horrifyingly seductive than the preced-
ing, each holding out to him a messianic promise. At the end, Antony is
saved by a vision of Christ, at exactly the same moment when Frank
Dell's troupe is reprieved by the prospect of a command performance.

The critic intent on discovering (as I was in my review) what this piece
is "about" may note what an extraordinarily astute and probing reading
of Flaubert the piece offers, not just of his hallucinatory *via negativa*, *La
Tentation de Saint Antoine*, but of the work's biographical and cultural
context. The critic may study how the piece, like Flaubert's letters, stages
the link between Flaubert, reading beside the corpse of his friend Alfred
Le Poittevin, who lay wrapped like "an Egyptian mummy," and the Orientalist fantasia he would begin six weeks later, which would be dedicated to
Le Poittevin's memory. He or she may also study how the Wooster Group's
adaptation (infinitely) displaces the written text, which, like the same
"horribly putrified" corpse,[3] is neither ever quite present in nor absent
from the performance. The critic may note, too, how the Group appropri-
ates *Saint Antoine* to examine the relationships among theater, magic, and
death,[4] identifying, for example, the narrator/huckster Frank Dell with
the broom handle corpse lying on the cot just behind him.

Although I believe the Wooster Group's *Saint Antony* offers rich opportunities to the hermeneutically inclined critic, I am here concerned less
to search for "meaning" than to delineate the politics of what is undeni-
ably a resplendent aesthetic experience. No other Wooster Group piece is
as richly sensuous as *Saint Antony*. No other uses the swirling mists, rap-
turous music, and battery of gorgeously colored lights—all to enchant
and inundate the spectator. At the same time, no other is as complex and
deeply intertextual; no other will as consistently frustrate any attempt to
fix the freeplay of references or to contain the plurality of signifiers. In so
doing, *Saint Antony* virtually fulfills Flaubert's dream of producing "a

book about nothing," an artifact sustained by its "style" rather than by any "external tie" or "subject." Like part III of *L.S.D.*—or, rather, its avatar after *The Crucible*'s erasure, *L.S.D. (. . . Just the High Points . . .)*— *Saint Antony* blurs the boundaries of both its seven episodes (by assiduously atomizing narrative) and its source texts (by insistently paraphrasing and interweaving them). Its principal sources (Flaubert's various texts, Albert Goldman's *Ladies and Gentlemen, Lenny Bruce!!*, and *The Magician*) are so subtly yet thoroughly transformed by the Group's verbal and gestural improvisations that they become "almost invisible." By so disappearing, they resist ascription to a single source and so would baffle any attempt by copyright lawyers to imitate Arthur Miller's success in closing *L.S.D.*

The various source texts for *Saint Antony* are aligned in part by the pivotal positioning of Ron Vawter as a central consciousness that conflates Lenny Bruce, Frank Dell, Flaubert, Saint Antony, and Bergman's Magician, Vogler. Standing downstage center for most of the piece, microphone in hand, Vawter mediates the performance, lip-syncing the Channel J videotape (the nude talk show) and doing all the voices, much as Antony's hallucinations articulate the "characters" in Flaubert's text. Willem Dafoe appears on videotape as antagonist to Vawter: as Channel J's cubby; as Hilarion (Antony's former disciple) on Vawter's "private" monitor, suspended over his head; as Alfred Le Poittevin; as the Devil and Christ.[5] In the Wooster Group's deeply ironic version of Flaubert's rather less ironic salvation narrative, the never-quite-present Dafoe looms both demonic and divine. He tortures Vawter from afar (on videotape the tempter, with his cocky, adolescent machismo, drives along a Los Angeles freeway) and yet, in a final apotheosis, proves the vehicle of his salvation (or maybe his damnation?) when he is revealed as Martin Scorsese's Christ on the cover of an Italian magazine—redeemer of the Wooster Group and bringer of fame, fortune, and stability. Alternately setting the scenes for Frank and taking the spotlight and microphones themselves, Kate Valk and Peyton Smith, as Onna and Phyllis, respectively, hover around this central male-male axis, functioning as would-be or ex-lovers (like members of Lenny Bruce's "harem"),[6] back-up singer/dancers, and stage assistants.

Although in performance I readily noted *Saint Antony*'s quasiexpressionist form and the relatively fixed relationships among the performer/

characters, I find my response to this piece very different from that to either *Route 1 & 9* or *L.S.D.* As my book *Breaking the Rules* demonstrates, I was always preoccupied with producing a thematic, structural, and political exegesis rooted in and at least provisionally bounded by the Group's deconstruction of two canonical texts, *Our Town* and *The Crucible*.[7] Watching *Saint Antony*, however, I found my exegetical desire alternately teased and mocked by the piece's nonsense, its hallucinatory fluidity, and its insistent fragmentation of plot and logical discourse, beginning with Ron Vawter's first line: "Underneath the apple leaves, down where the sugar patch grows, three dozen joints later. . . ."[8] My conflicted desire, both to produce and to cancel meaning, was redoubled by the four-page printed program, which seemed an attempt to stimulate and frustrate interpretation, simultaneously to engage the spectator's explicative skills and to make it impossible to master the piece's plurality. This plurality is even inscribed in the program's full-page presentation of the piece's "Argument," which uses a double-column format to run plot against plot (*The Magician* against *Saint Antoine*) and setting against setting ("A Hotel Room in Washington, D.C." against "Sunset in the Desert").

Even more telling is the inclusion of a glossary and information about source texts. For the first time in a program note, the Wooster Group explains its references and sources! And yet, in the same "user-friendly" gesture, the Wooster Group mocks the spectator by the very nature of the glossary, which (as Flaubert understood so well with his "Dictionnaire des idées reçues") underlines both the arbitrary character and the leveling effect of a list of terms produced in a purely alphabetical relation. The very form of the Wooster Group's glossary means that "Langley, Virginia" is given the same privileged status as the "Queen of Sheba" or "Arnie Schwarzenegger."[9]

In *Saint Antony*, this simultaneous enticement to and refusal of meaning is inflected most strikingly by a sequence of dialogue and business, introduced in episode 3, surrounding "groceries":

> FRANK: I can't talk to you right now, I just stepped out of the shower and I've got an armful of groceries.
> SUE: Was that a joke, Frank?
> FRANK: Yes . . . no, no, it's not a joke . . . it's a . . . J.J., what d'ya call it?

J.J.: Foreshadowing, Frank.

FRANK: Foreshadowing. You got a gun. You show it in the first act, it goes off in the third. You foreshadow the use of the gun. It's a stupid idea but it works.[10]

The "groceries" are broached two more times in the piece. At their second mention, the *Saint Antony* script glosses "groceries" with a footnote citing Goldman's biography of Lenny Bruce. There, in his narrative of the last day of Bruce's life, Goldman describes the concern of the woman he calls the Usherette with the dearth of food in Bruce's house. The dialogue Goldman ascribes to her ("Could you pick up some eggs and sausages and bring them up here? There's nothing to eat and I want to go out shopping") is echoed by Onna's line, "Why don't you go to the store and pick up some groceries? There's nothing to eat up here." In the biography the story of the groceries ends as the Usherette and another woman, "their trunk and back seat loaded with groceries," arrive at the house shortly after Bruce's fatal overdose, of which they are oblivious. In *Saint Antony*'s final moments Sue enters via the stage right ramp holding a bag of groceries and, after a pause, calls into the microphone, "Frank?" as Frank dons a gray Persian lamb coat and marches off theatrically.[11]

Goldman does not exploit the symbolic potential of the "groceries" and the motif functions as an arbitrary situational detail and formal device, used to provide one of many narrative threads to the story of Bruce's final day. In *Saint Antony*, as well, the "groceries" are articulated as a formal device, a random signifier deployed initially to incite and finally to satisfy the spectator's appetite for formal coherence. At the same time, however, the piece exploits the signified content of "groceries" as consumable commodities used to gratify a particular physical appetite. By so exposing the "content" of "form," the Wooster Group constructs a performance-text that is resolutely double: both pure signifier and pure signified; both irreducibly flat, banal, and material and irreducibly and impenetrably symbolic. The bag of groceries that Sue brings home at the end of the piece is a classic red herring: it produces the promised closure, but as for the hoped-for quantum of meaning or modicum of nourishment, "groceries" is just a random signifier.

But formal markers are not the only devices that *Saint Antony* manipulates and juggles. Relentlessly, the performance simultaneously exploits

Frank Dell's The Temptation of Saint Antony, *episode 6: The Magic Show. Ron Vawter and Peyton Smith. Photo: Louise Oligny.*

and exposes those tricksters and tricks on whose concealment the illusionistic stage depends. Both the scenic space and the characters are, like the "groceries," constructed as double, at once figurative *and* material, flagrantly literary *and* purely functional. Jeff Webster, for example, stands for the duration of the piece in the downstage trough as both the character Dieter and the technician running the soundtrack (and is credited with both functions in the program). This duplicity climaxes in the gloriously and ostentatiously fraudulent Magic Show in episode 6, in which a fog machine is used and the theatrical hocus-pocus is performed in full view of the audience. By exposing that which is normally hidden, by both filling and emptying signs, the Wooster Group also reproduces its audience as double (that is, in a contradictory relationship to the performance), both superbly omniscient and painfully obtuse, able to see through the illusion and yet incapable of making any sense.[12]

By so doubling the responses of its spectators, simultaneously seducing and alienating them, the Wooster Group seems to be replicating the contradictory posture of Flaubert vis-à-vis the culture of which he was a part and whose norms he despised. In opposition to both the socially committed and the bourgeois artist, Flaubert carefully constructed a position for himself as "the modern artist," in Pierre Bourdieu's words, a "full-time professional, dedicated to his work, indifferent to the exigencies of politics as to the injunctions of morality." [13] Embodying all the contradictions of his literary field, Flaubert took great delight in attacking the hypocrisy, vanity, and stupidity of the bourgeoisie—yet refused to side with the proletariat against them. Just two months before beginning work on *Saint Antoine*, Flaubert came to Paris during the abortive Revolution of 1848 and, in a letter to Louise Colet, described his malicious joy at the fall of the monarchy: "Well, it is all very funny. The expressions on the faces of the discomfited are a joy to see. I take the greatest delight in observing all the crushed ambitions. I don't know whether the new form of government and the resulting social order will be favorable to Art. That is a question. It cannot be more bourgeois or more worthless than the old." [14] For Flaubert, revolution was reconfigured insistently as theater, as a spectacle to be observed from afar, "from the artistic point of view." [15]

No work of Flaubert stages revolution as orgiastically as his sprawling *Saint Antoine*, which was greeted by the press with dismay when first published in 1874.[16] Scandalously, Flaubert had upset the norms of poetic drama and the canons of taste by parading a multitude of transgressions (assorted blasphemies and illicit sexualities) through the wild and fantastic Egypt of his invention. Although reveling in sensuous detail, this encyclopedic drama constructs the Orient, as Edward W. Said has pointed out, as impassive and overwhelming, and Saint Antoine as "a man for whom reality is a series of books, spectacles, and pageants unrolling temptingly and at a distance before his eyes." [17] Like Flaubert's perspective on the Revolution of 1848, his Orient is a spectacle of disorder scrupulously located in a wild and fantastic other realm which remains, finally, inscrutable, unapproachable, and elsewhere. Placed safely out of reach, in a theater of the imagination, his "closet drama" would appear ideal as the basis for a theater piece that would avoid the kind of controversies provoked by *Route 1 & 9* and *L.S.D.* At the same time, with startling prescience, it would seem to conform before the fact to the repressive standards advocated by a beleaguered National Endowment for the Arts in the wake of cutting its funding for exhibitions of work by Robert Mapplethorpe and Andres Serrano.

Speaking to the National Assembly of States Arts Agencies, the recently appointed chairman of the NEA, John E. Frohnmayer, has insisted that his agency will only fund work whose political message is subordinated to its "artistic content." By way of example, he draws a distinction between two kinds of activity, contrasting the production of a "political polemic" with the painting of a masterpiece, "a 'Guernica.'"[18] Although certainly aware of Guernica's political content, Frohnmayer presumably considers it subordinate to its artistry, or, in any case, believes the painting to be noncontroversial, that is, promoting political and moral values pronounced "universal" by most arbiters of taste and culture.[19] His statement (like the reading of Flaubert proffered above) is based on a binary opposition dear to the liberal humanist, who assiduously wrests the aesthetic from the political and the private from the public. For Frohnmayer, art is a privileged refuge from the turbulence of the political realm that is sullied and fatally compromised by its adoption of a "polemical" (read: counterhegemonic) stance.

In many ways, Flaubert's aestheticism marks a crucial moment in that marginalization of art to which the NEA is a monument. Flaubert, like Frohnmayer, has carefully separated the aesthetic from the social, as witnessed by his letters and other writings.[20] However, to hold Flaubert up as an aesthete, pure and simple, is to ignore the most radical dimension of his work, which deconstructs the opposition between art and political revolution. More literally than any other work by Flaubert, *La Tentation de Saint Antoine* is, in Benjamin's remarkable phrase, "shot through with chips of Messianic time," with the revolutionary promise of redemption.[21] Throughout the text, Antony swings wildly between hope and despair, waiting and praying for a deliverance of which he can never be sure. Finally, at the moment of peripety, as day begins to dawn, he has an apocalyptic vision of searing power in which he imagines himself absorbed into the very life of the universe: "I'd like to have wings, a carapace, a rind, to . . . divide myself up, to be inside everything, to drift away with odours, develop as plants do, flow like water, vibrate like sound, gleam like light, to curl myself up into every shape, to penetrate each atom, to get down to the depth of matter—to be matter!"[22]

Antony's desire for transfiguration—this dissolution of the individual subject into sound and light—is here congruent with Flaubert's own utopian impulse, that explosive force that dissolves the Revolution of 1848 into the minutiae of petty bourgeois relations in chapter 6 of *Bouvard et Pécuchet* and elsewhere imagines the disappearance of his words into a "book about nothing."[23] In both of these works, revolution is not merely one among a sequence of narrative events. More fundamentally, it is dispersed into the very body of the text, where it appears as a semiotic disorder, an orgy of signs that pulverizes both narrative and history. Revolution is the "almost invisible" subject of the almost unbounded play of signification that comprises Flaubert's much desired "book with no external tie." It is the most exhilaratingly "beautiful" of subjects. But, at the same time, this sign without a referent, this dehistoricized revolutionary hope, is only a sleight of hand, a terrifying "nothing."

Like Flaubert's contradictory works, *Frank Dell's The Temptation of Saint Antony* rejects the macropolitics of most committed theater artists (ranging from Emily Mann, George C. Wolfe, and the San Francisco Mime Troupe to Caryl Churchill and Howard Brenton) in favor of a radical micropolitics; it abjures what Frohnmayer would label the "polemical" and takes refuge in an almost fastidiously subtle ideological critique. This strategy is perhaps most clearly discernible in the piece's use of fragments of the extraordinary film *Flaubert Dreams of Travel But the Illness of His Mother Prevents It*, made by the Wooster Group and Ken Kobland in an unidentified Washington hotel. As shown on Ron Vawter/Frank Dell's "private" monitor (at once marginalized compositionally and granted a privileged cognitive status in regard to the dreaming, speaking subject), the film gently debunks Flaubert's Orientalism. By producing "Egypt" in a tacky hotel room and using Ron Vawter/Frank Dell, in a mustache, goatee, and turban, to impersonate the visionary writer, the film dislocates Flaubert's Orient, removing it from the realm of the Other to that of the Self, exposing the mythology that conceives the Orient, in Said's phrase, as a "surrogate and even underground self."[24]

The film's lucid debunking of Flaubert's Orientalism does not, however, guarantee *Saint Antony's* effectiveness as progressive theater. For despite this demythologizing gesture, despite a new level of integration of the political into the very sinews of performance, *Saint Antony's* reconfiguration of the macropolitical as the micropolitical seems finally to reas-

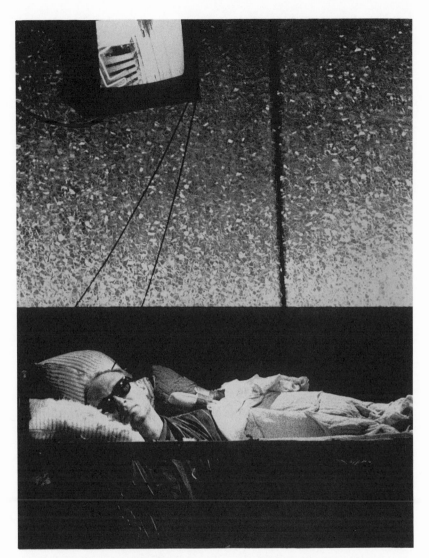

Frank Dell's The Temptation of Saint Antony, *episode 4: The Party. Ron Vawter. Photo: Louise Oligny.*

sert the separation between art and politics so urgently demanded by the agency that has been the largest single source of funding for the Wooster Group during the 1980s—the NEA. In its playful aestheticism and its re-luctance to bring home the "groceries," the piece has become, I believe, remarkably akin to a variety of deconstructive theater that has become increasingly fashionable and profitable, from which the Group's work was so easily distinguishable during the early 1980s. Like the recent pieces of Robert Wilson and Laurie Anderson, which have discarded politically charged images and rhetoric in favor of a postmodern shrug of the shoulders, *Saint Antony* stages both the self and the world as relentlessly textualized and paralytically undecidable. While it remains unlikely that most of the chic opening night audience that makes a pilgrimage to the Brooklyn Academy of Music's Next Wave Festival would crowd the Performing Garage, it would be no more vexed by *Saint Antony* than it was by Robert Wilson's *The Forest*.

Although I believe that *Saint Antony* reduces its politics almost to the point of invisibility, I am not prepared to argue that the piece thereby automatically becomes politically reactionary. Rather, I want to set it in relation to the whole of *The Road to Immortality*, to which it brings, if not closure, at least an end. Considered, as I have maintained, as a meditation on revolution, the trilogy begins by fomenting it, in *Route 1 & 9*; continues by textualizing it, in *L.S.D.*; and concludes by turning it into an aesthetic experience, in *Saint Antony*. In the course of the three pieces, action is gradually recast as contemplation, demonstration as discussion, and the combative as the solipsistic. *Route 1 & 9* forces confrontation, both inside and outside the theater, by using blackface comedy to deconstruct the racial stereotypes deployed by *Our Town* and ratified by liberal humanist discourse. *L.S.D.* reads a collection of documents from the countercultural revolution of the 1950s and 1960s to prove the unbridgeable gulf between history as a body of texts and history as a sequence of events. *Saint Antony* moves from historiography to aesthetics and reconstitutes revolution as theater, magic, and death, dissolving it, with sleight of hand, into a shimmer of language and swirl of theatrical fog. Revolution is collapsed into history, which is then collapsed into theater. In the last moments of the trilogy, the Wooster Group (following Flaubert's narrative) flashes the naked face of the savior. However, in *Saint Antony* (unlike Flaubert's work), this avatar of revolutionary hope is reconfigured as a deceptive image of a deceptive image of a deceptive image: a television still shot of a magazine cover across which is splashed a photograph of a Hollywood Christ. By so deriding the messianic promise, the Wooster Group snidely rewrites Antony's utopian vision as just another page in the book of commodity culture.

In *The Road to Immortality* the Wooster Group has produced a dazzling and perplexing double text that eludes any conclusive meaning. Read from one point of view, the trilogy stands as a "timeless" witness to the inevitable failure of revolution. Read from another, however, it becomes a chilling statement about success during the 1980s in America, where the road to immortality is the erasure of revolutionary politics. With its characteristic insouciance, the Wooster Group has withheld any indication whether this erasure is deliberate or accidental. I, certainly, am unable to determine whether this repositioning results from anxiety over government funding or marks a carefully considered change in direction, whether it represents a gesture of compliance with or an indictment of the aesthetic tide. I do know that in the years since I wrote *Breaking the Rules*, I have become increasingly uncomfortable with this giddy undecidability and a political posture that I identified (even then) as more Nietzschean than Marxist.[25] Given the ongoing success of an American foreign policy designed by thugs, the effective dismantlement of social programs, the demonstrably racist and genocidal indifference to AIDS and homelessness, and the attempt by the NEA to stifle the voices that decry these circumstances, I have become increasingly skeptical of those artists (and critics) who produce a cultural critique so subtle and so endlessly skeptical that it finally does little else than deconstruct itself. Reconfigured as Frank Dell's traveling troupe, at the end of a decade and the end of the *Road*, the Wooster Group has managed to turn even its revolutionary stance into a magic show: now you see it, now you don't.

NOTES

The author wishes to thank those who provided valuable feedback both on the Wooster Group and on this essay, especially John Emigh, Nelly Furman, Brian Herrera, David Hult, Neil Lazarus, Ronn Smith, and Paula Vogel.

1. David Savran, "Adaptation as Clairvoyance: The Wooster Group's *Saint Anthony*," *Theater* 18:1 (Winter 1986–1987): 36–41.

2. Walter Benjamin, "Theses on the Philosophy of History," in *Illuminations*, trans. Harry Zohn (New York: Schocken Books, 1969), 253–264.

3. Gustave Flaubert, *Letter to Maxime Du Camp, April 7, 1848*, quoted in Savran, 36. See also Eugenio Donato, "The Crypt of Flaubert," in *Flaubert and Postmodernism*, ed. Naomi Schor and Henry F. Majewski (Lincoln and London: University of Nebraska Press, 1984), 30–45.

4. My earlier article on *Saint Antony* explicitly aligned theater, magic, and death in its final three sentences (Savran, 41): "*Saint Anthony* [sic] thereby reidentifies theater with magic—the play of appearance and disappearance. It recovers the magical power of theater to cheat death, to commemorate what is no longer there. It marks the death of death: now you see it, now you don't." I now add revolution to that triad.

5. The presence of Ron Vawter at the center of the piece, as master of ceremonies, raconteur, and hallucinator, is in part produced by the absence of a "live" Willem Dafoe, his co-equal through most of *Route 1 & 9* and *L.S.D.* For most of the composition of *Saint Antony*, Dafoe was away from New York pursuing an extremely successful career in commercial films.

6. Albert Goldman, from the journalism of Lawrence Schiller, *Ladies and Gentlemen, Lenny Bruce!!* (New York: Ballantine Books, 1974), 752. All of the Wooster Group's previous work focuses on the spectacle of male subjectivity and (re)produces women as marginal to that spectacle in order to undermine this configuration. Thus, *L.S.D.* self-consciously quotes that marginality (through the figure of Nancy Reilly/Ann Rower) to deconstruct a masculinist notion of history. *Saint Antony*, in contrast, appears somewhat reluctant to problematize the marginalized position of women and, consequently, seems to reflect (rather than critique) the phallocentric organization of the Flaubert and Lenny Bruce texts.

7. David Savran, *Breaking the Rules: The Wooster Group* (New York: Theatre Communication Group, 1988), 9–45, 169–220.

8. The Wooster Group, *Frank Dell's The Temptation of Saint Antony*, unpublished manuscript, 2.

9. The Wooster Group, program for *Frank Dell's The Temptation of Saint Antony*, October 1989.

10. The Wooster Group, *Frank Dell's The Temptation of Saint Antony*, 27 October 1989.

11. Goldman, 789, 798; *Saint Antony* manuscript, 28 and 91. Vawter's final exit is almost exactly the same as that of the fur-wrapped Rose in the 1989 Broadway revival of the Styne-Sondheim-Laurents musical, *Gypsy*.

12. During the Magic Show the audience is doubled in the sense that it is repositioned without leaving its seats: the implied orientation of the stage reverses and the "front" that the audience has been watching is suddenly reconstituted as "backstage."

13. Pierre Bourdieu, "Flaubert's Point of View," trans. Priscilla Parkhurst Ferguson, in *Literature and Social Practice*, ed. Philippe Desan, Priscilla Parkhurst Ferguson, and Wendy Griswold (Chicago and London: University of Chicago Press, 1989), 223.

14. Gustave Flaubert, *The Letters of Gustave Flaubert, 1830–1857*, ed. and trans. Francis Steegmuller (Cambridge: Belknap Press of Harvard University Press, 1980), 93.

15. Quoted in Francis Steegmuller, *Flaubert and Madame Bovary: A Double Portrait* (New York: Farrar, Straus, 1950), 147.

16. See Gustave Flaubert, *The Letters of Gustave Flaubert, 1857–1880*, ed. and trans. Francis Steegmuller (Cambridge: Belknap Press of Harvard University Press, 1982), 212; also E. E. Freienmuth von Helms, *German Criticism of Gustave Flaubert, 1857–1930* (New York: Columbia University Press, 1939), 19–22.

17. Edward W. Said, *Orientalism* (New York: Vintage Books, 1979), 188.

18. Quoted in Grace Glueck, "Border Skirmish: Art and Politics," *New York Times*, 19 November 1989, section II, 25.

19. Frohnmayer's perspective is by no means unusual. In one of the first American reviews of *Guernica*, Henry McBride, while noting the "ferocity" with which Picasso, "an ardent communist," depicted the horrors of war, reassured his readers: "This sounds like propaganda and in fact the picture was intended to be such, but it ended in being something vastly more important—a work of art" (*New York Sun*, 6 May 1939; reprinted in Ellen C. Oppler, *Picasso's Guernica* [New York and London: W. W. Norton, 1988], 227).

20. Consider, for example, one of Flaubert's personal notes after visiting La Scala: "A theater is as holy a place as a church. I enter it with a religious emotion. It is there that the human mind, surfeited with itself, seeks to escape from reality" (quoted in Maurice Nadeau, *The Greatness of Flaubert*, trans. Barbara Bray [New York: Library Press, 1972], 212).

21. Benjamin, 263.

22. Gustave Flaubert, *The Temptation of Saint Antony*, trans. Kitty Mrosovsky (Harmondsworth: Penguin Books, 1980), 232.

23. The encyclopedic processional of Flaubert's last novel, *Bouvard et Pécuchet*, in effect, rewrites *Saint Antoine* in an ironic mode. These two most underappreciated of Flaubert's works face each other as distorting mirrors: the one secular, contemporary, and sober; the other religious, historical, and hallucinatory. For a cogent account of the textualization of the Revolution of 1848 in *Bouvard et Pécuchet*, see Antoine Compagnon, *La Troisième République des lettres, de Flaubert à Proust* (Paris: Editions du Seuil, 1983), 253–268.

24. Said, 3.

25. Savran, *Breaking the Rules*, 222.

Bernard Shaw

and the

Drama of

Imperialism

J. ELLEN GAINOR

It should not be possible to read nineteenth-century British
literature without remembering that imperialism, understood as
England's social mission, was a crucial part of the cultural
representation of England to the English. The role of literature in
the production of cultural representation should not be ignored.
These two obvious "facts" continue to be disregarded in the
reading of nineteenth-century British literature. This itself attests to
the continuing success of the imperialist project, displaced and
dispersed into more modern forms.
—*Gayatri Chakravorty Spivak, "Three Women's Texts and a*
    Critique of Imperialism"

In recent years, analysts of British fiction and poetry have acknowledged Spivak's 1986 critique of literary scholarship and begun to
incorporate her theoretical views into their work (along with those of
Edward Said and others noted for their studies of imperialism and literature).[1] This understanding of the influence of imperialism on British literature has not spread to studies of the drama, however. Although many other
aspects of nineteenth- and twentieth-century political thought have been

explored in their theatrical contexts, scholarly attention has yet to focus on the connection between the imperial enterprise and the drama, not only as a theme, but also as a structuring force guiding setting, plot, and characterization. Bernard Shaw's dramas from the late 1890s to 1919 exemplify this incorporation of imperial issues in the theater; through an examination of plays from this period, I hope to show both the significance of this topic to his dramaturgy and the variety of modes through which he developed it. Closely engaged politically with the progress of imperialism abroad and its impact at home, Shaw included these concerns in his dramas. From the late Victorian era through the early years of World War I, Shaw's plays filled the English stage with images of empire, bringing before his audience a range of views on the colonies and on England's role as an imperial power.

I want first to locate this aspect of Shavian dramaturgy in two visual images—two elements of Shaw's set and costume designs for *Misalliance* (1910) and *Heartbreak House* (1919). In the opening stage description for *Misalliance*, Shaw carefully depicts the upstage area of John Tarleton's country house in Hindhead, Surrey. He notes the supporting archway to be erected a bit off center, with more wall to the right than to the left, and then explains: "Just through the arch at [the right] corner stands a new portable Turkish bath."[2] The details here are important; according to Shaw's design scheme, the Turkish bath lies directly upstage center, where it remains throughout the play, the visual focus of the scene.[3]

Midway through act II of *Heartbreak House*, Hector Hushabye appears dressed for dinner "in a handsome Arab costume,"[4] which he wears throughout the entire second half of the drama, standing out markedly from the appearance of the rest of the cast, who sport elegant, English-country-weekend attire. Hector's outfit, like the Turkish bath, has both symbolic and dramatic functions within the play itself. Yet if we think of these design details as existing solely for their immediate plot functions, without considering their larger connotative and allusive potential as signs of imperial ideology, then we reproduce an obliviousness to the critique of imperialism that Shaw would preclude through his plays of this era. Edward Said's notion of the relation of empire to Oriental images in his study *Orientalism* is useful here for understanding this same connection in Shavian dramaturgy:

The Orient is not only adjacent to Europe; it is also the place of
Europe's greatest and richest and oldest colonies, the source of its
civilizations and languages, its cultural contestant, and one of its
deepest and most recurring images of the Other. . . . I doubt that it
is controversial . . . to say that an Englishman in India or Egypt in
the later nineteenth century took an interest in those countries that
was never far from their status in his mind as British colonies.[5]

That Shaw should place two Oriental images so centrally in these plays
suggests, albeit subtly, that his interest in British imperialism is likewise
central to his work.

Given the pervasiveness of this issue in Shaw's *oeuvre* (including such
early novels as *Cashel Byron's Profession*, set partly in Australia), it is
surprising that Shaw scholarship has touched so lightly on this topic.
Shavian critics have barely examined the imperial content of his plays,
although many have observed their historical references to the empire.
J. L. Wisenthal traces some of the elements in Shaw to contemporary imperial parallels. For example, he suggests that the name Hastings Utterword, the imperial governor in *Heartbreak House*, may have been derived from Warren Hastings, the eighteenth-century governor general of
India.[6] Martin Meisel finds imperial echoes in other earlier dramas in his
Shaw and the Nineteenth-Century Theatre.[7] Details like these help the
reader to trace the factual and artistic sources for Shaw's work, but scholars rarely go on to interpret these components of the plays. Even Margery
Morgan, one of the few critics to comment on imperial details, explains
them only marginally, in a footnote to her discussion of the late play *Too
True to be Good* (1932):

> Shaw's use of Lawrence of Arabia as his model for Private Meek
> is not irrelevant, even aesthetically, as the contemporary audience's
> awareness of it must have helped set the play in the context of de-
> bate on Britain's imperial role. The remote locales of both *Too
> True* and *The Simpleton* correspond to the turning of Shaw's politi-
> cal concerns beyond national confines to explore the relation of
> Britain to the rest of the world.[8]

However, Morgan's dating of this "turning" as late in Shaw's career
may demonstrate some assumptions about Shaw, his politics, and British

imperialism that merit investigation. Does Morgan mean that it is only with these late plays that Shaw overtly exposes the fallacies of certain imperial practices and beliefs? What, then, are we to make of Shaw's earlier work, which features these concerns and relationships just as centrally, but from a point of view more in line with some of the philosophical goals of British imperialism, if not necessarily its practice? In other words, it is not until Shaw seems to "oppose" the empire that critics can acknowledge the depth of his involvement with this issue and discuss his use of imperial details as something other than contextual set dressing. Finally, this form of analysis, which seeks to anatomize the drama into a political statement either "for" or "against" imperialism, eliminates the possibility of examining the contradictions, developments, or subtleties in Shaw's use of an imperial theme.

Shaw's use of imperial topics often coincided with historic events and/ or debates tied to Britain's imperial activities. At the time of the Boer War, for example, England was sharply divided over its involvement in South Africa, and the Fabian Society reflected this British conflict within its own ranks. Initially, Sidney Webb believed the Fabians should have no position at all with respect to foreign policy, but other members disagreed; in February 1900, a referendum was held to answer the question: "Are you in favour of an official pronouncement being made now by the Fabian Society on Imperialism in relation to the War?" [9] After lengthy debate and the resignation of a number of prominent members opposed to the pro-imperial direction in which the group was moving, the executive asked Shaw "to draft a manifesto on imperialism" for the society. [10]

As Michael Holroyd observes in the second volume of his Shaw biography, Shaw's attitude toward the empire and the Boer War "seemed completely to invert the traditional socialist standpoint—supporting pacifist permeation tactics at home while tolerating a good deal of bloodshed overseas." [11] In the manifesto *Fabianism and the Empire*, Shaw states:

> Great Powers, consciously or unconsciously, must govern in the interests of civilization as a whole; and it is not in those interests that such mighty forces as gold-fields . . . should be wielded irresponsibly by small communities of frontiersmen. Theoretically, they should be internationalized, not British-imperialized, but until the Federation of the World becomes an accomplished fact we must

accept the most responsible Imperial Federation available as a substitute for it.[12]

Imperial historian Harry Magdoff analyzes Shaw's argument as "but a variation of the dominant imperialist theme of his times and of his country: Great Britain's responsibility for empire arose from its obvious superiority in political administration; its manifest destiny was to civilize the heathens by teaching them the art of government." [13]

Shortly before drafting the manifesto, Shaw had written a play about teaching the art of government, *Caesar and Cleopatra*.[14] Although Shaw scholarship has not connected these writings, they seem to me to be closely linked. At the same time that Shaw was grappling with his political views on empire, he chose to write a play set in an imperial age, dealing directly with Rome's involvement in Egypt. Shaw's metaphor for the British empire fell right in line with the thinking of many Britons; according to Samuel Hynes, at the time of the Boer War, many Edwardians thought of the parallel between England and Gibbon's *The Decline and Fall of the Roman Empire*, and "the idea of imperial decline and fall haunted imaginations of the time." [15] Other writers chose to see the relation in a more positive light. In 1912, for example, Sir C. P. Lucas wrote a volume entitled *Greater Rome and Greater Britain*, in which he proposed "to examine some of the leading features of the British Empire, and to compare and contrast them with the characteristics of the Roman Empire, which was the greatest political system of the ancient world." [16]

Shaw added a second prologue to *Caesar and Cleopatra* in that same year, speaking to his British audience through the character of the Egyptian god Ra:

> Ye poor posterity, think not that ye are the first. Other fools before ye have seen the sun rise and set. . . . As they were so ye are; and yet not so great; for the pyramids my people built stand to this day; whilst the dustheaps on which ye slave, and which ye call empires, scatter in the wind even as ye pile your dead sons' bodies on them to make yet more dust. . . . Know that even as there is an old England and a new, and ye stand perplexed between the twain; so in the days when I was worshipped was there an old Rome and a new. (7–8)

The story of the older Caesar and the young Cleopatra which follows this prologue dramatizes Caesar's pragmatic methods of teaching leadership and sustaining power. It also depicts an idealized view of imperial rule and presents a model for British government. At the same time, however, Shaw's rendition of this narrative incorporates some of the tropes of imperial discourse identified by critics as components of an imperialist ideology. Like many narratives of the British empire, *Caesar and Cleopatra* focuses on a feminized Oriental Other—Cleopatra's Egypt is the feminine East that must learn to mirror the tactics of Rome. Cleopatra herself appears younger in the play than her historical age at the time of her meeting with Julius Caesar, a detail which coincides with colonizers' descriptions of colonized peoples as children, needing their superior experience and guidance.

Shaw published *Caesar and Cleopatra* together with *Captain Brassbound's Conversion* and *The Devil's Disciple* in 1901 as *Three Plays for Puritans*. The dramas can also be thought of as Shaw's "imperial trilogy," for each concerns issues of imperial expansion and colonization and is set in a foreign locale. *The Devil's Disciple*, like *Caesar and Cleopatra*, uses a historically distant milieu, this time the American colonial period.

Captain Brassbound's Conversion focuses on the present,[17] depicting a series of events in and around the Atlas Mountains of Morocco. The play opens with a humorous analysis of the role of missionaries in Africa, characterized by the Scot, Mr. Rankin, "a convinced son of the Free Church, and the North African Mission" (601). Shaw alludes to the serious involvement of Scottish missionaries against the slave trade (607), but also undermines their religious impact on the natives, revealing that after twenty-five years' residence in Morocco, Rankin has yet to make one convert (604). Two British tourists, Lady Cicely Waynflete and her brother-in-law, Sir Howard Hallam, an eminent judge, soon arrive. Shaw modeled Lady Cicely in part on Mary Kingsley, whose *Travels in West Africa* (1897) described her intrepid and unconventional voyages.[18] In notes and letters on the play, Shaw also refers to Henry Stanley's *In Darkest Africa* (1890), Sir Richard Burton's translation of *The Arabian Nights* (1885–1888), and R. B. Cunninghame Graham's *Mogreb-el-Acksa* (Morocco the Most Holy, 1898) as influential source texts which contributed to the tone of the drama and the exoticism of its setting.[19]

Shaw proceeds to establish Lady Cicely as an ideal imperialist, who, by counteracting all traditional procedures for dealing with the natives, succeeds in establishing superior, peaceful relations with everyone. "Why do people get killed by savages? Because instead of being polite to them, and saying, Howdyedo? like me, people aim pistols at them. Ive been among savages—cannibals and all sorts. Everybody said theyd kill me. But when I met them, I said Howdyedo? and they were quite nice. The kings always wanted to marry me" (617). Her actual encounters with Sheikh Sidi el Assif and the Cadi of Kintafi in act II are almost incidental to the main plot, however, for Shaw directs our attention primarily to the developing relationship of Lady Cicely and their guide in the Atlas Mountains, the dark and mysterious Captain Brassbound.

Through exposition, we learn that the Captain, also known as Black Paquito, is the son of a Brazilian woman who gave him this nickname as a child in the West Indies (606). Brassbound has also served under Charles Gordon, the recently martyred British antislave crusader, in Khartoum (607), giving him a colorful and romantic history. Through a series of slightly contrived coincidences of the well-made play variety, it turns out that Brassbound is the rightful heir to a West Indian sugar plantation seized by Sir Howard from dishonest agents after the untimely demise of his brother Miles. Brassbound is, in fact, Sir Howard's nephew, the son of Miles and his wife, the unnamed Brazilian woman. Brassbound's prime motive is now to seek revenge on Sir Howard for the disenfranchisement and subsequent death of his mother, while Lady Cicely's becomes dissuasion of Brassbound from this plan and his conversion to her form of civilized British attitudes and behavior.

Many critics of *Captain Brassbound's Conversion* have observed the historical connections of the play to British imperial concerns of the time,[20] having taken their cue from Shaw himself, who explained in a letter to Ellen Terry, the actress for whom he had written Lady Cicely:

> I . . . give you a play in which you stand in the very place where Imperialism is most believed to be necessary, on the border line where the European meets the fanatical African, with the judge on the one hand, and indomitable adventurer-filibuster on the other, said in-adv-fil pushing forward "civilization." . . . I try to shew you

fearing nobody and managing them all as Daniel managed the lions, not by cunning . . . but by simple moral superiority.[21]

Shaw's creation of Lady Cicely as a figure of moral superiority, upholding imperial values, stands unchallenged by scholars who see her as one of the playwright's strong, noble, independent women.[22] Critics accept Lady Cicely's views and techniques as idealized contrasts to the conventional modes of Christian crusaders and the legal system, represented by Rankin and Hallam. They do not question the conversion, its methods, its assumptions, or its implications. According to Maurice Valency, for example:

> The conversion of Captain Brassbound involves a comic reappraisal of justice and contrasts the working of private and public vengeance, to the obvious detriment of both. . . . In this play the hero is . . . in revolt against what he conceives to be a corrupt and evil system. . . . When the facts of Brassbound's life are examined in the cold light of reason, it turns out, however, that he is an avenger without a motive. The villain he is pursuing is not a villain; the stolen plantation was worthless; the oppressed mother was a woman unworthy of sympathy.[23]

The "cold light of reason" which Valency and other critics use to dismiss Brassbound's anger and the situation of his mother merits closer examination, however. In his notes to the play, Shaw claims the "story of the West Indian estate" came from "Mr Frederick Jackson of Hindhead . . . through an attempt to make the House of Commons act on [the case]. This being so, I must add that the character of Captain Brassbound's mother, like the recovery of the estate by the next heir, is an interpolation of my own. It is not, however, an invention" (690). Shaw tantalizingly does not clarify his comments further, suggesting that some other source lies behind these components of the drama.

Shaw does allude to Dickens's *Bleak House* (690) here, however, which raises the possibility that he may have been thinking of other nineteenth-century novels. His story of the mad West Indian wife provocatively echoes that of Bertha Mason, in Charlotte Brontë's *Jane Eyre*. Gayatri Spivak, in her reading of this novel, makes several observations equally pertinent for Shaw's play:

> . . . feminist individualism in the age of imperialism, is precisely the
> making of human beings, the constitution and "interpellation" of
> the subject not only as individual but as "individualist." This stake
> is represented on two registers: childbearing and soul making. . . .
> the second is the imperialist project cathected as civil-society-
> through-social mission. As the female individualist . . . articulates
> herself in shifting relationship to what is at stake, the "native fe-
> male" as such . . . is excluded from any share in this emerging
> norm. If we read this account from an isolationist perspective in
> a "metropolitan" context, we see nothing there but the psycho-
> biography of the militant female subject.[24]

In other words, with Shaw's play, as with criticism of Brontë's novel, the
"native female" is excluded from significant consideration, while the
"militant female subject," in this case Lady Cicely, appears to be the social and moral heroine. Spivak maintains that "Bertha's function in *Jane
Eyre* is to render indeterminate the boundary between human and animal
and thereby to weaken her entitlement under the spirit if not the letter of
the Law."[25]

Shaw's depiction of the nameless Brazilian mother surely functions
similarly. In act II, Brassbound is forced to reveal that his mother had "a
very violent temper" (646), that she went mad, and that she drank (641).
Sir Hallam, who did not help her regain the land that belonged to her
husband, although he later seized it for himself, acknowledges "her case
was a hard one—perhaps the hardest that has come within even my experience" (640). When Lady Cicely asks, "Couldnt you have helped her,
Howard?" he replies: "No. This man may be ignorant enough to suppose
that when I was a struggling barrister I could do everything I did when
I was Attorney General. You know better. There is some excuse for his
mother. She was an uneducated Brazilian, knowing nothing of English
society, and driven mad by injustice" (641). What Lady Cicely later reveals she "knows better" is that although he "says he couldnt" help the
woman, "perhaps the real reason was that he didnt like her" (647).

Lady Cicely tries to turn Brassbound away from maternal identification
and its code of vengeance. Although he claims, "I have no relations.
I had a mother: that was all" (644), she insists, "I daresay you have your
mother's complexion. But didnt you notice Sir Howard's temper, his dog-

gedness, his high spirit . . . Didnt you recognize yourself in that?" (644).
Lady Cicely hypocritically, yet unconsciously, uses the same attribute—
temper—employed to condemn the native mother to form a bond with
the British Hallams. At the same time, she attempts to convince him that
his preferred racial identity is no more than skin deep. Within the larger
framework of the play, Brassbound stands out as the greatest racial threat
to imperial dominance. Although Lady Cicely treats everyone the same,
she clearly recognizes difference, and her sense of British superiority facili-
tates this removed semblance of egalitarianism. But Brassbound, the symbol of racial indeterminacy, must be controlled—must be transformed
into a Hallam so that "proper" distinctions within the social order can be
maintained. As in *Jane Eyre*, there is here "the general epistemic violence
of imperialism, the construction of a self-immolating colonial subject for
the glorification of the social mission of the colonizer." [26]

In the final scene between Lady Cicely and Brassbound in act III, she
attempts to complete the conversion. She encourages him to come to England, "to make the most of [his] opportunities" (684). "Dont you understand that when you are the nephew of a great bigwig, and have influential connexions, and good friends among them, lots of things can be done
for you that are never done for ordinary ship captains? . . . In my world,
which is now your world—*our* world—getting patronage is the whole
art of life. A man cant have a career without it" (684–685). She also succeeds in manipulating him into the destruction of the last vestiges of his
maternal connection, the letters and the portrait, which he rips up, "now
that [Lady Cicely has] taken the meaning out of them" (682–683). Lady
Cicely leaves Brassbound in a void, having destroyed his sense of identity
through the elimination of the "native" component of his self. Shaw shifts
the tone of the final moments of the play with a proposal scene between
the two, but it is nevertheless an ambiguous ending. [27]

Reading *Captain Brassbound's Conversion* primarily as a study of conventions of justice and morality with an imperial backdrop recapitulates
the obliviousness to the colonial subject that inheres in the fate of the
nameless Brazilian mother within the play. Surely Shaw intends a certain
irony in his title, with the legal meaning of conversion, "the unlawful appropriation of another's property," [28] consciously present. Might we not
extend the sense of property to include one's sense of self and read the
play as a dark example of the imposition of British identity and values

on the Other, with its concomitant elimination of native culture, under imperialism?

Related issues of religious conflict and land conversion also inform *John Bull's Other Island* (1907),[29] Shaw's first dramatic work on the Irish Question. Set against a backdrop of Gladstonian politics and the issue of Home Rule, the drama explores the impact on Ireland of recent changes in the position of tenant farmers, tensions between Catholic and Protestant views of the country's future, and the relative merits of native, as opposed to English, leadership. In his lengthy "Preface For Politicians," attached to the play in 1906, Shaw seems very aware of the attitudes of British leaders, summarized later by historian James Morris: "In the imperial context, set beside the marvels of African expansion, . . . Ireland's anxieties seemed nagging and parochial."[30] Thus, Shaw takes care to establish parallels between events and conditions in Ireland and those in India and Egypt, including a long, graphic discussion of the Denshawai affair—the recent massacre of innocent Egyptian natives by British soldiers after a conflict during a pigeon-shooting party—presented "by way of object-lesson" for "countries [like Ireland] which are denied Home Rule" (38).

The play itself treats these concerns far less violently, focusing humorously on the colorful residents of Rosscullen. They welcome home Larry Doyle, the son of the local rent-turned-mortgage collector, after an eighteen-year absence spent establishing himself as an engineer in London. Doyle arrives with his business partner, Tom Broadbent, a robust Englishman who believes "there are great possibilities for Ireland. Home Rule will work wonders under English guidance" (81). Broadbent, swept away by the fantasy of Irish romanticism, quickly finds Doyle his opponent: the latter wants nothing to do with the Irish imagination and its avoidance of hard reality (81), which Shaw links in his preface to William Butler Yeats's neo-Gaelic movement and the Irish Literary Theatre (7).

Shaw weaves together two plot lines in *John Bull's Other Island*, one public and one private. The first centers on the selection of a candidate for Parliament in the upcoming Rosscullen election—a position Larry Doyle declines, but which intrigues Broadbent, who decides to run as a Liberal Home Ruler with plans to develop the area into a tourist attraction. Labeled by Father Keegan "the conquering Englishman" (155),

Broadbent epitomizes English hypocrisy and its imperial views toward Ireland, also suggested by the play's title.

Shaw pits Broadbent against Doyle in the private arena as well, structurally unifying the play on all levels. For all eighteen years of Doyle's absence, Nora Reilly has waited for him to return to marry her. Like Lopakhin in Chekhov's *Cherry Orchard*, Doyle has never quite been able to bring himself to propose, however, and Broadbent, unexpectedly smitten, begs Nora for her hand instead, clasping her delicate frame to his expansive chest and marveling at her simplicity and charm (146–148).

The love story clearly attracts audiences for its (melo)dramatic appeal, but there seems to be a more complex dramaturgical rationale for Shaw's incorporation of these two parallel stories. Margery Morgan proposes that Nora is "a figure of Ireland" at strategic points in the drama,[31] but I believe Nora and her relationships to Doyle and Broadbent are designed to function entirely on a symbolic, as well as literal romantic, level. Just as Broadbent stands for blustering British imperialism, so Nora represents the feminized Ireland that England wants to embrace, protect, and dominate, albeit benevolently. Shaw appears acutely aware of the tradition which depicts "the Celtic race . . . [as] an essentially feminine race."[32] His dramatization of Irish concerns corresponds to the theoretical parallels David Cairns and Shaun Richards have recently drawn between "Edward Said's statement of the relations of power inscribed in the discourse of Orientalism . . . [and] Celticism":[33]

> "Orientalism [Celticism] depends for its strategy on . . . flexible positional superiority, which puts the Westerner [Englishman] in a whole series of possible relationships with the Orient [Ireland] without ever losing him the upper hand" [Said, *Orientalism*, 7]. In the discourse of Celticism the positional superiority of the English was guaranteed by the strategic formation of philology and anthropology which both inscribed the Irish as members of a second-order race in relation to the first-order Teutons, represented by the English.[34]

Shaw returns to an English setting with *Misalliance* in order to explore other facets of imperialism from an entirely British perspective. The ar-

rival of Lord Summerhays, a colonial administrator who has just completed twenty-five years of duty in "Jinghiskahn" (134), prompts John
Tarleton, the pro-imperialist manufacturer of underwear and owner of
the above-mentioned Turkish bath, to tie imperialism to education, one
of the key themes of the play: "Good thing the empire. Educates us.
Opens our minds. . . . And civilizes the other chaps. . . . Look at what
the Romans did for Britain! They burst up and had to clear out; but think
of all they taught us! They were the making of us. . . . Thats the good side
of Imperialism: it's unselfish" (150). Behind Tarleton's diatribe here lies
Shaw's ongoing comparison of the Roman empire with current British
imperial activities. Later in the play, he characterizes this in a familiar
way when Gunner, in an obvious allusion to Gibbon, exclaims, "Rome
fell. Babylon fell. Hindhead's turn will come" (176).

In a letter to his friend and fellow Irishman Matthew Edward McNulty,
Shaw revealed, "Gunner is ME,"[35] a parallel that most critics confirm
through Gunner's socialist beliefs and his impecunious position as a low-
level clerk, which Shaw was in his youth. But I believe there is another,
deeper connection at work here that associates Gunner with the imperial
theme of the play. Gunner, the impoverished, lower-class young man, is
clearly an outsider in this world of wealthy week-enders. His manners,
tastes, and behavior have no connections with those of the Tarletons and
their friends, and the class distinction and cultural distance between them
correspond to the kind of apartheid found in colonized areas. Shaw
makes this tie explicit through staging, by involving the central set piece,
the Turkish bath. When Gunner sneaks into the Tarleton house, intent on
shooting Tarleton in revenge for slighting his recently deceased mother,
he hides in the bath to escape detection. When he emerges, he tries to
denounce these upper-crust Britons, but he is forcefully silenced.[36] Shaw
physically links Gunner with the image of the Orient, the bath, as he
transforms him into an oppressed Other. By connecting Gunner with
himself, Shaw also binds him to another colonized people, the Irish,
thereby establishing a network of polarized social groups that all feel the
force of imperial domination.

In this depiction of class division in *Misalliance*, Shaw echoes another
facet of the imperial discourse of his time—one which had begun to relate
conditions in the colonies abroad to the life of the poor at home. In 1890,
Henry Stanley published his views of native life, *In Darkest Africa*,[37] which

was extremely influential, spawning numerous corollaries throughout the late Victorian/Edwardian era, including General William Booth's study *In Darkest England*. Booth notes:

> This summer the attention of the civilised world has been arrested by the story which Mr Stanley has told of 'Darkest Africa.' . . . It is a terrible picture, and one that has engraved itself deep on the heart of civilization. But while brooding over the awful presentation of life as it exists in the vast African forest, it seemed to me only too vivid a picture of many parts of our own land. As there is a darkest Africa is there not also a darkest England? . . . May we not find a parallel at our own doors, and discover within a stone's throw of our cathedrals and palaces similar horrors to those which Stanley has found? [38]

Shaw shared his concern with the condition of the underclass with many of his fellow Fabians. Yet it is only in post-1900, post–*Fabianism and the Empire* dramas that the connection Booth draws also appears in Shaw's work. In the 1913 *Pygmalion*,[39] written only a few years after *Misalliance*, Shaw again depicts upper-middle-class domestic settings and a visiting colonial administrator. Colonel Pickering, recently returned from India, describes himself as "a student of Indian dialects" (21), a detail which links him with the tradition of Orientalist philologists that Edward Said describes as central to the long-lived images of the East. According to Said,

> As a scholarly attitude the picture of a learned Westerner surveying as if from a peculiarly suited vantage point the . . . seminal, feminine . . . East, then going on to *articulate* the East, making the Orient deliver up its secrets under the learned authority of a philologist whose power derives from the ability to unlock secret, esoteric languages—this would persist [well into the Victorian era].[40]

From a pragmatic viewpoint, imperial policy explicitly connected language with the successful transfer of the dominant culture: "The Education of the Native was one of the basic purposes of . . . imperialism, and the British had long ago decided that a Western education was the only kind worth giving him. . . . From this conception had sprung the use of English in public instruction in the Empire." [41]

Thomas Macaulay, the author of this educational mandate, believed that "the literature now extant in [English] is of far greater value than all the literature which 300 years ago was extant in all the languages of the earth put together."[42] This view is echoed in Henry Higgins's admonition to Eliza: "Remember . . . that your native language is the language of Shakespear and Milton and the Bible" (19–20). Eliza, the cockney guttersnipe, must learn *that* language—Standard British English—and its attendant culture if she is to succeed in her goal of attaining status in British society.

Shaw once again ties his drama to imperial concerns in his preface to the play, which tells the story of Henry Sweet, a phoneticist whom Shaw admired and on whom he partly based the character of Higgins. According to Shaw, "Once in the days when the Imperial Institute rose in South Kensington, and Joseph Chamberlain was booming the Empire, I induced the editor of a leading monthly review to commission an article from Sweet on the imperial importance of his subject" (6). The article Sweet produced, unfortunately, was not appropriate, having nothing to do with the proposed topic, and Shaw "had to renounce [his] dream of dragging its author into the limelight" (6). Or did he? In the refiguration of Sweet as Higgins, I believe Shaw realized the political behind the personal agenda, that is, producing a document on the imperial importance of linguistics and language education to promote and disseminate British culture. Positioned between the representations of colonial policy in India and domestic British culture, Eliza emerges as a lighter image of the parallel between underclass and colonial natives in "Darkest England" and "Darkest Africa," while the play as a whole suggests Shaw's ongoing concern with current imperial practices at home and abroad.

As world conflict, historically linked to Western imperial rivalries, appeared increasingly likely, Shaw began work on *Heartbreak House*, his class-specific study of "cultured, leisured Europe before the war" (7). Suffused with an aura of imminent upheaval, *Heartbreak House* depicts the lives of upper-crust Britons at the outbreak of the Great War. In the preface to the play, Shaw notes, "When the play was begun not a shot had been fired; and only the professional diplomatists and the very few amateurs whose hobby is foreign policy even knew that the guns were loaded" (7). Historian Bernard Porter presents a similar analysis of British foreknowledge of the impending conflict: "Via Turkey and Morocco and the Balkans, Germany since the 1890s had steered a steady course, which was bound eventually to bring her into collision with Britain. Imperialists had been warning their countrymen of this for some time."[43] Porter goes on to put the war in a specifically imperial context:

> . . . the war when it broke out was clearly . . . a war for the preservation of the empire. . . . There were campaigns outside Europe which were overtly colonial . . . in the middle east against Germany's ally, the Ottoman empire. . . . If the Allies won, large areas of the underdeveloped world would come again on to the open market: the German colonies, and the remaining dominions of the Ottoman empire.[44]

Shaw, who may well have considered himself one of these "amateurs in foreign policy," shows clear cognizance of the relative distance in his characters' minds between these imperial issues and their own comfortable lives. "Sir Hastings Utterword, who has been governor of all the crown colonies in succession" (55), is offstage "in a remote part of the Empire" (53) throughout the play, indicating his degree of remove from their consciousness. Yet, as noted earlier, Shaw places Hector Hushabye in Arab costume for half the play, a detail which suggests he wants imperial concerns to have greater centrality.

Hector's outfit, which he finds "ridiculous" but wears because his wife "thinks [him] absurd in evening dress" (132), symbolically represents his position at the center of an inverted seraglio fantasy, the "Arab" male surrounded by a bevy of desirous English women.[45] But at this historical moment, with its conflicting European interests in the Arab world and the potential impact of that conflict's proximity to British colonies, Shaw surely intends a greater meaning in his choice of costume. By bringing an image of the Arab world into the latter half of *Heartbreak House*, just as the realities of the war begin to have an impact on the characters, Shaw demonstrates how awareness of imperial issues must come into prominence, despite their seeming disruption of the insularity of British taste, thought, and concerns.

Shaw criticism thus far seems to reflect traditional scholarly assumptions about imperialism as an unproblematic element of Western history; Shavians have not discussed the wealth of imperial details in his writing because they have not considered them anything other than backdrops for the domestic concerns they feel dominate his dramaturgy and thus merit their analysis. But an examination of Shaw's preoccupation with the empire may disrupt conventional views of his role as a political iconoclast and progressive socialist. Charting the development of Shaw's attitudes toward British imperialism may necessitate a revised view of the politics of his drama: the evidence from *Fabianism and the Empire* and these and other plays suggests a more complicated, conflicted, and conservative position within the political status quo.

NOTES

I wish to express my thanks to David A. Faulkner for his editorial assistance.

1. Gayatri Chakravorty Spivak, "Three Women's Texts and a Critique of Imperialism," in *"Race," Writing and Difference*, ed. Henry Louis Gates, Jr. (Chicago: University of Chicago Press, 1986), 262–280.

2. George Bernard Shaw, *Misalliance*, in *Misalliance and the Fascinating Foundling* (Harmondsworth: Penguin Books, 1984), 113. All references are to this edition, hereafter cited in the text.

3. Shaw's fellow Irishman James Joyce used a roughly contemporaneous setting for the "Lotus Eaters" chapter of *Ulysses*, which links the exotic Orient with a Turkish bath. Bloom muses on "the far east" with its "Cinghalese lobbing about in the sun" and its "waterlilies," then decides it is "time to get a bath round the corner. . . . Turkish," details which suggest the strong ongoing connection of the object with its European origin (Joyce, *Ulysses* [New York: Vintage Books, 1986], 58–69). For a discussion of the relation of Turkish and European material culture, including details about Turkish baths, see V. G. Kiernan, *The Lords of Human Kind: Black Man, Yellow Man and White Man in an Age of Empire* (New York: Columbia University Press, 1986), 133–134.

4. George Bernard Shaw, *Heartbreak House: A Fantasia in the Russian Manner on English Themes* (New York: Penguin Books, 1977), 114. All references are to this edition, hereafter cited in the text.

5. Edward W. Said, *Orientalism* (New York: Vintage Books, 1979).

6. J. L. Wisenthal, *Shaw's Sense of History* (Oxford: Clarendon Press, 1988), 158–159.

7. Martin Meisel, *Shaw and the Nineteenth-Century Theatre* (New York: Limelight Editions, 1984).

8. Margery Morgan, *The Shavian Playground: An Exploration of the Art of George Bernard Shaw* (London: Methuen, 1972), 271n.

9. Michael Holroyd, *The Pursuit of Power 1898–1913*, vol. 2 of *Bernard Shaw* (New York: Random House, 1989), 40.

10. Holroyd, 40.

11. Holroyd, 40.

12. George Bernard Shaw (ed.), *Fabianism and the Empire: A Manifesto by the Fabian Society* (London: Grant Richards, 1900), 23–24.

13. Harry Magdoff, *Imperialism: From the Colonial Age to the Present* (New York: Monthly Review Press, 1978), 151.

14. George Bernard Shaw, *Caesar and Cleopatra* (Baltimore: Penguin Books, 1974). All references are to this edition, hereafter cited in the text.

15. Samuel Hynes, *The Edwardian Turn of Mind* (Princeton: Princeton University Press, 1968), 17.

16. Sir C. P. Lucas, *Greater Rome and Greater Britain* (Oxford: Clarendon Press, 1912), 9.

17. George Bernard Shaw, *Captain Brassbound's Conversion: An Adventure in Three Acts*, in *Complete Plays with Prefaces* (New York: Dodd, Mead, 1962), 1:599–694. All references are to this edition, hereafter cited in the text.

18. For a detailed analysis of the relationship of Lady Cicely to Mary Kingsley, see Stanley Weintraub's "Shaw's Lady Cicely and Mary Kingsley," in *The Unexpected Shaw: Biographical Approaches to G. B. S. and His Work* (New York: Frederick Ungar, 1982), 105–110.

19. George Bernard Shaw, *Collected Letters 1898–1910*, ed. Dan H. Laurence (London: Max Reinhardt, 1972), 98; *Captain Brassbound's Conversion*, 653, 688.

20. See Holroyd, 21; Meisel, 206–211; and Ina Rae Hark, "Lady Cicely, I Presume: Converting the Heathen, Shavian Style," *Shaw* 1 (1981): 57–73.

21. Shaw, *Collected Letters 1898–1910*, 98–99.

22. See, for example, Barbara Bellow Watson, *The Shavian Guide to the Intelligent Woman* (New York: W. W. Norton, 1972), 68–74. Watson categorizes Lady Cicely as a "Saving Woman," highlighting her "spiritual independence" and her "intelligent virtue . . . puritan virtue . . . [and] aristocratic virtue."

23. Maurice Valency, *The Cart and the Trumpet: The Plays of George Bernard Shaw* (New York: Oxford University Press, 1973), 192.

24. Spivak, 263–264.

25. Spivak, 268.

26. Spivak, 270.

27. Valency, 192.

28. William Morris (ed.), *The American Heritage Dictionary of the English Language*, s.v. "conversion" (Boston: Houghton Mifflin, 1969), 291.

29. George Bernard Shaw, *John Bull's Other Island* (Harmondsworth: Penguin Books, 1984). All references are to this edition, hereafter cited in the text.

30. James Morris, *Pax Britannica: The Climax of an Empire* (New York: Harcourt, Brace and World, 1968), 461.

31. Morgan, 128.

32. Ernest Renan, quoted in David Cairns and Shaun Richards, *Writing Ireland:*

Colonialism, Nationalism and Culture (Manchester: Manchester University Press, 1988), 46.

33. Cairns and Richards, 47.

34. Cairns and Richards, 47–48.

35. George Bernard Shaw, *Collected Letters 1911–1925*, ed. Dan H. Laurence (London: Max Reinhardt, 1985), 233.

36. Note the similarity of plot here to that of *Captain Brassbound's Conversion*, with the parallel outcome for the outsider figure.

37. One of the texts referred to in Shaw's commentary on *Captain Brassbound's Conversion*.

38. William Booth, "Why Darkest England?" in *In Darkest England and the Way Out* (1890), reprinted in *Into Unknown England 1866–1913: Selections from the Social Explorers*, ed. Peter Keating (Manchester: Manchester University Press, 1976), 141–142, 145.

39. George Bernard Shaw, *Pygmalion: A Romance in Five Acts* (New York: Penguin Books, 1982). All references are to this edition, hereafter cited in the text.

40. Said, 137–138.

41. Morris, 140.

42. James Morris, *Heaven's Command: An Imperial Progress* (New York: Harcourt Brace Jovanovich, 1973), 76.

43. Bernard Porter, *The Lion's Share: A Short History of British Imperialism 1850–1983*, 2nd ed. (London: Longman, 1987), 233.

44. Porter, 234–235.

45. I am grateful to Stanley Kauffmann for suggesting this interpretation. For a discussion of European male fascination with the Arab harem, see Kiernan, 131–138.

Deconstruction

Constructing Patroclus

The High and Low Discourses of Renaissance Sodomy

GREGORY W. BREDBECK

My attitude toward anyone's sexual persuasion is this: without deviation from the norm, progress is not possible.
—Frank Zappa

Sodomy during the Renaissance was both done and written; frequently it was written more interestingly than it was done. For while the act of sodomy is constrained by certain physical exigencies—one can only *do* so much with what one *has*—the discursive encoding of it reveals a vast and sometimes self-contradictory canon of writing that spans arenas from law and lexicography to arcadian romance, biblical exegesis, and broadside pornography. Much criticism has reduced this transversal canon to its most rarefied or conservatively controlled ideologies.[1] Even an enlightened scholar such as Alan Bray, who recognizes a plurality of ways that homoeroticism was expressed during the Renaissance, posits this plurality as a response to one impetus, a monolithic and unavoidable ideological inscription of moral stigmatism: "[The individual drawn to homosexuality] was faced with more than the naked fact of that intense disapproval: he had also to contend with its widely accepted integration into the way the scheme of things was understood and into the Christianity of his time. It was this dimension which was the iron in the problem, especially as that view of things was probably something he shared himself."[2] For Bray, the rhetoric of Renaissance sodomy is fully inscriptive—fully able both to mandate and to control the possible meanings of its subject.

There is a strong case to be made for this stigmatized reading of Renaissance sodomy. Throughout the Renaissance, a large number of derogatory terms became associated with homoeroticism: pathic, cinaedus, catamite, buggerer, ingle, sodomite;[3] and legal writings of the time express a definite attitude of abhorrence. James I, in advising his son on the ideal tenets of a prince, labels sodomy (along with witchcraft, willful murder, incest, and counterfeiting) as one of the "horrible crimes that yee are bound in conscience never to forgive."[4] Edward Coke, in the *Reports*, ascribes sodomy to the realm of "sorcerers, sodomers, and heretics."[5] Francis Meres's *Palladis Tamia* labels sodomy as "unlawful, because it is against kinde,"[6] and the prosecutor in the trial of Mervin Touchet, the earl of Castlehaven, who was tried for sodomy in 1631, states, "As for the *Crimen Sodomiticum*, in the second Indictment, I shall not Paraphrase upon it, since *it is of so abominable and Vile a Nature*, that as the Indictment truly expresses it, *Crimen inter Christianos non nominandum*, it is a crime not to be named among Christians."[7] In all of these examples, as in much criticism written about them, homoeroticism is contained within a mythology of the unnatural, the alien, and the demonic.

Certainly this mythology is what is said, but the means of saying it indicates the peculiar epistemological status of Renaissance homoeroticism. *Contra naturam*: against nature—this legal codification current throughout the sixteenth and seventeenth centuries suggests more than condemnation. For if nature is, as Thomas Browne would later summarize the commonplace, "the universall public manuscript of God,"[8] then to be against nature is to be against significance, against, in its most philosophical form, signification and meaning. The rhetoric of Renaissance sexual legislation ascribes a devalued position to sodomy within the hierarchy of sexual meaning, but at the same time also suggests the limited margins of this hierarchy by metaphorically associating sodomy with spaces uninscribed by these social schemata. While the language of sodomy attempts to territorialize illicit behavior in behalf of such normative schemata as nature and language, it at the same time betrays these schemata by suggesting epistemological realms that remain Other to their own totalizing goals. When at play within a culture, subjected to, as Michel Foucault would call them, the "apparatuses" that solidify power and efface discrepancies,[9] the importance of this epistemological double-bind fades. But when *dis*played on the stage—that is, both anatomized through performance and cut free from the social cables that moor it—the rhetoric of sodomy becomes a powerful hermeneutic tool for examining the relationship between the raw material of society and the process of cultural self-narration that arises from it.

My topic in this essay is one such theatrical example, Shakespeare's *Troilus and Cressida*. This play exploits the bifurcated potentiality encoded in Renaissance sodomy, for it at once teaches us to read the stigmatized sodomite of Renaissance ideology and at the same time teaches us to reread ideology through the figure of sodomy; in the process it demonstrates that the language of Renaissance sodomy was neither absolute nor monolithic, but rather encoded discrepancies and contradictions that were subject to exploitation by the very culture it sought to contain.

SATIRE AND THE CONSTRUCTION OF SODOMY

In the play, Thersites, the "scurrilous and deformed" Greek, labels Patroclus as "Achilles' brach," "Achilles' male varlet," and Achilles' "masculine whore" (V.i.14−16).[10] Coming from the base railer of the Greeks, such gibes, perhaps, are easily elided or attributed to the deformities of the cur's mind. Thersites is, after all, the first to call Cressida a whore, the first to associate Pandarus the man with the derogatory term "pander," and the first to remove Menelaus and Paris from the level of military heroes to the level of "the cuckold and the cuckold-maker" (V.vii.9); the mind of Thersites is as he describes the world of the play: "Lechery, lechery, still wars and lechery! Nothing else holds fashion" (V.iii.163−165). Despite this propensity for the base, Thersites' participation in the rhetoric of Renaissance sodomy has seldom been noted.[11] The silencing of Thersites' sodomitical gibes is more than the *ex post facto* moralizing of current criticism; it is also a process of emendation that disengages the play from the cultural constructions it seeks to critique. For Thersites' rhetoric specifically draws on the tropics of Renaissance satire—a genre that vividly displays the interrelatedness of sodomy and the construction of social order.

The prevalence of homoerotic allusions within Renaissance satires is easily documented. Richard Brathwaite, for example, dedicates his *Strappado for the Divell* to "Ladies, Monkies, Parachitoes, Mar- / mosites, and Catamitoes." [12] His *Heroycke Embleme upon the Warriour Called Honora* also derides "Romane Catamites, / Inventresses of pleasures." [13] John Donne, in his first satire, returns to these sodomitical tropics to slur the dandy "that dost not onely approve, / But in ranke itchie lust, desire, and love / The nakedness and bareness to enjoy, / Of thy plumpe muddy whore, or prostitute boy." [14] The two Middletons, Richard and Thomas, each engage the mode; Thomas's *Blacke Booke* chastises "this neast of Gallants" who "keepe at every heele a man, beside a French Lackey, . . . and an English Page which filles up the place of an Ingle," and Richard's *Epigrams and Satyres* describes the drunken Longatoe who, "like a Catamite, kist all the men about him, / While they laught at his follie and did flout him." [15] The writer who is today perhaps the most famous of all the Renaissance satirists, John Marston, also provides the most numerous examples of satire's affinity for sodomitical allusions. *The Scourge of Villanie* attacks at various points "some pedant Tutor" who "in his bed / Should use my frie, like Phrigian *Ganimede*," "yon effeminate sanguine *Ganimede*" who "is but a bever, hunted for the bed," Luscus, who "hath his *Ganimede*, / His perfum'd she-goat, smooth kembd & high fed," "yon gallant in the sumptuous clothes" who shows a propensity for "sodome beast-lines," and another gallant who has a "*Ganimede* . . . that doth grace / [his] heeles. . . . / One *who for two daies space / Is closely hyred.*" [16]

In all of these examples the recourse to homoeroticism is part of a larger strategy of social exclusion. Through the pejorative display of social deviance, satires such as these attempt to isolate and expel elements that threaten the integrity of orthodox social structures. [17] Satires are, as Richard Brathwaite terms them, "Carefull preservers of our Memorie" that preserve orthodox social order: [18] "When the natures of men are deere perverted, then it is high time for the Satyrist to pen something which may divert them from their impietie, and direct them in the course and progresse of Vertue."[19] Satire becomes, then, a genre that seeks to preserve, to use Thomas Middleton's phrase, "the civil Ranck of sober and continent Livers."[20] In all of these formulations satire is a social regulator that vividly displays exemplars of "low" or deviant modes that, by contrast, solidify the "high" or orthodox modes that are not present, but are clearly invoked through a contradistinction; and in the process it enacts a social stratification, a system in which "bad" is ascribed, "good" is implied, and order is achieved.[21]

It is helpful to think of the satiric mode as something similar to what Stephen Mullaney has recently termed "a rehearsal of culture,"[22] in that these satires provide spaces in which the Renaissance culture could manipulate or "play" with its own self-constructed identity. Satires provide a particularly effective stage for such rehearsals, for, in addition to their internal stratification of high and low, they also situate themselves within such a hierarchy, clearly labeling themselves as Other to the higher realms of order and orthodoxy; while satires label what *is* base, they also label themselves *as* base.[23] Brathwaite claims that his poems are "portraide by a lesse art-ful fist," and further claims of every satirist that "th'lines he writes (if ought he writes at all) / Are drawne by inke that's mixed most with gall."[24] Marston, at various places, derides his poetry as "base ballad stuff," "serius iest, and iesting seriosnes" written in "rough-hew'd rimes," and "idle rimes" "in such shapeless formes, / That want of Art."[25] Established as the base, gross, and low, satire in turn becomes a discursive arena in which the low can be constructed with no possibility whatsoever that it will infiltrate the high.

The parallels between satire as a genre and Thersites as a character are obvious, and it is probably not too farfetched to label Thersites as a personification of satire. Thersites' penchant for lechery manages to replicate almost the entire inventory of standard satiric topics. Moreover, Thersites himself offers an explanation of his purpose that seems to imitate those of other satirists. As he says, "With too much blood and too little brain these two may run mad, but if with too much brain and too little blood they do, *I'll be the curer of madmen*" (V.i.47–49, my emphasis). Most importantly, while Thersites doggedly pursues the identification of the low, he himself is also devalued. Like the grotesque genre of satire, Thersites is a grotesque character, a bastard "scurrilous and deformed," a "vinewd'st leaven" and "whoreson cur" (II.i.14, 42), as Ajax calls him. The importance of Thersites' physical appearance is clarified by the words of another satirist, Philip Stubbes, who, in *The Anatomie of Abuses*, offers this formula that is a commonplace in satires: "If the least or meanest member of thy whole body be hurt, wounded, cicatrized, or brused, doeth not the heart, and every member of the body, feele the anguish and payne of the greeved parte, seeking and endevoring, by all meanes possible . . . , to repaire the same, and never ioying untill it be restored againe to his former integrity and perfection?"[26] The deformed outward shape is symbolic of an *entire* deformity. Like satirists, who cast their poems as devalued discourses, the play casts Thersites as a devalued speaker, a character whose very body imitates the decayed and bilious genre of the satire.[27]

Thersites, then, is presented in discursive and generic terms specifically designed to draw attention to the sodomitical references that criticism has effaced. Moreover, the play uses this association to critique the strategies of hierarchicalization implicit in the genre. Initially this critique consists of engendering a space between the rhetoric of Thersites' accusations and the events they propose to explain. Thersites' gibes label Patroclus as a catamite, but the actuality of the play's world more frequently finds him heroic, or at least politic. The play presents Patroclus in the role of mediator, placating Thersites and arbitrating Ajax's headstrong combat with the railer (II.i). Moreover, when Patroclus dies, he dies in an almost epic catalogue of heroes presented by Agamemnon (V.v.6–14). The juxtaposition of Thersites' sodomitical Patroclus to this more heroic Patroclus begins to suggest a critique of satire and its strategies of social hierarchicalization. For if the image of a debased Patroclus is false, then the hierarchy of high and low achieved in Thersites' railing must also be false. This skepticism toward stratification assumes an even more important level in the play than simply casting doubt on Thersites' commentary. Thersites constructs an image of Patroclus that is an absolute Other to orthodox order—an otherness achieved through the construction of Patroclus as a sodomite—and the play in turn radically critiques this order by demonstrating that this image is not just a part of the low satiric idioms, but is also central to the high political machinations of the Greeks.

SODOMY AND THE DECONSTRUCTION OF ORDER

The intersection of Thersites' low discourse and the high orders of the
Greek world occurs, importantly, in the most discursively ordered scene
in the play, the famous Greek Council scene (I.iii). It begins with a speech
by Agamemnon that echoes political primers of the Jacobean and Elizabethan eras:

> The ample proposition that hope makes
> In all designs begun on earth below
> Fails in the promis'd largeness: checks and disasters
> Grow in the veins of actions highest rear'd,
> As knots, by the conflux of meeting sap,
> Infects the sound pine and diverts his grain
> Tortive and errant from his course of growth. (I.iii.3–9)

In contrast to Thersites' genre, which focuses specifically on deviations
and affronts to order, Agamemnon speaks a language of absolute order, one in which seemingly gratuitous "checks and disasters" are, like
knots in a pine, part of a divine design. Aberrations are puzzling only
from the "earth below"; from a proper vantage point, the hierarchy gov-
erning the world is a perfectly coherent text; for, as Agamemnon further
states, the problems facing the Greeks are "but the protractive trials of
great Jove / To find persistive constancy in men" (I.iii.20–21).

Agamemnon's speech has been compared to any number of possible
sources—Elyot's *The Governour*, the homily *Of Obedience*, Aristotle's
Ethics, Boethius's *De Consolatione Philosophiae*.[28] Yet the specific source
of the oration is not as important as its status as an example of a topos
that permeated the Elizabethan and Jacobean ethos. Importantly, the
structure of the oration also presents the topos as a contradictory and
inconsistent discourse. In describing the necessity of such "protractive
trials," Agamemnon also unintentionally validates the possibility of a re-
lationally (rather than absolutely) defined world:

> . . . for when the bold and coward,
> The wise and fool, the artist and unread,
> The hard and soft, seem all affin'd and kin;

> But in the wind and tempest of her frown,
> Distinction, with a broad and powerful fan
> Puffing at all, winnows the light away,
> And what hath mass or matter by itself
> Lies rich in virtue and unmingled. (I.iii.23−30)

The strong allegiance to order in Agamemnon's speech masks a recognition of its antithesis: the possibility that all is but chance; as Nestor phrases it, "In the reproof of the chance / Lies the true proof of men" (I.iii.33−34). The end to this "tale of length" about degree is a startlingly relativistic formulation: "Troy in our weakness stands, not in her strength" (I.iii.136). Agamemnon's speech, so often taken as one of the great Shakespearean statements of universal teleology,[29] actually destabilizes the order it professes: there is the precept of order, the praxis of a war unwon, and no way to cohere these disparate themes.

This slippage in the rhetoric of order is also present in the most famous speech of the play, Ulysses' 63-line *amplificatio* of Agamemnon's theme:

> . . . O, when degree is shak'd,
> Which is the ladder of all high designs,
> The enterprise is sick. How could communities,
> Degrees in schools, and brotherhoods in cities,
> Peaceful commerce from individual shores,
> The primogenity and due birth,
> Prerogative of age, crowns, sceptres, laurels,
> But by degree stand in authentic place?
> Take but degree away, untune that string,
> And hark what discord follows. (I.iii.101−110)

Ulysses' rhetoric betrays the same potentiality for slippage present in Agamemnon's speech; for if degree is the necessary precondition for divine hierarchy, then men should be dependent on it, not it on men. Yet Ulysses' formulation seems to imply that order is a function of men's will to have it exist. As he says, "Degree being vizarded, / Th'unworthiest shows as fairly in the mask" (I.iii.83−84). Implicit in this statement is a hidden problem of agency: who does the vizarding? For if Jove controls degree, then it is never vizarded, but only changed into a further "protractive trial"; but if Jove does not control degree, then not everything is ascribed a place in divine hierarchy, and the manifest validity of the hierarchy is negated. This question, indeed, is the simple but fatal indeterminacy underlying the entire scene; the question is: does hierarchy inscribe men, or do men inscribe hierarchy; is order a matter of precept or of praxis? The philosophical problem underlying the Greek council scene, then, is the anxious possibility that precept and praxis are not separate epistemological realms, but rather are arbitrary divisions that randomly intermingle and exist coterminously.

The Greeks' problem, then, is one of muddled ideology, and their strategy for redividing the tenets of their epistemology is, importantly, a recourse to the base idioms of Thersites' sodomitical discourse. The only solution offered to "the sickness found" (I.iii.141) is Ulysses' (re)construction of the catamitical Patroclus:

> The great Achilles, whom opinion crowns
> The sinew and the forehand of our host,
> Having his ear full of airy fame,
> Grown dainty of his worth, and in his tent
> Lies mocking our designs: with him Patroclus
> Upon a lazy bed the livelong day
> Breaks scurril jests,
> And with ridiculous and awkward action,
> Which slanderer, he imitation calls,
> He pageants us. (I.iii.142–151)

This oration depicts Achilles as a debauched man entertaining a minion who basks on the couch and bitchily derides the Greek order. Like Thersites' construction of Patroclus, Ulysses' accusation clearly focuses on homoeroticism as an absolute base Other to the world of order. His condemnation relies on images of imitation and pageantry, all theatrical in nature and hence suggesting a fake or artificial dimension. To him Patroclus is "like a strutting player," one who speaks "with terms unsquar'd" and who uses the stuff of politic order only "to make paradoxes" (I.iii.153, 159, 184). Ulysses' recourse to theatrical metaphors fully inscribes his discourse within the low arenas of satiric sodomy, for throughout the Renaissance satirists intervalidated theatrical derogation and sodomitical stigmatism;[30] Edward Guilpin, to note but one example, derides the "fine fellow" "who is at every play, and every night / Sups with his *Ingles*. . . ."[31]

Ulysses' construction of Patroclus on one level replicates the intentions of Renaissance satire. Like, say, Marston or Brathwaite, Ulysses is "mirroring" a "sickness found" in the hopes of isolating and expelling it. However, the play's careful correlation of Thersites' satiric railing and Ulysses' ordered oration also collapses the empowering division between high and low discursive arenas: Ulysses is not speaking the language of politic order, but rather can be seen as speaking the language of Thersites; Thersites' debased rhetoric, by extension, can be seen not as an Other to order, but as a constituent of it. This collapse is further apparent in the council scene. After Aeneas delivers the battle challenge from Hector, Ulysses begins to form his plan in a distinctly different rhetorical mode: "I have a young conception in my brain: / Be you my time to bring it some shape" (I.iii.311–312). He is no longer delivering an oration about the shape of Platonic order but is now attempting to order a shape for the exigencies of the present moment. Moreover, like Thersites' construction of Patroclus, which ultimately is undercut by the action of the play, Ulysses' construction is also revealed to be at most false, and at least misplaced:

> Blunt wedges rive hard knots; the seeded pride
> That hath to his maturity blown up
> In rank Achilles must or now be cropp'd,
> Or shedding, breed a nursery of like evil
> To overbulk us all. (I.iii.315–319)

The problem is no longer, nor has it ever been, the sexual behavior of Patroclus. The problem is Achilles' "pride"—at least according to Ulysses—and the foregrounding of Patroclus' catamitical possibilities has been merely a convenient "use" of sodomy designed to destroy Achilles.

The personal motive underlying Ulysses' construction of Patroclus, as well as its arbitrariness, is continually foregrounded as Ulysses improvises his plan, and the Greek council gradually abandons its original allegiance to divine order. Nestor recognizes that in the "sportful combat . . . much opinion dwells" (I.iii.335–336), and Ulysses knows that "the lustre of the better shall exceed / By showing the worse first" (I.ii.361–362). Degree is no longer a precept, but is a matter of praxis; in a remarkable tour de force of sophistry, Ulysses explains how the *mutability* of meaning can serve the Greeks in battle:

> What glory our Achilles shares from Hector,
> Were he not proud, we all should share with him;
> But he already is too insolent,
> And it were better parch in Afric sun
> Than in the pride and salt scorn of his eyes,
> Should he 'scape Hector fair. If he were foil'd,
> Why then we did our main opinion crush
> In taint of our best man. No, make a lott'ry,
> And by divide let blockish Ajax draw
> The sort to fight with Hector. Among ourselves
> Give him allowance for the better man;
> For that will physic the great Myrmidon,
> Who broils in loud applause, and make him fall
> His crest that prouder than blue Iris bends.
> If the dull brainless Ajax come safe off,
> We'll dress him up in voices: if he fail,
> Yet go we under our opinion still
> That we have better men. (I.iii.367–384)

Again, this use of teleological slippage serves more of a purpose than merely saving face, for Ulysses ends his advice with his by now redundant theme: "Ajax employ'd plucks down Achilles' plumes" (I.iii.386). And the idea of a rigged lottery provides an ironically deflating embodiment of Nestor's earlier theoretical position that "in the reproof of chance / Lies true proof of men" (I.iii.33–34).

Ulysses' construction of Patroclus leads the Greek world of precept into the mutable world of improvised praxis—the very world that the construction of Patroclus originally sought to efface. The point of Ulysses' "solution," then, is clear: behind the rhetoric of order rests a reliance on chaos; beyond the precept of politic theory is a praxis of mutability and individual difference. Precept and praxis conflate in the play's figure of homoeroticism, for Patroclus the catamite is at once what the Greek world does not want and what it can most fortuitously use. Sodomy and related areas of homoerotic meaning, then, do not just delineate the division between high and low—do not just make the stuff of satire and condemnation; rather, they also demarcate the point at which high and low meet and may be transversed. There is an affinity between the representation of sodomy and the depiction of politic failure, for homoeroticism, a category that both creates and destroys a division between high and low, exists in the artificial but crucial space that teleological theory inserts between precept and praxis, between order and chaos, and between Man and men.

The (re)construction of Patroclus begins to suggest the possible role that stigmatized sodomy might play in the construction of order and, by extension, also suggests the place it might have in current critical practice. The structure of the play presents the discursive construction of order from two perspectives—the low idiom of satire and the high order of politic theory—and then deconstructs the assuredness of these perspectives by demonstrating how they intersect in their uses of sexual difference—an intersection vividly marked by the figure of sodomy. The construction of Patroclus demonstrates the simple but central principle that the articulation of order demands means of accounting for disorder—and these means frequently involve issues of sex, sexuality, and eroticism. Sexual difference functions as an epistemological space that can easily be contorted to account for discrepancies; and this variability of sexual significance is deflatingly exposed in Shakespeare's play. *Troilus and Cressida*, then, might best be thought of as a critical primer: it at once teaches us to read the stigmatized sodomy of Renaissance ideology and at the same time teaches us to recognize the dependency implicit within ideology on what it attempts to banish. And in the process it also empowers us to re*write*, to articulate the forces ordering Renaissance culture in their most fragmented and plural form, to create a hermeneutic that can demonstrate the margins within the centers, the lows within the highs, and the sodomy that helps make "history."

NOTES

Research for this essay was supported by a University of Pennsylvania Dean's Fellowship, a University of Pennsylvania Department of English Penn-in-London

Fellowship, and Intramural and Field Research funds provided by the University of California. I am grateful for helpful comments from Stephen Orgel, Jonathan Crewe, Rebecca Bushnell, Stuart Curran, Phyllis Rackin, and Peter Stallybrass.

1. To date the most comprehensive account of Renaissance homoeroticism is Alan Bray's *Homosexuality in Renaissance England* (London: Gay Men's Press, 1982). Additionally, several critics have begun the lengthy process of situating the topic within the literary and aesthetic dynamics of England and Europe: James Saslow, *Ganymede in the Renaissance: Homosexuality in Art and Society* (New Haven: Yale University Press, 1986)—cf. Francis Ames-Lewis, "Ganymede on Dangerous Ground," *European Gay Review* 4 (1990): 128–134; Joseph Pequigney, *Such Is My Love: A Study of Shakespeare's Sonnets* (Chicago: Chicago University Press, 1987); as well as Stephen Orgel, "Nobody's Perfect: Or Why Did the English Stage Take Boys for Women"; Jonathan Goldberg, "Colin to Hobbinol: Spenser's Familiar Letters"; and Joseph A. Porter, "Marlowe, Shakespeare, and the Canonization of Heterosexuality"—all in *Displacing Homophobia: Gay Male Perspectives in Literature and Culture*, ed. Ronald R. Butters, John M. Clum, and Michael Moon (Durham: Duke University Press, 1989). Throughout the essay I use the terms "homoeroticism" and "sodomy" as they apply to male-male sexual behavior. I am intentionally excluding female-female eroticism so as not to imply that the variable of sexual difference subsumes the material differences engendered in a culture by the man/woman dichotomy. For a fascinating example of the potentialities posited by the historical placement of lesbianism, see Judith Brown's *Immodest Acts: The Life of a Lesbian Nun in Renaissance Italy* (Oxford: Oxford University Press, 1986).

2. Bray, 63.

3. Bray, 13–32.

4. James I, *The Political Works of James I, Reprinted from the Edition of 1616*, ed. Charles Howard McIlwain (Cambridge: Harvard University Press, 1918), 20.

5. Edward Coke, *An Exact Abridgement of the Two Last Volumes of Reports, Entitled the 12th & 13th Parts* (London: Henry and Timothy Twyford, 1670), 36.

6. Francis Meres, *Palladis Tamia, or, Wits Treasury: Being the Second Part of Wits Commonwealth* (London: P. Short, 1598), 322.

7. Anon., *The Tryal and Condemnation of Mervin, Lord Audley Earl of Castle-Haven, at Westminster, April the 5th 1631* (London: n.p., 1699), sig. C2.

8. Thomas Browne, *Religio Medici and Other Works*, ed. L. C. Martin (Oxford: Oxford University Press, 1964), 15.

9. Michel Foucault, *Politics, Philosophy, Culture: Interviews and Other Writings, 1977–1984*, ed. Lawrence D. Kritzman (New York: Routledge, 1988), 111. See also Foucault's *The History of Sexuality, Volume One: An Introduction* (New York: Random House, 1980), 15–50.

10. William Shakespeare, *Troilus and Cressida*, ed. Kenneth Palmer (London:

Methuen, 1982). All citations are hereafter noted in the text by act, scene, and line numbers.

11. Ironically, some very conservative criticism affirms the relationship between Thersites and the discourse of sodomy through the very strength of its denials. Kenneth Palmer's glosses to the Arden edition, for example, eloquently note the sodomitical possibilities of the speeches in their effort to demonstrate how they are invalid (cf. 156, 263). The desire to "read out" the catamitical possibilities of the play is further undermined by the occurrence of both Achilles and Patroclus in the Renaissance lexicography of homoeroticism; see Thomas Cooper's *Bibliotheca Eliotae* ([Londini: n.p., 1552], sig. TTTiii) and Christopher Marlowe's *Edward II*, I.iv.395–396 (*Christopher Marlowe: Complete Plays and Poems*, ed. E. D. Pendry and J. C. Maxwell [London: J. M. Dent and Sons, 1976]).

12. Richard Brathwaite, *A Strappado for the Divell: Epigrams and Satyres Alluding to the Time, with Divers Measures of No Lesse Delight* (London: Richard Redmer, 1615), sig. A9.

13. Brathwaite, 32.

14. John Donne, *Complete Poetry and Selected Prose*, ed. John Hayward (London: Nonesuch Press, 1962), 122.

15. Thomas Middleton, *The Blacke Booke* (London: Ieffrey Chorlton, 1604), sig. C3; Richard Middleton, *Epigrams and Satyres* (London: Nicholas Okes, 1608), 9.

16. John Marston, *The Scourge of Villanie* (London: I. R., 1599), sigs. C5, F3, C4, E6v–E7r, 51.

17. More than almost any other genre, satire has provoked prolonged rumination on the relationship between literary production and social purpose. Even Alastair Fowler, who consistently views literature as a self-referential discourse, recognizes that "a radical moral stance is perhaps the most striking feature of the satiric repertoire" (*Kinds of Literature: An Introduction to the Theory of Genres and Modes* [Cambridge: Harvard University Press, 1982], 110) and additionally claims that it is the social referentiality of satire that has made it one of the most frequently censored genres (215). A similar view can be found in Harry Levin's "The Wages of Satire," in *Literature and Society: Selected Papers from the English Institute, 1978*, ed. Edward W. Said (Baltimore: Johns Hopkins University Press, 1980), 5, 1–14, *passim*.

18. Brathwaite, sig. L5r.

19. Brathwaite, sig. A2.

20. Middleton, *Blacke Booke*, sig. A3.

21. The model of satiric stratification I am proposing is reminiscent of—and indebted to—the model of cultural formation proposed by Mikhail Bakhtin (*Rabelais and His World: Symbolic Inversion in Art and Society* [Ithaca: Cornell University Press, 1981]) and the similar model of cultural maintenance proposed by Mary Douglas (*Purity and Danger: An Analysis of Concepts of Pollution*

and Taboo [London: Routledge and Kegan Paul, 1973]). These theories are elo-quently and influentially synthesized in Peter Stallybrass and Allon White, *The Politics and Poetics of Transgression* (London: Methuen, 1986), which is an ex-tended elaboration of the central thesis that "a fundamental rule [of cultural for-mation] seems to be that what is excluded at the overt level of identity-formation is productive of new objects of desire" (25).

22. Stephen Mullaney, "Strange Things, Gross Terms, Curious Customs: The Rehearsal of Culture in the Late Renaissance," *Representations* 3 (Summer 1983): 53–62.

23. This structure is not original to the Renaissance. It dates at least as far back as Horace, who, in the *Satires* (I.4.39–39), derogates satire as being alien to the *mens divinior*. Cf. C. O. Brink, *Horace on Poetry: Prolegomena to the Literary Epistle* (Cambridge: Cambridge University Press, 1963), 161–163.

24. Brathwaite, 2–3.

25. Marston, sigs. D8, F5, E4v–E5r.

26. Philip Stubbes, *The Anatomie of Abuses* (London: Richard Jones, 1585), 6.

27. Thersites' affinity for the tropics of satiric sodomy is again reinforced by the recurrence of Troy and of Troilus and Cressida as the topics of satires during the Renaissance. For example, Thomas Middleton's *Micro-cynicon* includes a lengthy satire on "Ingling *Pyander*," a title that immediately draws a correlation between the story of Troilus and Cressida and the language of sodomy.

28. Cf. E. M. W. Tillyard, *The Elizabethan World Picture: A Study of the Idea of Order in the Age of Shakespeare, Donne and Milton* (New York: Random House, n.d.), 9–17.

29. Cf. Tillyard, 9–10.

30. In addition to the associations with satire, Ulysses' theatrical metaphor would have carried particularly indecorous connotations in Renaissance minds, since Ulysses quite literally derides Patroclus for being a "boy actor," a problem-atic occupation that carried with it numerous sexual connotations (Lisa Jardine, *Still Harping on Daughters: Women and Drama in the Age of Shakespeare* [Brighton: Harvester Press, 1983], 9–33; Orgel, 7–30).

31. Edward Guilpin, *Skialethia, or, A Shadowe of Truth in Certaine Epigrams and Satyres* (London: Nicholas Ling, 1598), sig. B1.

The

Politics

of

Metamora

JEFFREY D. MASON

The American Indian is a myth. When the first European refugees arrived on North America's eastern shore, they were exiles from their own geography and history and so had to find a new identity. In spite of the diverse peculiarities of religion, nationality, or economic circumstance that had driven each group here, they all shared the experience of dislocation to a certain destination, and they sought a characterization of their consequent sense of homogeneity. They arrogated for themselves the title of "American," but they then required a means to justify this self-construction as denoting more than just a transplanted European; they needed to define the new name in terms of the new land. They solved that problem by asserting a classic binary opposition, positing themselves as one element and finding the other in "Indian," a conflation of the many cultures native to their new home.[1] This strategy rested on an assumption of essential and comprehensive difference, so the whites proceeded with an ongoing diacritical examination of both signs, "American" and "Indian," and the cultures they allegedly represented. In the eyes of the colonists, the natives (the unwitting and subsequently unwilling objects of the European gaze) lost whatever self-created identity they had and became, according to the demands of the moment, either a band of savages or the fabulous inhabitants of the Western terrestrial paradise that Old

World legend had promised. So constructed, the natives consequently became an obscure mystery to the interlopers, who, because they seldom sought to understand them on their own terms, failed to find a sensible manner of coexistence. The American Indian is a myth, therefore, not only in the sense of representing a people's attempt to express, in symbolic terms, the nature of their experience, but also in being more a product of white imagination than a metaphor for an actual culture—being a fiction.

Both myth and theater create fictions that can displace the actualities—the putative referents—that inspire them. Any fictional process, through selection and interpretation, both obscures and reveals its subject, but myth is exceptionally powerful because it creates and wields fictions in an attempt to transcend the personal and particular and to convey the experience of an entire culture. Richard Slotkin describes myth as "a complex of narratives that dramatizes the world vision and historical sense of a people" and goes on to say that "the narrative action of the myth-tale . . . reduces both experience and vision to a paradigm."[2] In so doing, myth can eclipse not only the relevant history but also our perception of the interaction between that myth and that history; we seek to see the object, but the myth acts as a veil, hiding the object from view and even usurping its place in our gaze, luring us into misprision. Likewise, theater offers the potential for universality in that an actor on the stage can, in the minds of the audience, represent *all* people. Thus, the actor is a virtual myth-maker, one who can either reinforce or challenge the fictions that the audience cherishes.

John Augustus Stone's *Metamora* (1829) was more than an "Indian" play, more than a travesty of the history of King Philip's War, and more than a highly popular vehicle for the touring star, Edwin Forrest. It was a political instrument, a means of delicately balancing several components of the American sensibility, projecting the passionate nationalism of the new nation by incorporating, incongruously, an emblematic Native American into white narrative, presenting him as an idealized hero who embodied sentimental values—but without suggesting an inconsistency with Andrew Jackson's policy of Indian removal. How Forrest's audiences perceived the play as theatrical event was partly a function of the ideology consequent to their perception of the Indian as fiction and the native as reality and of themselves as Americans.[3]

KING PHILIP'S WAR

Up to the time of his death (1661?), the Wampanoag sachem Massasoit had succeeded in nurturing a fragile peace with Plymouth Colony. His elder son, Wamsutta, apparently intended to carry on the policy of co-existence with the settlers, but died under suspicious circumstances in an English home after the General Court ordered him to Duxbury. Meta-comet, Wamsutta's younger brother, whom the English called "Philip" after the Macedonian king, assumed the leadership of his people.[4] As early as 1667, the English summoned him to court to answer accusations of conspiracy with the French and the Dutch; after further such encoun-ters, they demanded, on 10 April 1671, that he sign a statement of sub-mission to king and colony: "I having of late through my Indiscretion, and the Naughtiness of my Heart, violated and broken this my Covenant with my Friends, by taking up Arms, with evil intent against them, and that groundlessly; I being now deeply sensible of my Unfaithfulness and Folly, do desire at this Time solemnly to renew my Covenant with my ancient Friends."[5]

On 29 January 1675, a Wampanoag named John Sassamon was found dead, apparently murdered. He was a "praying" or Christian Indian who had served as an interpreter for the English during the Pequot War and later taught school in Natick. He switched allegiance to become one of Metacomet's advisors, but he may have been acting as a double agent, for he subsequently returned to the English fold and informed the governor that the sachem was forming a conspiracy. Some believed that Meta-comet then exerted his prerogative under tribal law and ordered the rene-gade's execution, a possibility which introduced the tricky question of whether native or English authority should prevail. The settlers accused three men of the Wampanoag tribe of murder and, after a trial probably staged for political effect, put them to death in June. The natives became increasingly unruly; the settlers complained of vandalism on 20 June and retaliated on 23 June by killing a looter. On 24 June at Swansea, the na-tives killed nine Englishmen, and the war began.[6]

From the summer of 1675 through the summer of 1676, King Philip's War decimated the New England colonies; in proportion to the popula-tion, it was the bloodiest conflict in American history.[7] The devastation inspired in the colonial historians a grim rage, which they focused on

Metacomet, who was, in spite of the war's misnomer, not a supreme military leader but only one of several independent chieftains leading warriors into battle. Nonetheless, the settlers soon relegated to him the role of whipping boy for their fear and hatred.

By 1677, three New England clerics had published accounts of the war in London and Boston. Increase Mather opens his version by describing the natives as "heathen" and later draws the significant distinction between the "praying Indians" and the "profane Indians."[8] He assures the reader that "one reason why the *Indians* murdered *John Sausaman*, was out of hatred against him for his Religion, for he was Christianized and baptiz'd . . . and was wont to curb those *Indians* that knew not God, on the account of their debaucheries."[9] He refers to Metacomet as "the perfidious and bloody Author of the War and woefull miseryes that have thence ensued."[10] Nathaniel Saltonstall reviles Metacomet as a "heathen" because he would not listen to Christian gospel and defends the English right to prosecute the war, asserting that, while they paid a low price for their lands, they did indeed purchase them.[11] He relates the natives' atrocities in sensuous detail, claiming that "many have been destroyed with exquisite Torments, and most inhumane barbarities; the Heathen rarely giving quarter to those that they take, but if they were women, they first forced them to satisfie their filthy lusts and then murdered them; either cutting off the head, ripping open the Belly, or skulping the head of skin and hair, and hanging them up as Trophies; wearing men's fingers as bracelets about their necks, and stripes of their skins which they dresse for Belts."[12] William Hubbard describes Metacomet as Satan's tool, asserting that "the Devil, who was a Murderer from the Beginning, had so filled the Heart of this savage Miscreant with Envy and Malice against the English, that he was ready to break out into open War against the Inhabitants of Plimouth."[13] He later calls him a "treacherous and perfidious Caitiff" and compares him with a savage beast.[14]

The colonists destroyed Metacomet because he impeded and defied their zealous enterprise; but, in order to justify the war according to their own ethical standards, the historians had to define him as an agent of evil whose villainy transcended temporal concerns. They condemned him (and, by implication, all refractory natives) for rejecting English religion and denying English authority—in essence, for maintaining a tenacious hold on his cultural identity. As Slotkin has pointed out, the war narratives expressed the Puritan vision of the Indian/white dichotomy as barbarism vs. civilization.[15] The writers were members of the ruling theocracy, forging myth in the service of an ideology which sought to bolster their society's hegemony over nonbelievers, both red and white.[16] Puritan theology gave them an anomalously theatrical cosmic vision: God was a superdirector who had entrusted the colonists with a sacred mission and then permitted Satan to lead a series of antagonists against them in an apparently endless divine melodrama. They had little doubt as to where Metacomet fit into this casting structure.

THE ROMANTIC WARRIOR

With the establishment of the republic in the late eighteenth century, those who had once identified themselves as European colonists sought to create a new image. Their perspective had reversed: as Europeans, they could reject anything American as Other; but as Americans, European values and symbols were the alien antagonists against which they defined their national identity. Furthermore, anything incontrovertibly American offered attractive raw material for the (re)formation of myth. Although the concept of Indian as satanic villain had survived most of the colonial period, the nation's apologists now sought a native heroism and so reconsidered the Indian.

The problem was how to confer literary nobility on those who were historical enemies not only of westward progress, but of civilization itself. The poets embraced the idea of the noble savage, locating it in the distant past, a nostalgic image that Americans accepted with increasing ease as the frontier receded, putting more and more distance between the hostile tribes and the eastern cities. This Romantic revision not only rejected the Puritan model but returned to the dream of the uttermost West as a primitive idyll, a tradition as old as Hesiod.

In Philip Freneau's "The Prophecy of King Tammany" (1782), the Lenni Lenape chieftain contemplates the proliferating aggressive Europeans who have invaded his land and weeps for his people's loss. He mourns the Indians' inability to resist the whites militarily, but as he resigns himself, he delivers a dire warning to his enemies:

When struggling long, at last with pain
You break a cruel tyrant's chain,
That never shall be joined again,
    When half your foes are homeward fled,
    And hosts on hosts in triumph led
    And hundreds maimed and thousands dead,
    A sordid race will then succeed
        To slight the virtues of the firmer race,
        That brought your tyrant to disgrace . . .[17]

The chief then climbs onto his funeral pyre and smiles to think that his troubles are nearly over—another "last" Indian making way for the inevitable onslaught of white civilization. Freneau helped to reconstruct the concept of the Indian and to make room for a new image of Metacomet.

In 1814, Washington Irving published "Philip of Pokanoket," a delicately ironic piece of propaganda contrived to discredit the settlers and establish the Indians as a noble, wronged race. He begins with a wistful gaze back into the days before civilization, then describes the seventeenth-century chieftains as "a band of native untaught heroes, who made the most generous struggle of which human nature is capable; fighting to the last gasp in the cause of their country, without a hope of victory or a thought of renown."[18] He attacks the Puritan narrative directly, accusing its authors of interpreting comparable incidents as English triumph on the one hand and Indian outrage on the other and suggesting that the settlers, victims of "the gloom of religious abstraction," were given to superstitious fears. Irving lays the foundation for *Metamora* by depicting Philip as a patriot in the Revolutionary War tradition who proceeds with a daring guerrilla war on the settlements and miraculously eludes capture again and again to hide in the New England swamps, where the hapless English cannot follow. Finally, Philip retreats to Mount Hope.

> Even in this last refuge of desperation and despair, a sullen grandeur gathers round his memory. We picture him to ourselves seated among his careworn followers, brooding in silence over his blasted fortunes, and acquiring a savage sublimity from the wildness and dreariness of his lurking-place. Defeated, but not dismayed—crushed to the earth, but not humiliated—he seemed to grow more

> haughty beneath disaster, and to experience a fierce satisfaction in draining the last dregs of bitterness. Little minds are tamed and subdued by misfortune; but great minds rise above it.[19]

Irving construes Philip as "a patriot attached to his native soil . . . proud of heart, and with an untamable love of natural liberty," fighting at the head of a band of freedom fighters, seeking against hope to "deliver his native land from the oppression of usurping strangers."[20]

James Fenimore Cooper elaborated on Irving's model in his 1829 novel, *The Wept of Wish-ton-Wish*, which presents Metacomet as an Indian avatar of George Washington, presiding over a postbattle council with dignity in spite of a fresh wound.

> The least practised eye could not mistake the person of him on whom the greatest weight of authority had fallen. The turbaned warrior . . . occupied the centre of the group, in the calm and dignified attitude of an Indian who hearkens to or who utters advice. . . . He had thrown a light blanket . . . over his left shoulder, whence it gracefully fell in folds, leaving the whole of the right arm free, and most of his ample chest exposed to view. From beneath this mantle, blood fell slowly in drops, dyeing the floor on which he stood.[21]

Metacomet is a visionary, a prophet who listens politely as an English ambassador makes his case, although privately intuiting the present and future truth about the inevitable dealings between red and white.

In his poem "Metacom" (1829), John Greenleaf Whittier presents the sachem as a warrior who can find meaning only in death. He stands in the red light of sunset, telling his advisor that he has foreseen his own demise at dawn and that he seems to see his father's spirit beckoning. He mourns the inevitable doom of his people:

> A few more moons, and there will be
> No gathering to the council tree;
> The scorched earth—the blackened log—
> The naked bones of warriors slain,
> Be the sole relics which remain
> Of the once mighty Wampanoag![22]

He leaves his dying curse to the English and predicts the chaos of the Revolutionary War; with dawn comes a volley and he falls with "one vengeful yell." Whittier and the other myth-makers had transformed Metacomet from demon to Romantic warrior.

FORREST'S PLAY

Edwin Forrest commissioned *Metamora* as part of a nationalist agenda which supported his personal ambitions as the first major American touring star. He operated like a politician today, working to convince the members of his audience that he was common like themselves, yet still claiming the heroic stature that earned their applause. His career made him an icon of American masculinity—forthright, muscular, and upstanding—and it was no mere coincidence that he attracted the enthusiasm of the nativist societies of the mid-forties and became the excuse for the jingoistic Astor Place Riot of 1849.[23] In 1834, he wrote, "In a country like ours, where all men are free and equal, no aristocracy should be tolerated, save that aristocracy of superior mind, before which none need be ashamed to bow. . . . The parasitical opinion cannot be too soon exploded which teaches that 'nothing can be so good as that which emanates from abroad.' Our literature should be independent. . . ."[24] Later that year, he announced, to repeated cheers, "I feel grateful for the honorable support I have received in my anxious endeavors to give to my country, by fostering the exertions of our literary friends, something like what might be called an American national drama."[25] In a Fourth of July speech delivered in 1838, he asked, "Where does the sun, in all his compass, shed his beams on a country freer, better, happier than this?" and went on to wonder, "What bounds can be set to the growth of American greatness?"[26]

When Forrest announced his first playwriting prize on 22 November 1828, he specified a Native American hero, so Stone adjusted the historical raw material in order to elevate his protagonist.[27] While the actual Metacomet signed a capitulation in 1671, Metamora meets with the English only to scorn them and reinforce his personal and tribal pride. Metacomet was never clearly linked to Sassamon's assassination, but Metamora welcomes personal responsibility. The actual war evolved through a series of subtle, escalating provocations, but Metamora defies the English in open council, declaring and initiating the war on the spot, then mustering his warriors as the charismatic leader of his people. Metacomet's wife and son were captured and later sold into slavery, but Stone spares Metamora's family such indignities, presenting the sachem as a tender father and family man by including the sensational scene where he mourns his slaughtered boy and then stabs Nahmeokee himself to protect her from their enemies. Metacomet died in a scramble as Benjamin Church's men surprised his camp, but Metamora anticipates the soldiers' arrival, challenges them to fight him singly, and invites the volley that kills him, a champion to the last. Like Irving's Philip, Metamora is more a patriot than a savage, exhorting his warriors in the manner of Patrick Henry: "If ye love the silent spots where the bones of your kindred repose, sing the dread song of war and follow me! . . . Call on the happy spirits of the warriors dead and cry, 'Our lands! Our nation's freedom! Or the grave!'"[28]

INDIAN REMOVAL

Metamora might now be considered just one more embarrassing white exploitation of Native Americans were it not for its concurrence with Indian removal. Like King Philip's War, removal was an intense expression of the gulf separating two cultures, the natives perceiving the land as a resource that all share, and the whites defining it as private property, the foundation of liberal society and the *raison d'être* for their new nation.[29] The American concept of freedom depended on a constant supply of unoccupied land that offered individuals the chance to repeat the Lockean experience of the first immigrant and found their own society, producing a nation of self-created, independent individualists living freely under a minimal government. Native presence therefore came to be seen as an unacceptable obstacle to white aspirations, and American energy—and therefore American law—precluded coexistence of red and white nations within the same territory.[30]

When Thomas Jefferson first proposed removal in 1803, he saw only two possible futures for the natives, and the ensuing debate found no others: first, to assimilate, that is, to adopt Christianity and an agricultural society, which the whites accepted as the hallmarks of civilization; second, to sustain the old way of life beyond the reach of white influence.[31] As early as 1817, Jackson himself saw citizenship or removal as the only two viable alternatives open to the Cherokee, and he wrote a treaty that helped legitimize treating the natives as individuals, not nations.[32] From colonial times on, the whites had treated the natives not as the sovereigns of their land but as its owners; by reducing the natives' claims to matters of deed and purchase, the whites could confer a comfortable legality on their encroachments.[33] Even the most benevolent leader could adopt the preservationist rationale in order to justify the dispossession and transportation of tens of thousands of people; certain missionaries supported removal on the grounds that exposure to white culture tended to corrupt the natives.[34] On the other hand, some white response to the "Indian problem" displayed a certain exasperated perplexity that the natives had not already eagerly adopted the customs and practices of white civilization and apparently needed to be persuaded and educated into doing so; those less inclined to respect native feelings typically cited their intransigent barbarism as justification for abuse.

President Monroe presented his plan for removal and civilization on 7 December 1824, hoping to establish an Indian region beyond the Mississippi. The issue moved slowly until July 1827, when the Cherokee nation raised the political temperature to a critical level by adopting a constitution modeled after America's own and by declaring sovereignty over parts of Georgia, North Carolina, Tennessee, and Alabama. As soon as Jackson was declared victor in the 1828 election, Georgia, Alabama, and Mississippi formally extended their jurisdiction over natives within their boundaries and abolished the tribe as a legal entity.[35] At his first inauguration, Jackson announced that "it will be my sincere and constant desire to observe toward the Indian tribes within our limits a just and liberal policy, and to give that humane and considerate attention to their rights and their wants which is consistent with the habits of our Government and the feelings of our people."[36] Yet, in his first annual message to Congress, he warned against the existence of the Indian nations as a threat to states' rights.[37] Bills were proposed in both houses of Congress in February 1830. They passed, and Jackson signed removal into law on 28 May 1830. In his second annual message, on 6 December 1830, he asked, "What good man would prefer a country covered with forests and ranged by a few thousand savages to our extensive Republic, studded with cities, towns, and prosperous farms, embellished with the improvements which art can devise or industry execute, occupied by more than 12,000,000 happy people, and filled with all the blessings of liberty, civilization, and religion?"[38] In a series of treaties beginning in 1830, the tribes ceded their homes in exchange for land west of the Mississippi; the recurring phrase is "to them and their heirs forever," an empty promise that became the hallmark of white/native relations. Ultimately, about 70,000 people, mostly from the Southeast, were transported.

THE PERCEPTION/RECEPTION OF METAMORA

The debate that led to removal reached its critical phase during the three years following the adoption of the Cherokee constitution and found at least an official resolution when Jackson signed the bill. *Metamora* first appeared during this crucial period, opening at the Park Theatre in New York City on 15 December 1829, and the timing raises the question of how Forrest's audience perceived the Indian hero in the context of native/white politics.

Theatrical representation does not, of course, take place in a vacuum or even in the isolation of an aesthetic preserve, but as part of a cultural fabric to which it contributes and of which it is a part.[39] To seek to describe the meaning of *Metamora* or, to propose the problem more fully, of Forrest-as-Metamora in a given historical and political framework is to confront the theoretical question concerning the source of that meaning (in text, character, actor, audience, or the interactions among them) and then to contemplate the more fundamental issue of *how* theater produces meaning, which is a matter of ideology. Raymond Williams has explained that one usage of "ideology" holds that it is "the general process of the production of meanings and ideas," while Terry Eagleton has argued that a text *produces* ideology rather than *expressing* it, suggesting that the same claim is valid for theatrical performance as distinct from text.[40] The search for meaning therefore requires an examination of the process that produces it, which in the case of theater involves a complex interaction between text and participants amid the codes and conventions of a given social context. In the case of *Metamora*, although the text, the character, the actor, and even some of the details of the performance are more or less accessible to historical inquiry, there is little record of audience response, so the reconstruction of the spectators' collective point of view presents a methodological challenge.[41]

In order to establish that Forrest's audience did, to a demonstrable extent, associate his Indian hero with the natives of the time, and to describe the popular image of both "Indian" and "native," I have examined two New York newspapers of the 1830s.[42] The federal government's resolution of the native problem required a certain rationale, a set of values that was conceived and promoted not only in Congress but also in public print. The newspapers in question enjoyed substantial circulation in their communities, and their articles and editorials are susceptible to Eagleton's axiom that text produces ideology. Therefore, the popular press produced a certain view of "native" for the consumption of their readership and the community at large, and that view informed the community's production of the meaning of *Metamora* (that is, version/perception of that meaning) in interacting with and completing Forrest's performance. Ultimately, the newspapers and the play worked to reinforce each other in validating the politics (of white treatment of native populations) and the myths (of the Indian) of their time.

At one level, the natives were a source of amusement. In 1837, the *Morning Herald* was given to making fun of them—how they superstitiously refused to have their portraits painted, how they found the umbrella a fascinating invention, and how their conversation consisted principally of grunts.[43] This derision sets up an incongruity with Forrest's Indian hero, but the more serious articles offer deeper contradictions.

In 1829, the *Evening Post* (edited by Forrest's friend William Cullen Bryant) interpreted the Indian problem simply as a question of states' rights, asserting that, while the tribes clearly had the right to possess and occupy their lands because the constitution prohibited the founding of a new state within the boundaries of an existing one without the consent of its legislature, they could not expect Washington to intervene.[44] The writer assured his readers that the natives had a free choice—to stay in the South and submit to white law, or to move west to lands whose permanent possession was guaranteed. Six months later, on the day that Jackson signed the removal bill, another article analyzed the law and concluded that "the very title of the bill itself,—'a bill to provide for an *exchange* of lands with the Indians,' &c. shows that no undue exercise of power is intended . . . there is nothing arbitrary, nothing tyrannical, nothing calculated to tarnish the honor of the country, and make our want of faith a byword in other lands." [45] The writer went on to ask "whether it would not be for the ultimate advantage of the Indians, as well as conducive to the interests and happiness of the whites, to remove the former from within the limits of the states, to a tract of country west of the Mississippi . . . the removal only to take place with the free consent of the Indians themselves." This argument rests on the assumption that the whites and the natives were equal parties entering into bona fide negotiations, and that the natives, whether as tribes or as individuals, had an opportunity to choose, without coercion, between viable alternatives; others bypassed such subtlety to affirm simply that the natives were doomed and that no one could prevent their demise. During the 1830s and 1840s, schoolbooks, leading literary magazines, and political journals took for granted the march of white civilization and justified removal in the name of providence or progress. [46] In 1837, the *Herald* described the natives as a "noble and unhappy race" which "is rapidly becoming extinct." [47] The writer conceded that "they are rapidly sinking into the stream of oblivion, and soon nothing of them will remain but the memory of their past existence and glory"—yet he avoided considering the causative connection between white politics and native ruin. In December 1831, possibly in response to the National Republican party's attack on Jackson's policy, the *Evening Post* referred to the "Indian question" as "settled," a judgment offered when removal was only just beginning. [48] These various responses all worked to absolve society, and those individuals who held political power, of responsibility.

The articles on *Metamora* drew a distinction between the actual natives and the poetic Indian of the play. In 1837, the *Morning Herald* referred to the title figure as "an excellent representative of the Indian of poetry" and acclaimed Forrest's performance:

> He has a large fund of that *sang froid* and self-sufficiency requisite
> to portray the stoicism of the red man. Endowed with a few set
> phrases about revenge, truth, lying, friendship, liberty, and the
> Manitou; the Indian carries us back to the heroic ages of
> Greece. . . . For the portraying of such personages, we say again

Mr. F is peculiarly suited.—His hoarse voice, uncontrolled by art—his sullen features, his dogged walk, his athletic frame, and his admirable personations of the transitions of the mind from calmness to passion, are lofty and enviable qualifications for the attainment of excellence in this range of the drama. . . . He is truly the impersonation of the Indian of romance. The Indian in his *true* character never *can* find a representative among the whites. Disgust, rather than admiration, would ensue, but if the author made him successful, our prejudices would revolt at the scene.[49]

In 1834, the *Evening Post* described a dinner given in Forrest's honor, where, in a lengthy toast, William T. McCoun referred to *Metamora* as "wholly American in its character and incidents" and described the title figure as "a strong and natural portrait of one of the most remarkable warriors of a race, the last relics of which are fast melting away before the advancing tide of civilization."[50] Three years later, an article in the same newspaper asserted that Metamora was "a faithful and spirited portraiture of one of the most heroic of that aboriginal race of men who were once the sole denizens of this continent, but of whom now but few and degenerate relics remain."[51] These perceptions disempower Native Americans, reserving respect for the Romantic fiction of the past, virtually making the case that they should embrace their own luxuriously melancholy demise, and leaving only contempt for the disappointingly real natives of the present, who, if mere relics, probably deserved to melt away.

Metamora served the political exigencies of its time. Melodrama provides a means of resolving fundamental contradictions; the form polarizes its elements but then sustains their interdependent relationship within a shared structure. Because white writers typically defined native culture as Other—whether through Puritan denunciation or Romantic panegyric—the narratives about Metacomet offered strong melodramatic potential.[52] The key element in this chemistry was Forrest himself, playing the role of "Indian" while signifying Euro-American values, his mimesis at odds with his semiosis. He and Stone appropriated the poetic Indian in order to promote whites' inaccurate concept of themselves as free, lonesome hunters, living in harmony with the land, a myth that was mostly humbug. Yet they also redefined Metacomet as a paragon in the sentimental tradition, inscribing the Indian with just those male virtues that white

Americans admired and that the actor portrayed so effectively. Their version of the mythic Indian set a standard that no actual native—no person of any background—could hope to match, and so vindicated both nostalgia and removal.

NOTES

1. It should by now be axiomatic that there is no neutral term that refers generically to the many original peoples of the territory now known as the United States of America. Although "native" seems to connote "primitive" and evokes echoes of drums and the rattling of bone-bead necklaces, I am using it (and occasionally the phrase "Native American") when I wish to refer, in as objective a voice as possible, to those in question as actual people, reserving the word "Indian" to signal a white, Euro-American construct, perception, or perspective. Throughout, "American," if used without "Native," conforms to current common usage, however hegemonic, referring to the United States, its culture, and its people.

2. Richard Slotkin, *Regeneration through Violence: The Mythology of the American Frontier, 1600–1860* (Middletown, Conn.: Wesleyan University Press, 1973), 6.

3. B. Donald Grose has also considered *Metamora* in the context of Jackson's policies; see "Edwin Forrest, *Metamora*, and the Indian Removal Act of 1830," *Theatre Journal* 37 (1985): 181–191, based on portions of his "Here Come the Indians: An Historical Study" (Ph.D. diss., University of Missouri, 1979).

4. As with "Indian" vs. "native," the sachem's name offers a semantic problem. Although most whites today know him as King Philip, I call him "Metacomet" when I refer to the actual man; when discussing him as fiction, I use whatever name the relevant author conferred.

5. Quoted in William Hubbard, *The History of the Indian Wars in New England, etc.* (1677; ed. Samuel G. Drake, Roxbury, Mass.: W. Elliot Woodward, 1865; rpt., New York: Kraus, 1969), 54.

6. For more detailed information on the relevant events of King Philip's War, see Douglas Edward Leach, *Flintlock and Tomahawk: New England in King Philip's War* (1958; rpt., New York: Norton, 1966), 23–43, 231–235; and Francis Jennings, *The Invasion of America: Indians, Colonialism, and the Cant of Conquest* (Chapel Hill: University of North Carolina Press, 1975), 289–296.

7. The war survives in white memory and imagination. After nine generations, my family still takes an interest in the fact that on 26 March 1676, while the citizens of Marlborough were attending Sunday services, the natives attacked the village and a warrior fired on Moses Newton, my ancestor, as he attempted to carry

an old woman to the safety of a garrison house. The shot shattered his elbow and disabled him for life. As in the official histories of the war, this family tradition presents the colonist as a heroic victim of unprovoked aggression.

8. Increase Mather, *A Brief History of the Warr with the Indians in New England* (1676), in *The History of King Philip's War, by the Rev. Increase Mather, D.D.; also, A History of the Same War, by the Rev. Cotton Mather, D.D.*, ed. Samuel G. Drake (Boston and London: n.p., 1862), 35, 47.

9. Mather, 48–49.

10. Mather, 193.

11. Nathaniel Saltonstall, *The Present State of New-England with Respect to the Indian War* (London: Dorman Newman, 1675), and *A New and Further Narrative of the State of New-England: Being a Continued Account of the Bloody Indian War* (London: Dorman Newman, 1676), in *The Old Indian Chronicle*, ed. Samuel G. Drake (Boston: Antiquarian Institute, 1836), 5–7.

12. Saltonstall, 100–101.

13. Hubbard, 53.

14. Hubbard, 57, 265.

15. Slotkin, 21.

16. See Richard Slotkin and James K. Folsom (eds.), *"So Dreadfull a Judgment": Puritan Responses to King Philip's War, 1676–1677* (Middletown, Conn.: Wesleyan University Press, 1978), 6.

17. Philip Freneau, *The Poems of Philip Freneau*, ed. Fred Lewis Pattee, 3 vols. (1903; rpt., New York: Russell and Russell, 1963), 1:189. "The Prophecy of King Tammany" first appeared in the *Freeman's Journal*; Freneau subsequently published similar treatments of the material in "The Dying Indian" (*Freeman's Journal*, 1784) and "The Indian Convert" (*Time-Piece*, 1797). In the quoted passage, Freneau must have been referring to the Revolutionary War, but with an obscure, brooding pessimism regarding the future.

18. Washington Irving, "Philip of Pokanoket," in *The Sketch Book of Geoffrey Crayon, Gent.* (1819; New York: Dodd, Mead, 1954), 299. First published in *Analectic Magazine* 3 (June 1814): 502–515, Irving's piece was again laid before the public when, on 19 December 1829, the *New-York Mirror, and Ladies' Literary Gazette* reprinted excerpts in honor of the opening of *Metamora* at the Park Theatre on 15 December.

19. Irving, 314–315.

20. Irving, 316, 306.

21. James Fenimore Cooper, *The Wept of Wish-ton-Wish*, 2 vols. (Philadelphia: Carey, Lea and Carey, 1829; rpt., New York: AMS, 1972), 2:106.

22. John Greenleaf Whittier, *The Complete Poetical Works of Whittier*, Cambridge edition (Boston: Houghton Mifflin, 1894), 489.

23. One indication of the resonance between Forrest and the nativists is the fact that the president of the Order of United Americans was given the title of

"sachem" (Richard Moody, *The Astor Place Riot* [Bloomington: Indiana University Press, 1958], 132).

24. Letter dated 8 January 1834 and addressed to Henry Hart, officer of a literary society in Albany, quoted in William Rounseville Alger, *Life of Edwin Forrest, The American Tragedian*, 2 vols. (Philadelphia: Lippincott, 1877; rpt., New York: Benjamin Blom, 1972), 1:179–180.

25. Forrest addressing the audience after his farewell performance as Lear at Arch Street on 2 April 1834, just before commencing his first trip to Europe, quoted in James Rees, *The Life of Edwin Forrest* (Philadelphia: T. B. Peterson, 1874), 104.

26. Edwin Forrest, *Oration Delivered at the Democratic Republican Celebration of the Sixty-Second Anniversary of the Independence of the United States, in the City of New-York, Fourth July, 1838* (New York: J. W. Bell, 1838), 13, 24.

27. In the *New York Critic*, Forrest offered $500 and half of a benefit performance "to the author of the best Tragedy, in five acts, of which the hero or principal character shall be an aboriginal of this country." Stone's was not the first dramatic treatment of King Philip; the anonymous *Philip; or, the Aborigines* appeared in 1822; Robert Montgomery Bird's lost *King Philip; or, The Sagamore* and James Kennicott's *Metacomet* both appeared in 1829. For discussions of the first of these, see Paul Ronald Cox, "The Characterization of the American Indian in American Indian Plays 1800–1860 as a Reflection of the American Romantic Movement" (Ph.D. diss., New York University, 1970), 121–125; Marilyn Jeanne Anderson, "The Image of the American Indian in American Drama: From 1766 to 1845" (Ph.D. diss., University of Minnesota, 1974), 327–328, 387–389; and Kathleen A. Mulvey, "The Growth, Development, and Decline of the Popularity of American Indian Plays before the Civil War" (Ph.D. diss., New York University, 1978), 87.

28. John Augustus Stone, *Metamora; or, The Last of the Wampanoags*, in *Dramas from the American Theatre, 1762–1909*, ed. Richard Moody (Cleveland: World, 1966), 224. For the Henry parallel, see Priscilla Sears, *A Pillar of Fire to Follow: American Indian Dramas, 1808–1859* (Bowling Green: Bowling Green University Popular Press, 1982), 51.

29. See Michael P. Rogin, *Fathers and Children: Andrew Jackson and the Subjugation of the American Indian* (New York: Knopf, 1975), 8.

30. See Robert F. Berkhofer, Jr., *The White Man's Indian: Images of the American Indian from Columbus to the Present* (New York: Knopf, 1978), 154–155.

31. In its *First Annual Report* of 1824, the American Board of Commissioners for Foreign Missions expressed its skepticism that the natives could find any place on earth to continue in a "savage and hunter state," and so recommended that they be civilized to save them from perishing, quoted in David Brion Davis, *Antebellum American Culture: An Interpretive Anthology* (Lexington: D. C. Heath, 1979), 236.

32. Rogin, 181; Ronald N. Satz, *American Indian Policy in the Jacksonian Era* (Lincoln: University of Nebraska Press, 1975), 10–11. Jackson offered land to Cherokees who remained in the East and became United States citizens; the agreement shattered the tribe into isolated individuals.

33. "In a well-publicized majority opinion in 1823, Marshall ruled that the Indians held their land by 'right of occupancy' which was subordinate to the 'right of discovery' that the United States had inherited from the British" (Satz, 3).

34. Robert F. Berkhofer, Jr., *Salvation and the Savage: An Analysis of Protestant Missions and American Indian Response, 1787–1862* (Lexington: University of Kentucky Press, 1965; New York: Atheneum, 1972), 100–102.

35. Rogin, 212–213.

36. Satz, 12.

37. Satz, 19.

38. *A Compilation of the Messages and Papers of the Presidents, 1789–1897*, ed. J. D. Richardson, 2:520–521; quoted in Roy Harvey Pearce, *The Savages of America: A Study of the Indian and the Idea of Civilization* (1953; rev. ed., Baltimore: Johns Hopkins University Press, 1965), 57.

39. Raymond Williams considers this issue in the introduction to *Drama from Ibsen to Brecht* (London: Hogarth, 1968, 1987), where he discusses the "structure of feeling" (17–20).

40. Raymond Williams, *Marxism and Literature* (Oxford: Oxford University Press, 1977), 4; Terry Eagleton, *Criticism and Ideology: A Study in Marxist Literary Theory* (London: NLB, 1976), 64.

41. The best-known report of audience reaction to *Metamora* in the context of removal is James E. Murdoch's anecdote about Forrest's appearance before an angry crowd of Georgians in Augusta in 1831 (*The Stage; or, Recollections of Actors and Acting* [Philadelphia: J. M. Stoddart, 1880], 298–300). I am not including this story in my discussion because I have been able to corroborate neither the incident nor the date. Richard Moody says that the actor spent the 1831–1832 and 1832–1833 seasons in New York, Boston, and Philadelphia, and he does not place him in Augusta until 1847 (*Edwin Forrest: First Star of the American Stage* [New York: Knopf, 1960], 104), thus raising the possibility that the tale is either apocryphal or inaccurately dated.

42. Although these newspapers may reflect the concerns of those who had the most opportunity to see Forrest's work, the eastern urban audience, it is possible that rural and/or southern periodicals would present significantly different perspectives. At this writing, I am still searching for concurrent discussions of *Metamora* and the Indian question in newspapers published in southern and border cities where Forrest is known to have performed the play during the 1830s: Natchez on 25 March 1839, New Orleans in 1834 and 1839, and St. Louis on 10 May 1839.

43. *Weekly Herald*, 7 October 1837, 355; 2 December 1837, 421. The *Morn-*

ing Herald acknowledged the inevitability of the whites eventually forcing the Indians out of their new territories (11 October 1837, 1). (The *Weekly Herald* was a collation of articles reprinted from the daily *Morning Herald.*)

44. *New-York Evening Post*, 11 December 1829, 2. Bryant joined the editorial staff in 1826, probably in July, and became editor-in-chief in July 1829. From 1823 to 1832, he wrote five "Indian" poems, three of which mourned the lost life of the "noble red man": "The Indian Girl's Lament" (1823), "An Indian Story" (1824), "An Indian at the Burial-place of his Fathers" (1824), "The Disinterred Warrior" (1832?), and "The Prairies" (1832), all collected in *The Poetical Works of William Cullen Bryant*, ed. Henry C. Sturges and Richard Henry Stoddard (1903; rpt., New York: AMS, 1969).

45. *New-York Evening Post*, 28 May 1830, 2.

46. Satz, 55.

47. *Weekly Herald*, 4 November 1837, 386.

48. *New-York Evening Post*, 14 December 1831, 2.

49. *Morning Herald*, 28 December 1837, 1.

50. *Evening Post*, 29 July 1834, 2. On 25 July 1834, Forrest's friends and admirers gathered to celebrate the actor's career before he left on his first trip to Europe. (The name of the newspaper had evolved to this truncated version.)

51. *Evening Post*, 11 October 1837, 2.

52. The writers in question (as well as all the writers of the period mentioned in this article) were not only white but male, and they also defined woman as Other, but that fact introduces issues beyond the scope of this piece.

The Eurocolonial

Reception of

Sanskrit Poetics

SUE-ELLEN CASE

The Orient functions as a theater, a stage on which a performance is repeated, to be seen from a privileged standpoint.

I treat ethnography itself as a performance emplotted by powerful stories.
—*James Clifford,* Writing Culture

Research in contemporary feminist criticism has focused, in part, on what are termed "differences." A refinement of earlier identity politics, these differences operate to situate both the perspective of the critic/historian and the object of research within specific institutional, historical, sexual, gender, race, and class affiliations. This focus has occasioned a new critical theory, a new historicism, and even a new epistemology. Both the scholar and the object of study are now configured within a multiple, shifting, often self-contradictory identity made up, as Teresa de Lauretis has phrased it, of "heterogenous and heteronomous representations."[1] This new construct of positionality came primarily from women of color working within ethnic communities in the United States. More recently, Third World women and men have brought a new dimension to "differences" and positionality through Edward Said's critique of *Orientalism,* the postcolonial critique of history, and literature written by Indian scholars working in subaltern studies.

Within intercultural studies, this new notion of positionality has transformed the way in which the critic/historian confronts a text or tradition from another culture. Here the title of James Clifford's book speaks directly to the re-vision of the project: *Writing Culture*. In his introduction, Clifford describes the interdisciplinary intersection of studies that is producing a new methodology and epistemology for intercultural work, containing, among others: historical ethnography, cultural poetics, cultural criticism, the critique of hegemonic structures, the semiotics of exotic worlds and fantastic spaces, the study of scientific communities, and, a category Clifford elides, feminist theory.[2] The compound of literary studies with ethnography, in conjunction with techniques of materialist history and materialist culture, and the postcolonial critique has produced the kinds of strategies deconstructed or otherwise employed in the following analysis of ellipsis, concealment, and partial disclosure. Thus, as a feminist scholar, this critique of differences, along with an awareness of the politics of First World study of the Third World, turned my studies to the postcolonial critique. More immediately, Avanthi Meduri's performance and critique in the Women and Theatre Program and the high visibility of Peter Brook's *Mahabharata* prompted me to review theatrical scholarship of what is deemed "classical" Indian theater.

To this end, I would like to execute a preliminary application of some strategies within the postcolonial critique to the reception of Sanskrit poetics and Brook's *Mahabharata* in order to illustrate the way in which these studies alter the methodology and received knowledge of the theater critic/historian. As this approach illustrates, this reception is marked with a colonialist ideology which originated near the beginning of the nineteenth century and carries into contemporary times. It hinges upon the reception of Sanskrit in European studies and the studied promulgation of the English language and literature in colonial India.

"DISCIPLINING" SANSKRIT

The project of creating Sanskrit as a "classical" language entails all of the presuppositions informing periodization that Thomas Postlewaite critiques in his article "The Criteria for Periodization in Theatre History": causality, narrativity, and unity.[3] But even more importantly here, this notion of the "classical" displaces the phenomenon of Sanskrit drama from its indigenous ground of meaning to a eurocentric one. The notion abounds with resonances of nineteenth-century German Romanticism, British empiricism, and the British systems of a "classical" and a colonial education.

Intimations of a glory long past—an aesthetic plenitude now spent—mark the German Romantic reception of both Sanskrit drama and the language itself. Heine, Schiller, Wilhelm von Humboldt, and Goethe praised the recently translated Sanskrit play *Sakuntala*. Goethe rhapsodized about its plenitudinous powers in this oft-quoted little poem:

> If I want the first blooms, the late-ripening fruits
> What charms and enchants; what nourishes and fulfills
> Heaven and earth—in one name—
> Sakuntala, I call you, and that says it all.[4]

Likewise, Sanskrit itself was situated as the source of grammatical plenitude. The assimilative project began in the late eighteenth/early nineteenth century with the new science of linguistics, founded, in part, by Friedrich Schlegel. Schlegel's *Über die Sprache und Weisheit der Indier*, written in 1808, asserts the common origin of Sanskrit and the principal European languages, creating the now-familiar notion of "Indo-European languages." Schlegel proposed that inflected languages, such as Sanskrit and German, have the same root and, further, that their common grammatical structure indicates similarities in the kinds of meanings and culture they produce. This so-called linguistic study was, in fact, a way of recuperating the Sanskrit tradition into Romantic values of the time. Written in the year of Schlegel's conversion to Catholicism, the treatise asserts that inflected languages are of "spiritual" origins, while noninflective ones are of "animal" origins.[5] Sanskrit, then, which Schlegel identified as the source of inflected languages, thus operated as an Edenic image of grammatical spirituality that constituted a spiritual culture.[6] Schlegel's notion of "spiritual" as distinct from "animal" rested upon the Romantic valuing of subjectivity and his own religious goals. This Romantic inscription had little to do with the cosmology within which the language historically operated.

Moreover, the role of "classical" Sanskrit's "spirituality" was constructed to operate against another "classical" language—Greek. In his preface, Schlegel calls for a new Renaissance based on Indian texts that would correct the pagan Greek cultures and that would lead one back to a better notion of the "Divine."[7] The other side of this Edenic past was, of course, the expulsion into the "fallen" present: languages with linguistic structures that rely upon suffixes and other helpers. In other words, lending Sanskrit a classical status inscribed it with subtextual Romantic and Christian metaphors that displaced its own ground of meaning with eurocentric goals and conflicts. Further, as a "classical" language, it is situated in comparative terms with the "classical" language of Greece. These appropriative operations have haunted the reception of this language until the contemporary period.

Yet these colonial operations do not necessarily occur directly in the texts, but are cloaked by a scientism in this new linguistics—a play for objective truth that mimics empirical methods by borrowing metaphors from the other sciences. Schlegel establishes Sanskrit as a source language by metaphorizing terms from the biological sciences—the sense that languages have roots and stems. Thus, Sanskrit becomes an organic, spiritual root of meaning.[8]

Nietzsche later employed this same appropriative process in his *Birth of Tragedy*. Once again, in a study of the "classical" age of Greece as a wish fulfillment of Romantic Idealism, Nietzsche combined philology and a longing for a potent, plenitudinous drama-gone-by with reconfigured Sanskrit terms to create the titanic struggle of the Dionysian/ Apollonian.[9] For Nietzsche, "the veil of maya" could be "torn aside . . . before the mysterious primordial unity" in the Dionysian.[10] Moreover, in Dionysian music "the annihilation of the veil of maya" would reveal "oneness as the soul of the race and of nature itself."[11] The German Romantics, then, marked the Sanskrit tradition as plenitudinous, salvational, subjective, and totally Other in a struggle with "fallen" grammars and forms.

OXFORD

In Britain, the institutionalization of Sanskrit was interwoven with East India trade policies and the overall project of colonizing India. The importation of Sanskrit into Oxford, in the early to mid-nineteenth century, was concurrent with the exportation of English into India. Both projects served the same end.

The study of the classics at Oxford both legitimatized British imperialism by elevating the Greek and Roman empires and offering them up comparatively to the British empire and by reading the classics as a source—even entirely imaginary—of imperial motives and projects. As Gilbert Murray offered: "at home England is Greek. In the Empire she is Roman." [12] Plato's educational system for the Guardians of his Republic was considered a model for the education of British colonists. Richard Symonds, in *Oxford and Empire*, cites the writings of prominent administrators in the century who kept the classics by their bedsides, carried them through exotic and dangerous lands, or identified themselves as characters from the classics in their writings. [13] This tradition carried into the twentieth century with people like Lord Bryce, a former cabinet minister and ambassador, who wrote *The Ancient Roman Empire and the British Empire in India* (1914). "Classics," then, offer appropriate mental constructs for imperialists and train their imagination and thought for administration.

Sanskrit as a "classic" had a slightly different assignment—to turn scholars away from its own system of meanings. The first chair of Sanskrit was endowed by Colonel Boden of the East India Company, "being of the opinion that a more general and critical knowledge of that language will be a means of enabling my countrymen to proceed in the conversion of the native of India to the Christian religion." [14] Somehow, Sanskrit had to be made a literary language that could be cut, by aesthetics, from its Hindu roots and then employed to suppress its own tradition. This project illustrates the way in which processes of assimilation and exclusion work together. Sanskrit, as a classical language, also served to strengthen a eurocentric notion of the class system in India—enfranchising a certain class of educated Indian necessary to the colonial process. After all, it was a "dead" language known only by the *literati*; thus, its inclusion in the British system allowed a certain mutual identification between the British and Indian educated classes.

At the same time, the teaching of English in India, particularly English literature, aimed at a similar assimilative goal. As Gauri Viswanathan details in "The Beginnings of English Literary Study in British India," to train the upper class in the ways of thinking and the values embedded in English literature was, in part, to utilize that class's assimilation to provide "a buffer zone for absorbing the effects of foreign rule." [15] In other words, the functional goal was to control the native population through literary persuasion and identification with British values. In her article on the importation of Shakespeare into India as an entertainment for that same class, Jyotsna Singh carefully traces the use of theater in this process. [16]

The teaching of English also aimed at creating an able labor force for bureaucratic and administrative affairs. The hope was to train the Indian mind, through the English language and its literature, for efficient administration—a capability attributed to the English character and considered missing in the Indian. [17] Under this assumption lay the notion of the efficacy of empiricism and rationalism, embedded in English literature, in contrast to the insufficiencies of indigenous systems of thought. For while the Indian worldview was characterized as imaginative, that same attribute mitigated against its knowledge of the "real world," creating the sense of the dreamer, or the Indian philosopher as mystic. [18]

THE CRITICAL RECEPTION OF SANSKRIT POETICS

The nineteenth-century reception of Sanskrit as a language and its relation to the status of "classic," along with the role of English, laid the ground for twentieth-century texts on Sanskrit poetics written in English. The following brief survey is designed to show how these older colonial ideologies still operate in theater criticism and history.

Sanskrit poetics are represented by the central work ascribed to Bharata, entitled *The Natyasastra*—a treatise on performance, reception, and texts. A typical frame for situating the treatise may be found in the Indian critic Adya Rangacharya's *Introduction to Bharata's Natya-Sastra*: "Like Aristotle among the Greeks, Bharata in India stands as one of the greatest law-givers for good taste in literature and drama. . . . If Bharata actually lived, then on his death his disciples might have shouted 'Bharata is dead, long live Bharata.'" [19] Note how proximate are both the British educative focus on the Greeks and the British imperial pathos in this author's triangulation between Aristotle, the revision of "Long live the king!" and a Sanskrit treatise on the drama. The author swiftly compounds the comparative mode of introducing Sanskrit in the context of Greek as a "classic" and the imperial majesty lent to such a work. This economy of language rests upon the secure, received colonial assumptions that facilitate such comparative modes.

Ironically, in the preface, the author pleads for the importance of the treatise as an indigenous work in postcolonial India, but within a similar colonial frame: "Even after Independence I found no signs of any University or any Akademi (Central or State) recognising the importance of research work on the Natya-Sastra. . . . On the other hand, a foreign Professor of Dramatics in a Foreign University . . . once highly recommended to me Bharata's wisdom. As an Indian scholar I felt proud, as a Sanskrit scholar I felt sorry that this sincere foreigner was apparently misguided by some cultural delegation type of Indian scholar. My reaction to what I felt then is these few pages." [20] In other words, his work was prompted by a foreign scholar and his resolve hardened by an "outside," even though misguided, perception.

As in Rangacharya, the comparison of the *Natyasastra* to Aristotle's *Poetics* runs through most of the critical and historical work on it. Its placement as both ancient and "classic" echoes the assumptions of British scholarship and situates it within a comparative Greek frame. This comparative model then locates Sanskrit drama as the foreign, invisible drama that can be perceived only through the central, seemingly transparent model of "classical" Greece. This comparative mode sometimes produces an insidious comparison, in which Indian drama is described as inferior. For example: "Indian drama is thus deprived of a motif which is invaluable to Greek tragedy, and everywhere provides a deep and profound tragic element. . . ." [21] Here, the drama is described as "deprived" of a universal element of drama, the fall of the individual, as constructed by the Greeks. What this means in the overall discussion is that the worldview, which brings human subjectivity, nature, and the forces of time into play, does so in a manner that is not of the highest dramatic use. This eurocentric notion of the dramatic suppresses the description of that dynamic in the Sanskrit tradition. This comparative mode, producing description through difference, often relegates the *Natyasastra* to negatives—how it is unlike. Even Richard Schechner, who, advised by anthropology, effectively situates his discussion of the treatise within its own metaphor of Indian food meanings and ceremonies, writes, "Unlike Aristotle . . . the *Natyasastra* is so full of details. . . ."[22]

When it comes to interpreting or culturally translating the treatise, the comparative displacement of the indigenous context redefines key concepts to fit eurocentric meanings and practices. Two prime examples of this practice may be found in the descriptions of the central dynamic in Sanskrit drama, *rasa,* and the treatment of the structure of the narrative that concludes in what is perceived as a "happy ending." *Rasa* is often described in comparison to catharsis. One Indian critic introduces the discussion this way: "Aristotle, while defining tragedy, enunciated a theory which is akin to the rasa-theory."[23] From this base, the critic's description of *rasa* operates within a discussion of the purgation of pity and fear; although the critic admits that this does not occur in *rasa,* she further insists that it does produce a state *similar* to the bliss produced by *rasa.* This discussion confuses unlike emotions and even unlike resulting effects through its insistence on the comparison. Bliss, a transcendental state of collective cohesion in *rasa,* seems wildly different from the effects of pity and fear.

Another Indian critic entangles the description of *rasa* in the negatives of difference, obscuring its dynamics: "*Rasa* does not involve, like the tragic *katharsis,* the idea of an emotional relief alone, even though this is one of its effects."[24] While this critic proceeds to describe the resonances of bliss, it is once more seemingly produced through a purgation as consonant with the Sanskrit sense of the disengagement of ego from the world. Thus, the individual struggle in Greek tragedy is perceived as similar to the operations of destiny in the Sanskrit drama—two quite different senses of agency made proximate under the umbrella notion of the "classic."

Richard Schechner, in his illustration of the dynamics of *rasa,* offers two charts for clarification, comparing the Greek and Indian systems.[25] Another Indian scholar, B. K. Thakkar, quotes Susanne Langer in defining *rasa.*[26] No doubt, in addition to colonial practices of reception, this comparative mode is produced because the authors are writing in English, with the European or American reader in mind. Nevertheless, the veil of negative description drawn over the phenomenon often completely obscures it, as in the following example: "the reaction is neither progression, nor montage nor marked by either the rise or fall of excitement. . . ." The author continues, as he places *rasa* in an Indian drama, that it "dispenses with . . . characterization, naturalism, heroic accomplishments, etc."[27]

The comparative model has cut so deep that several historians have insisted that Sanskrit drama actually had Greek roots. The most noted work in this historical tradition, *Der griechische Einfluß im indischen Drama*, insists that, although the epic form seems indigenous, the classical form with acts, exits, and stock characters seems Greek. It further argues that, since Indian drama arose after the time of Menander's conquests, when there is evidence of Greek productions in the provinces, the New Attic Comedy was the actual source of Indian drama.[28]

It is clear by now that the indigenous worldview that produced the notion of *rasa* has been displaced. Yet its absence prompts the question: what, specifically, is the target of this suppression? From the missionary projects at the beginning of the nineteenth century, through the Boden chair at Oxford, into the present, it seems that the worldview denoted as pagan was perceived as in a competitive mode to Christianity. Moreover, the Hindu system was perceived as the opposite of reason and empiricism. Its descriptions in the nineteenth century deploy metaphors of the jungle—"a wild tangle of overlapping and merely juxtaposed pieces . . . uncentered . . . unstable . . . and lacking in uniformity. . . . If Hinduism had a positive essence, it consists of its feminine imaginativeness, its ability to absorb and include. . . ."[29] This notion maps out a perfect ground for the conquering, masculine eurocentric Christian empiricism to take hold of and order. Such a system begged for colonialization.

In criticism, several strategies seek to suppress this tradition. One way to disregard it is to relegate it to the margins of the text, as in the J. L. Masson and M. V. Patwardhan edition of *Aesthetic Rapture*, the most authoritative early commentary on *rasa* by Abhinavagupta. Although the authors note that Abhinavagupta set the model of perceiving *rasa* as a combination of aesthetic and religious experience,[30] they relegate his so-called mystic beliefs to a footnote. In other words, in this English edition of the most famous commentary on the *Natyasastra*, the religious worldview that produces it—that makes sense of the theater experience—is suppressed to a footnote. However, when the authors cannot ignore certain religious explanations for specific theatrical effects, they report them with disclaimers. For instance, when Abhinavagupta's text ties empathy to a specific, carefully worked out notion of rebirth and certain intimations of rebirth that lead to *rasa*, the authors note that "we do not need to accept this in order to appreciate the idea."[31]

These are minor strategies, however, that still maintain the notations of the original system. The major displacement in this reception is to impose the eurocentric category of the aesthetic onto the original tradition. The category of art severs the interconnected set of ceremonies and practices of daily life from one another. Then performance and effect are severed from their cosmology to inhabit the category of theater. Finally, subjective dynamics such as *rasa* become an aesthetic response and its description becomes a poetics. The above treatment of Abhinavagupta's notion of *rasa* serves as an example of this process. Cutting away the notion of past lives and their role in the reception of Sanskrit drama, along with Hindu notions of desire (*kama*) and destiny (*dharma*), the bliss of *rasa* becomes an aesthetic function, comparable to Aristotle's notion of catharsis. Taking this displacement to an extreme, Anita Ratnam Rangaraj concludes that "the *Natyasastra* views theatre primarily as a recreational, leisure-time activity resembling a game or sport with sacred undertones."[32]

Establishing the category of the aesthetic as the frame for the Sanskrit drama tradition retranslates all of its elements into eurocentric categories. For example, the category of the spectator is constructed. This entails constructions of subjectivity and of seeing that are inscribed with eurocentric ideology. Particular to *rasa* is a certain kind of subjectivity that, when translated into English and aesthetics, sounds like a familiar class bias regarding the spectator. As Appa Rao describes the spectator capable of *rasa*, "The refined alone can have this experience." Yet this is not the refinement of an Oscar Wilde, nor of the select citizens of Athens; Rao explains it as a subjective capacity: "Refinement is a state of mind which can intuitively experience. . . ."[33] For this intuitive experience, this "spectator" must have what, in English, are called "dormant emotions." Once again, this subjectivity rests upon past lives and a complex of elements outside the category of aesthetic response. To the degree that this person may also necessarily be of a certain *varna* (estate) or *jati* (caste), the complex history and euro-anthropological reception of the caste system mark this sense of the spectator. In Rangacharya's study of Sanskrit drama, this "refined" spectator becomes "kings and rich persons" who "helped the development of drama" move from a "vulgar medium." [34] The overlay of class onto the notion of refinement, or of estate, sets up a eurocentric hierarchy that also reinscribes certain ideologies about art and class, completely foreign to this system. Thus, the construction of spectatorship becomes entangled in the history of colonial proscriptions, Christian interdictions, and "democratic" ideologies. [35] One might conclude that the notion of spectator so confounds the issue that it is perhaps best elided.

Finally, in addition to the transcultural translation of *rasa*, the reception of the structure of the plays marks the colonial reception. The Sanskrit plays all have what has now been constituted as a "happy ending." As one critic put it, "Indian themes have ended on a happy note while the Greek ones have ended in a tragic note." [36] In other words, this idea of "happy endings" comes basically out of the sense that great classical drama is tragedy; the Sanskrit drama is classical but without tragedy and thus, in contrast, has a happy ending. Once again, the comparative mode causes a defensive posture and an explaining away rather than an investigation of the nature of the form from its own perspective. From there, lengthy interpretations of the plays' structures investigate why the hero does not die and why there is no tragedy. Once more, the negatives dominate and descriptions of the actual processes are displaced by figuring the tradition as a vacant Other.

Although Sanskrit poetics in the *Natyasastra* can be successfully displaced to Aristotle, the failure of the plays to match the Greek model causes some authors to turn to other classics for comparison. In part, this motive leads to the production of books such as *Kalidasa and Shakespeare* or a general sense of the classic that controls contemporary production. [37]

CONTEMPORARY LEGACY

The colonial reception of Sanskrit traditions is not limited to interpretive and historical studies. Recently, a major international production manifested similar strategies: Peter Brook's production of *The Mahabharata*.

Brook employed all of the strategies of aesthetic displacement to obscure indigenous grounds of meaning and performance. His aesthetic universalizing is captured in this statement he made in an interview with Richard Schechner in 1987: "At this absolute and pregnant moment . . . geography and history cease to exist."[38]

From this vantage point, Brook and Jean-Claude Carrière began work on *The Mahabharata*. The politics of cultural translation and historical accuracy gave way to the eternal values of art. According to Carrière, "As far as we were concerned, this immense poem, which flows with the majesty of a great river, carries an inexhaustible richness which defies all structural, thematic, historic or psychological analysis."[39] Once again, the plenitude of the classic-age-gone-by, illustrated above in Goethe's reception of *Sakuntala*, provides an aesthetic excess that justifies the suppression of historical or structural indigenous meanings. Carrière's sentiment, grounded securely in the aesthetic, salves the initial European anxieties about the epic, as expressed by the missionary William Carey in 1796: "were it like [the] Iliad, only considered as a great effort of human genius, I should think it is one of the first productions in the world, but alas! it is the ground of Faith to Millions of men; and as such must be held in the utmost abhorrence."[40]

In contrast to Brook's and Carrière's gleeful universalizing, Gautam Dasgupta, an Indian steeped in the theater of Europe and the United States and one of the long-time editors of *Performing Arts Journal*, replied to their framing in this way:

> the epic in our time has come to symbolize, through its interconnected tales and legends and the morals attached to each, a virtual exegesis on the Hindu way of life. The *Mahabharata* I grew up with in India is a vital source of nourishment, a measure of one's thoughts and deeds. It is no mere epic constrained by literary and narrative strategies, but a revelatory injunction, ethical and theological in purpose, that determines and defines the social and personal interactions of millions of Indians.[41]

What Brook and Carrière suppressed, then, is the world of indigenous beliefs that organize the narrative. The displacement of the religious is most blatant in Carrière's process of necessary cuts from the 90,000 stanzas. In addition to eliminating a vocabulary that "would bring foreign ghosts into the work,"[42] Carrière focused on the "main story," cutting many "secondary tales."[43] Primary among these "secondary tales" was the entire *Bhagavad-Gita*—what Dasgupta calls "the epicenter of the poem, the fulcrum on which rests the entire thrust of this monumental drama of humanity."[44] Brook and Carrière reduced this text to a few unheard stage whispers. By cutting away the *Bhagavad-Gita*, a "classical" play could be fashioned, untroubled by foreign traditions—a play that Brook described as "Shakespearean in the true sense of the word."[45] Thus, Brook's so-called international project brought *The Mahabharata* securely back to the British sense of classic theater, imported like tea for the eurocentric stage. In fact, Brook's production seemed Shakespearean in delivery style, relation of plot to subplot and comic scenes to tragic ones, mise-en-scène, and the style of meaning.

At least at this point in history, with the aid of a growing postcolonial critique, there was a critical reception of this production that raised historical and ethnic issues. Philip Zarrilli produced an interview for the *Drama Review* entitled "The Aftermath: When Peter Brook Came to India." Probir Guha, director of the Living Theatre in India, describes it this way: "some foreigners they just come here and grab something . . . take it and go . . . I would call it cultural piracy."[46] Zarrilli concludes:

> When this happens, what makes it any different from political or military colonialism? Where do we draw the line between the value of a work of art, and the license that one takes or the means one uses to create it? In intercultural theater work we're not talking about simply extracting a piece of marble from a mountain (which may create its own environmental problems) but about extracting pieces of *lived culture*. The question we all have to face is: does the end justify any means used to create it?[47]

However, the above critique does not mean to imply that there is a way to know some pure indigenous culture. My choice not to include any seemingly objective information about the subject here foregrounds its absence—focuses narrowly on the colonial markings of its reception without suggesting a false/real binary. This deconstructive process, appropriate to a First World scholar, does not suggest that Third World scholars have direct access to pure indigenous traditions. Gayatri Chakravorty Spivak deconstructs the sense of a pure indigenous model in many of her articles.[48] In fact, she disrupts the organization of colonizing/colonized: "I am critical of the binary opposition coloniser/colonised. I try to examine the heterogeneity of 'colonial power' and to disclose the complicity of the two poles of that opposition as it constitutes the disciplinary enclave of the critique of imperialism."[49]

In one sense, I have operated here in somewhat "monolithic figures" of colonialism, themselves decentered in the new analysis.[50] Moreover, by foregrounding the absence of any method of knowing the Sanskrit tradition, I have maintained its category as Other and left it as a monolith. Having no access to the Sanskrit tradition through language acquisition or formal training, however, I cannot disrupt this resulting bipolarity with any success. What I could foresee as a continuation of this project, and something I have fragmentarily begun, is to investigate more deeply the vested interests of those eurocentric theater critics, historians, and practitioners who received the tradition. Part of this project would entail situating the reception of this tradition within the context of translations and publications of other Indian "classical" texts in this century. For example, one part of the dynamic of *rasa* hangs on the notion of *kama*, translated as desire. The English word "desire" entangles this word in all kinds of ideologies that displace its function in the drama. The reception and popular uses of the *Kama Sutra* offer only one blatant example of how that transcultural translation works.

Yet this singular focus on the colonial effect also lends all power to the colonizer, displacing once more any strategies of resistance on the part of the colonized. Jyotsna Singh, in her article on Shakespeare in India, not only traces the abuses of power, but the ways in which Shakespeare was translated, resisted, and appropriated. Perhaps I have erred in not compiling or locating those instances—this elision is based, in part, on the shortcomings in my training.

Nevertheless, I still find it useful, at this point in theater studies, to untie seemingly objective descriptions from their empirical shorings and reveal, instead, their collusion with colonial, imperial practices. At least it disrupts what Timothy Murray has called the "unmediated gaze, the absorptive eye of the world-picture."[51] At this time when cultural studies, in a different way, draw our focus back to intercultural performance/drama traditions, a preliminary review of the literature can serve to alert the reader to strategies of concealment, suppression, and displacement.

NOTES

1. Teresa de Lauretis (ed.), *Feminist Studies/Critical Studies: Issues, Terms, and Contexts* (Bloomington: Indiana University Press, 1986), 9.

2. James Clifford, *Writing Culture*, ed. James Clifford and George E. Marcus (Berkeley: University of California Press, 1984), 3.

3. Thomas Postlewaite, "The Criteria for Periodization in Theatre History," *Theatre Journal* 40:3 (1988): 299–318.

4. Johann Wolfgang Goethe in a letter to F. H. Jacobi, 1 June 1791.

5. See Sebastiano Timpanaro, "Friedrich Schlegel and the Beginnings of Indo-European Linguistics in Germany," in Schlegel, *Über die Sprache und Weisheit der Indier* (Amsterdam: John Benjamins B. V., 1977), xviii.

6. Schlegel, 62–68.

7. Schlegel, x.

8. Schlegel, 35–36.

9. See Friedrich Nietzsche, "The Birth of Tragedy," in *The Birth of Tragedy and the Case of Wagner*, trans. Walter Kaufmann (New York: Vintage Books, 1967), 35, 40.

10. Nietzsche, 37.

11. Nietzsche, 40.

12. Quoted in Richard Symonds, *Oxford and Empire* (London: Macmillan, 1986), 32.

13. Symonds, 32–33.

14. Symonds, 103.

15. Gauri Viswanathan, "The Beginnings of English Literary Study in British India," *Oxford Literary Review* 9:1–2 (1987): 8.

16. Jyotsna Singh, "Different Shakespeares: The Bard in Colonial/Postcolonial India," *Theatre Journal* 41:4 (1989): 445–458.

17. See Symonds, 250–253.

18. For a complete discussion of this colonial prejudice, see Ron Inden, *Imagining India* (Oxford: Basil Blackwell, forthcoming).

19. Adya Rangacharya, *Introduction to Bharata's Natya-Sastra* (Bombay: Popular Prakasgan, 1966), 8.

20. Rangacharya, v.

21. A. Berriedale Keith, *The Sanscrit Drama in Its Origin, Development, Theory and Practice* (Oxford: Clarendon Press, 1924), 277.

22. Richard Schechner, *Between Theater and Anthropology* (Philadelphia: University of Pennsylvania Press, 1985), 136.

23. P. S. R. Appa Rao, *A Monograph on Bharata's Naatya Saastra*, trans. P. Sri Rama Sastry (Khairatabad: A Naatya Maalaa Publ., 1967), 31–32.

24. Anita Ratnam Rangaraj, *Natya Brahman Theatric Universe* (Madras: Society for Archaeological Historical and Epigraphical Research, 1979), 17.

25. Schechner, 141.

26. B. K. Thakkar, *On the Structuring of Sanskrit Drama* (Ahmedabad: Saraswati Pustak Bhandar, 1984), 36.

27. Henry W. Wells, *The Classical Drama of India* (New York: Asia Publication House, 1963), 43.

28. See a full discussion of this controversy in Keith, 57–68.

29. Inden, 87.

30. J. L. Masson and M. V. Patwardhan, *Aesthetic Rapture*, 2 vols. (Poona: Deccan College, 1970), 1:7.

31. Masson and Patwardhan, 33.

32. Rangaraj, 11.

33. Rao, 27.

34. Rangacharya, 46.

35. For a treatment of the issue, though itself a controversial text, see Louis Dumont, *Homo Hierarchicus: The Caste System and Its Implications* (Chicago: University of Chicago Press, 1979). For a history of the colonial reception of caste and estate, see Inden.

36. Rao, 33.

37. Mayadhara Mansinha, *Kalidasa and Shakespeare* (Delhi: Motilal Banarsidass, 1969).

38. Richard Schechner, Mathilde La Bardonnie, Joël Jouanneau, and George Banu (interviewers), "Talking with Peter Brook," *Drama Review* 30:1 (Spring 1986): 55.

39. Jean-Claude Carrière, introduction to *The Mahabharata* (New York: Harper and Row, 1985), ix.

40. Quoted in Viswanathan, 19.

41. Gautam Dasgupta, "The Mahabharata: Peter Brook's Orientalism," *Performing Arts Journal* 30, 10:3 (1987): 10.

42. George Banu (interviewer), "Talking with the Playwright, the Musician, the Designer," *Drama Review* 30:1 (Spring, 1986): 74.

43. Carrière, 74.

44. Dasgupta, 12.

45. Brook in interview with Banu, 64.

46. In Philip Zarrilli, "The Aftermath: When Peter Brook Came to India," *Drama Review* 30:1 (1986): 96.

47. Zarrilli, 97–98.

48. See Spivak, "French Feminism in an International Frame" and "Subaltern Studies: Deconstructing Historiography," in *In Other Worlds* (New York: Methuen, 1987).

49. Spivak in Angela McRobbie, "Strategies of Vigilance: An Interview with Gayatri Chakravorty Spivak," *Block* 10 (1985): 9.

50. See Benita Perry, "Problems in Current Theories of Colonial Discourse," *Oxford Literary Review* 9:1–2 (1987): 27–58.

51. Timothy Murray, "Subliminal Libraries: Showing Lady Liberty and Documenting Death," *Discourse* (1987): 117.

Revealing
Surveillance
Strategies

_____

The Artificial Eye

Augustan Theater and the Empire of the Visible

JOSEPH ROACH

In Robert Hooke's *Micrographia* of 1665, there is a fold-out plate nearly two feet long when it is fully extended. On this plate Hooke engraved the exhaustively detailed, superenlarged image of a common flea. This astonishing tableau, oft-reproduced as a milestone of scientific observation, could compete for laurels in the literary genre of the mock-heroic. Jonathan Swift was not the last author to have found it all but inexpressibly revolting. Showing the public what a microscope could do, Hooke elevated to the status of academic wonder the previously invisible and indescribable surfaces of the everyday world. He captured what the naked eye could not see in a form that words alone could not express.[1]

The power of the microscopic sublime resides in the definitive articulation of its details. Its very tangibility resists allegorization. Hooke's rendering reveals each formidable flap of the martially armored thoracic segments. It luxuriates the busy liaison of six appendages rooted in hairy pods. Most alarmingly, it emphasizes the belligerent tilt of the proboscis, lowered in apparent determination to alight and to suck. To say that it resists allegory is not to say that it is without style. Its wonder, its alterity, and its threat reside in the immediacy of its rendering. Poised at the balance point between stillness and motion, the flea's attitude suggests the aesthetic design of the "pregnant moment," the instant in which the figures in a pictorial composition seem ready to leap into decisive action. In

131

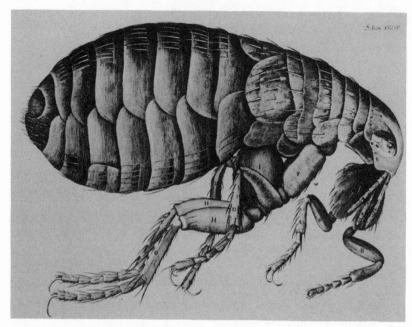

Robert Hooke, Micrographia, *1665, plate xxxiv. Northwestern University Photo Services.*

terms of theatrical history, the micrographic flea might be thought of as the inciting incident of a domestic drama à la Diderot and Greuze, a scene of everyday life enlarged into an imposing tableau of bourgeois crisis.

As self-contained as the hyperenlarged specimen appears, its very impact as a graphic design refers the beholder to another kind of power. This is the power of the artificial eye that fixed the image of the flea upon the page. Behind the engraved image lies the scrutiny of the microscopic gaze. Behind that gaze operates the enormously successful optical technology of the late seventeenth century. It was this mature science of vision that opened newly discovered territories of the quotidian to graphic conquest. It enlarged the explorer's map of the visible world to delineate even the local topographies of vermin. A reproof to metaphysics, optics appeared to advance a science of what was really there to see. Hooke illustrates an insect, but he also stakes a claim to a realm of knowledge that is only possible within the limits of specialized instruments. These instruments create new knowledge by manipulating the scale of the objects they view.

The micrographic image presents a paradox of scale. To appreciate it the beholder must alternate in wonder between a perception of its actual smallness and commonplace familiarity, on one hand, and its gigantic appearance, on the other. The effectiveness of Hooke's presentation depends upon micrography's power to construct and then to reconstruct a sense of scale in the mind of the viewer, whose imagination must oscillate between reassurance (by the small and familiar) and alienation (by the large and the strange). The technology Hooke deploys extends the beholder's concept of the range of nature to encompass previously unknown varieties, replete with unprecedented features, opulent with the wealth of heretofore unimagined details.

The visual discovery of these exotic new realms of nature and the dissemination of knowledge about them through graphic reproduction illuminate, I believe, the contemporaneous practices regulating the representation of intercultural encounters. These were marked by the ambitious collection and display of physical specimens, artifacts, descriptive accounts, and illustrations, gathered from the far reaches of empire and empire-to-be. Visual display and illustration impelled expansion of the system of classification known as natural history. Such an expansion might further be said to characterize the modern emergence of what Martin Jay, summarizing the antiocular theology of Jacques Ellul's *Humiliation of the Word* (1985), has termed "ocularcentrism." Through the manifold advances in the means of the production and reproduction of images has come the irreversible "privileging of vision."[2] At the same time, voyages of discovery and encounter further stimulated ocularcentric practices—as ways of dealing with racial and cultural Others. At least this is the argument of Michel de Certeau's chapter on ethnography in *The Writing of History*:

> The eye is in the service of a "discovery of the world." It is the front line of an encyclopedic curiosity that during the sixteenth century "frenetically heaps up" materials in order to posit the "foundations of modern science." The rare, the bizarre, the unique . . . are apprehended in the fervor of an englobing ambition: "that nothing will remain foreign to man and that everything will be at

his service." . . . The frenzy of knowing and the pleasure of looking reach into the darkest regions and unfold the interiority of bodies as surfaces laid out before our eyes.[3]

The maturation of optical science in the seventeenth century, however, repositioned the conceptual linkages among vision, knowledge, and conquest in their relationships to technology, on one hand, and to rational taxonomy, on the other. The historical location of these developments suggests that new historicists, attempting to match eurocolonial power and Renaissance theatrical representation, may have dated the "Empire of the Gaze" too early.[4]

In the same year that Robert Hooke published *Micrographia*, John Dryden produced *The Indian Emperour; or, the Conquest of Mexico by the Spaniards* (1665). A sequel to *The Indian Queen* (1664), it represented Aztec culture at the crisis of its eurocolonial encounter. Through the magnifying lens of the Restoration heroic play, *The Indian Emperour* dramatized both sides in a conflict of imperial expansion and intercultural discovery. It remained very popular for the next seventy years, coinciding with the consolidation of the British empire in the home islands and overseas, including America. As Dryden noted in the dedication, "[Montezuma's] story is, perhaps the greatest, which was ever represented in a Poem of this nature; (the action of it including the Discovery and Conquest of the New World)."[5] Unlike Shakespeare's *Tempest*, however, with which it shares a common source in the ethnographic essays of Montaigne, *The Indian Emperour* localizes and particularizes the geography and peoples of the conquest.

Dryden varies history to suit his dramaturgical needs: first, by attaching a villainous and greedy Pizarro to the expedition of the noble and selfless Cortez; second, by interweaving the cultural politics of the story with a triple love plot. But Dryden also makes use of the detailed accounts of the early European witnesses of the conquest in order to people his brave new world with the closest thing he could approximate to authentic specimens:

> I have neither wholly followed the story nor varied from it; and, as near as I could, have traced the Native simplicity and ignorance of the *Indians*, in relation to *European* Customs: the Shipping, Armour, Horses, Swords, and Guns of the *Spaniards*, being as new to

them as their Habits and their Languages were to the *Christians*.
The difference of their Religion from ours, I have taken from the
Story it self; and that which you find of it in the first and fifth Acts,
touching the sufferings and constancy of *Montezuma* in Opinions,
I have only illustrated, not alter'd from those who have written
of it. (27–28)

I shall return to *The Indian Emperour* in greater detail, but first I want to
establish a context for the continuing success of Dryden's play, especially
on the early eighteenth century stage, which was increasingly the theater
of the "artificial eye."

The theater, like the microscope, is an instrument of highly selective
enlargement. The analogic status of microscopy and theater appears in
the new illustrated encyclopedias of the early eighteenth century. Mediat-
ing between the arts and sciences, these practical dictionaries of technology and nature testify to the importance of optics, or at least metaphors
of optics, in the systems of knowledge they advanced. When the encyclopedist John Harris says in the preface to the *Lexicon Technicum*
(1704) that words must give way to things in the new priority of scientific
representation, he sets an agenda for the enlarging and recording of visual
impressions that resembles the contemporaneous humiliation of the word
by a scenically opulent Augustan stage. When Ephraim Chambers, in his
celebrated *Cyclopaedia; or, an Universal Dictionary of the Arts and Sciences* (1727; 5th ed. 1741–1743), enthuses over the *Camera Obscura* ("in
optics, a machine, or apparatus representing an artificial eye; whereon
the images of external objects received through a double convex glass, are
exhibited distinctly and in their native colours"), he summarizes the appeal of the device in terms appropriate to theatrical representation: "[The
artificial eye] affords very diverting spectacles; both by exhibiting images
perfectly like their objects, and each cloathed in their native colours; and
by expressing at the same time, all their motions: which latter, no other
art can imitate."[6] Chambers expresses a heightened sense of entitlement
bestowed, it would seem, by the power to render visible, to reproduce,
and to illustrate actions as well as images in ever more rigorously elaborated detail.

Proliferation of detail stimulated advances in classification. It did so by
promoting the division of natural phenomena into categories on the basis

of those differences and similarities that lent themselves especially well to illustration. This was true of botany, as in Linnaeus's exquisite delineation of the varieties of plants by their sexual organs. It was true of the passions, as in Charles Lebrun's depiction of distinctive physiognomical expressions under the stress of strong emotions. And it was also true of the eighteenth-century theater, the stage on which new standards of specialized gesture redefined the actor's art, in which new conventions of scenic illusion intensified the relative value of spectacle, and for which the wider realms of visible nature provided a growing abundance of strange and amusing objects, localities, and cultures for discovery and categorical appropriation.

In these particularizing systems of organization and representation, all the folds and crevices of nature's visible surfaces seemed to become potential signifiers within a grid of phylogenetic difference. As Hooke's flea celebrated the conquests of the artificial eye, so natural history proudly enlarged the empire of the visible to the eurocolonial frontiers. As it surveyed and aggregated human societies and cultures, however, it entered a different realm than the elucidation of objects. In this project, the artificial eye scrutinized and attempted to represent classes of visible behaviors with the same confidence with which it had illustrated classes of insects and plants. It examined alien cultures as it explored tactile surfaces, microscopically, as if the infinite clarity of its vision ensured that races needed only to be discovered, not encountered. When Linnaeus, for example, turned his attention from plants to people in the *Natural History* of 1735, he extended his observations of physical difference to the fine particulars, equally clear and unproblematic to him, of habits, customs, and actions. In the order of primates of the phylum of Mammalia, he located *Homo sapiens* as "diurnal; varying by education and situation," exemplified by the differences between, say, Africans and Europeans:

> [Europeans] Fair, sanguine, brawny. *Hair* yellow, brown, flowing, *eyes* blue; *gentle*, acute, inventive. Covered with close vestments. *Governed* by laws.
> [Africans] Black, phlegmatic, relaxed. *Hair* black, frizzled; *skin* silky; *nose* flat; lips tumid; *crafty*, indolent, negligent. Anoints himself with grease. *Governed* by caprice.

While the "Asiatic" is "*governed* by opinions," the American is "*regulated* by customs."[7] Here the great optical and taxonomic project of the Enlightenment beholds the oscillating constructedness of cultural meanings of difference and Otherness, but it does not blink. The peoples of the world offer themselves for discovery and illustration, like flowers and insects, as far as the artificial eye can see.

In the early eighteenth century, certainly no European eye saw further than the English-speaking mercantile one. In the taxonomy of Chambers's *Cyclopaedia*, by far the richest network of cross-indexed articles systematically subordinates world geography to British commercial and imperial interests. Its cross-references speak directly to its ideological imperatives: INDIA: see EAST-INDIA COMPANY; ORIENTAL: see OCCIDENTAL, "a term used chiefly in commerce, to distinguish commodities brought from the West-Indies, i.e. America, from those brought from the East-Indies, which are said to be *oriental*"; NEGRO: see SLAVE; SLAVE: see COMMERCE; COMMERCE: see COLONY; COLONY: see AMERICA; AMERICA: see CANNIBAL.

As the Augustan encyclopedist surveyed and illustrated the march of empire, the Augustan dramatist staged images of the fabulous varieties, human and material, of the new world beyond the seas. In George Lillo's *The London Merchant* (1731), for instance, Thorowgood, the title character, outlines for Trueman, his worthy apprentice, the duties incumbent upon them as captains of commerce in the world system. In act III, scene i, they speak of the economic macrocosm as Thorowgood examines Trueman's inventory accounts:

> THOROWGOOD: Methinks I would not have you only learn the
> method of merchandise and practice it hereafter merely as a
> means of getting wealth. 'Twill be well worth your pains to study
> it as a science, see how it is founded in reason and the nature of
> things, how it has promoted humanity as it has opened and yet
> keeps up an intercourse between nations far remote from one
> another in situation, customs, and religion; promoting arts,
> industry, peace, and plenty; by mutual benefits diffusing mutual
> love from pole to pole.
> TRUEMAN: Something of this I have considered, and hope, by

your assistance, to extend my thoughts much farther. I have observed those countries where trade is promoted and encouraged to not make discoveries to destroy but to improve mankind—by love and friendship to tame the fierce and polish the most savage; to teach them the advantages of honest traffic by taking from them, with their own consent, their useless superfluities, and giving them in return what, from their ignorance in manual arts, their situation, or some other accident, they stand in need of.

THOROWGOOD: 'Tis justly observed. The populous East, luxuriant, abounds with glittering gems, bright pearls, aromatic spices, and health-restoring drugs. The late-found western world glows with unnumbered veins of gold and silver ore. On every climate and on every country Heaven has bestowed some good peculiar to itself. It is the industrious merchant's business to collect the various blessings of each soil and climate and, with the products of the whole, to enrich his native country.

Theirs is truly a multinational corporate vision. They speak as if they walk together, Gulliver-like, upon an outspread map of the world, trying not to step on any deserving trading partners. Trueman's almost evangelical ambition "to tame the fierce and polish the most savage" consecrates his commercial interests. Gold and silver have value, but less than people, for gold and silver do not consume, do not band together as markets, do not organize themselves into systems of dependency and commerce. Lillo set his play at the time of the Spanish Armada, contrasting the English mercantile empire with the cruel Spaniard's "slow return of wealth from his New World."[8] Their critique of Hispanic imperialism restates a dramatic stereotype embodied in Dryden's play, especially in the role of Pizarro, which derives from other heroic plays and operas of the period, beginning with William Davenant's *The Cruelty of the Spaniards in Peru* (1658).

The Indian Emperour opens with the Spaniards alone in an exotic landscape, "The Scene a pleasant Indian *Country*" (30). This setting was reused, along with some evidently very special costumes, from *The Indian Queen* of the previous season (prologue, 29). In 1664, Aphra Behn returned from South America bearing native specimens suitable to a cabinet of curiosities, including snake skins, rare flies, baskets, aprons, weapons, and, above all: "Feathers, which they order into all Shapes, make themselves little short Habits of 'em, and glorious Wreaths for their Heads, Necks, Arms and Legs, whose Tinctures are unconceivable. I had a Set of these presented to me, and I gave 'em to the King's Theatre, and it was the Dress of the *Indian Queen*, infinitely admired by Persons of Quality, and was inimitable."[9] The power of these vestments resides in the authenticating particularity of their visible details—feathers for every appendage, as copious as insect hairs enlarged by the micrographic eye, exhibitions of the natural history of the New World.

The conquistadors admire the native topography with eyes that marvel in discovery and with language that speaks in images of infancy and new birth:

> CORTEZ: On what new happy Climate are we thrown,
>   So long kept secret, and so lately known;
>   As if our old world modestly withdrew,
>   And here, in private, had brought forth a new! (30)

But these eyes also explore every detail of the surface, probing the geological tissues, mapping the landscape as if to mark the very particulates of favored minerals in the soil:

> VASQUEZ: Methinks we walk in dreams on fairy Land,
>   Where golden Ore lies mixt with common sand;
>   Each downfal of a flood the Mountains pour,
>   From their rich bowels rolls a silver shower.
> CORTEZ: Heaven from all ages wisely did provide
>   This wealth, and for the bravest Nation hide,
>   Who with four hundred foot and forty horse,
>   Dare boldly go a New found World to force. (31)

Like Thorowgood and Trueman, then, Cortez and Vasquez take inventory as far as the eye can see. Although they differ to some extent in the level of coercive force they are ready to project, what they see is vast amounts of raw materials in the hands of childlike peoples, "all untaught and salvage," denizens of the "Infant world" (30).

The following scene (I.ii) shows a remarkable transformation of the image of the Indians. It is set in a temple where high priests, ritually burning incense, announce the bloody sacrifice of five hundred human victims. Montezuma enters, attended by members of his family and court, who *"place themselves"* with solemn formality and discuss the intricacies of dynastic succession. The oscillation in the scale of the image from the previous scene is striking: the artless children the Spaniards described now appear as the regal executors of a powerful and subtle culture. They speak in rhymed couplets, the language of Dryden's Titans, and, like his Herculean heroes, they must struggle to govern complex passions and to accommodate conflicting loyalties. Montezuma, semidivine potentate, is rendered helpless by his unrequited love of Almeria:

> My Lyon-heart is with Loves toyles beset,
> Strugling I fall still deeper in the net. (38)

Here the meaning of the representation depends upon the imaginative acquiescence of the viewers to the dual nature of the image—small and familiar one moment, large and strange by turns.

This reading is supported by a visual record of a particular event in theatrical history. William Hogarth depicted an amateur performance of *The Indian Emperour* (c. 1731). His painting shows a small stage set up in the house of Conduitt, master of the mint, and a cast of four young children taking the parts in Dryden's play. The contradiction in scale is readily apparent. The children act formally, imitating the large gestures, stern expressions, and heroic poses illustrated in the acting manuals of the period. They represent the struggle to govern the adult passions that surely cannot be contained within their diminutive bodies. As the children of the household, they are small and familiar. In the foreground, however, a mother in the audience greatly admonishes a fidgeting child who has dropped her miniature fan. This vignette heightens by contrast the magnifying effect of the child performers onstage. As heroic figures on a stage representing dynastic struggle and imperial conquest, they are large and strange. Hogarth thus captured the double operation of the artificial eye, manipulating the scale from microcosm to macrocosm, enlarging the quotidian into the global, shrinking the imperial into the domestic.

In a world made smaller by trade and more readily visible by exhibition and representation, such differences and such contradictions could, to an unprecedented degree, be collected as phenomena of natural his-

William Hogarth, The Indian Emperour; or, The Conquest of Mexico, *c. 1731.*

tory. On the level of daily consumption of the fantastic diversity of the world, Augustan London teemed with human exhibits that traded upon the accommodation of the commonplace to the strange. There was the "Indian King" from Jamaica, who, "redeemed from slavery by a London merchant," could be viewed for twopence at the Golden Lion, Smithfield. There was the "Painted Prince" from Mindanao, who exhibited a map of the world tattooed on his "Admirable backparts," viewable daily at the Blue Boar's Head, Fleet Street. Arrayed upon a taxonomic grid of difference, such racial novelties were juxtaposed to the normative attractions provided by Anglo-Saxon freaks: "giants and dwarfs exhibited together, masculine women, persons without arms and legs, monstrous births, strange formations and diseases . . . fire eaters, stone eaters, eaters of raw flesh—cats, etc.," and, by the projection device of the magic lantern, Robert Hooke's micrographic flea.[10]

There was much indeed for the artificial eye to behold. No less mercenary than the circuslike fair booths, but somewhat more calculatingly decorous in its choice of specimens, the Augustan theater traded on racial and cultural differences in its audiences, when it could arrange them, and in its play selections, when it could produce them. It capitalized on the occasional visits of foreign embassies, for instance, from the proliferating outposts of empire-in-the-making. These royal progresses included heavily advertised appearances at the London theaters, suggesting that the exotic princes proved powerful competitors to the common run of curiosa. In 1702, *The Emperour of the Moon* played "for the entertainment of an African Prince, Nephew to the King of Banjay." In 1703, it was repeated for "the entertainment of His Excellency Hodgha Bowhoon, Envoy to Her Majesty [Queen Anne] from the Great King of Persia." In 1708, *Othello* played "for the entertainment of the Ambassador of the Emperour of Morocco"; and in 1710, the opera house served up Davenant's musical version of *Macbeth* for the delectation of four Mohawk "Kings," representing the great Iroquois Confederacy of North America.[11] The crowd at this event insisted that the Native Americans be placed onstage— the better to be seen against a backdrop of flying witches and boiling cauldrons. The ambassadors, invited to attend the spectacle, became the spectacle themselves.[12] Their physical presence in public view onstage reinforced the role of theater as the illustrator of brave new worlds and the strange creatures in them. This role proved congenial to some of the most popular plays of the period—Shakespeare's *Othello* and Thomas Southerne's *Oroonoko* come to mind. In their scenes of intercultural encounter, the artificial eye cast its magnifying gaze on visible behaviors, illustrating them, measuring them, fixing them, in relation to European norms.

Dryden alerted his public that his characterization of Montezuma, the titular hero of *The Indian Emperour*, would show the authentic sufferings of "an *Indian Prince*, and not to expect any other Eloquence from his simplicity, then that which his griefs have furnished him" (25). As victim, Montezuma represents natural man, spokesperson for a natural religion, the elaboration of which includes the aforementioned exotic rites, chanting priests, and human sacrifice. The most extraordinary scene of *The Indian Emperour* is that in which Pizarro and a "Christian Priest" torture Montezuma on the rack to force disclosure of the location of his gold (V.ii). Dryden points up Montezuma's unnerving serenity by having an "Indian High Priest" tortured at the same time. His cries and eventual death show by contrast the Emperour's preternatural self-possession:

INDIAN HIGH PRIEST: I faint away, and find I can no more:
Give leave, O King, I may reveal thy store,
And free my self from pains I cannot bear.
MONTEZUMA: Think'st thou I lye on Beds of Roses here,
Or in a Wanton Bath stretch'd at my ease?
Dye, slave, and with thee, dye such thoughts as these.
[High Priest turns aside and dyes.] (101)

Here there is a precise and terrible magnification. Dryden locates the Indian Emperour's behavior among the phenomena of natural history. The strength of Montezuma's "Natural Religion" becomes visible in his wonderful ability to endure pain. This Dryden examines in exquisite detail, as Linnaeus might delineate the web of venous tissue on the underside of a leaf. As the ropes tighten, as his "veines breake" and "sinews crack," the Indian Emperour serenely expounds in rhyming couplets his native theology on the insubstantiality of the body (98–101). The rack on which he is stretched is an ocular instrument that magnifies pain in visible increments, not unlike the gradations of enlargement of the microscopic lens, each turn of the wheel a measurement of his cultural and racial identity in ever finer resolution. In Dryden's staging of the categories of nature, Montezuma finds his niche in the phylum of the Noble Savage, earnest as a child, as invulnerable as a demigod, and apparently fixed forever as either smaller or larger than the dominant culture's vision of the norm. Such dramas demonstrate how nature becomes what the artificial eye creates and thinks it has seen.

I have attempted to interpret the Augustan theater as an instrument, closely analogous to contemporary optical instruments, especially suited to the magnification of behavior. Used within a system of observation and implicit classification, such an instrument disseminates, I believe, powerful constructions of social and cultural difference. Perhaps this instrument, circumscribed within the contingencies of a particular historical moment, might suggest some of the ways in which the infinitely more pervasive instruments of magnification of more recent times operate. The proscenium stage in the age of Dryden, like the microscope in the age of Hooke, is a paltry thing in comparison to what has followed. In view of the intercultural struggles of the telecommunications age, it seems quaint to think in terms of the singular form, the artificial eye, to describe an ocularcentric technology that has multiplied its images, like the inside of an insect's eye, magnifying and reconfiguring human difference as it consolidates a global empire of the visible.

NOTES

1. Robert Hooke, *Micrographia; or Some Physiological Descriptions of Minute Bodies Made by Magnifying Glasses* (London: Royal Society, 1665), plate xxxiv. For commentary on the import of microscopy in Augustan literature, see Marjorie Hope Nicolson, *Science and Imagination* (1956; rpt., Hamden, Conn.: Archon Books, 1976), 155–234; and Paul Fussel, *The Rhetorical World of Augustan Humanism* (London, Oxford, New York: Oxford University Press, 1969), 233–261.

2. Martin Jay, "The Rise of Hermeneutics and the Crisis of Ocularcentrism," in *The Rhetoric of Interpretation and the Interpretation of Rhetoric*, ed. Paul Hernadi (Durham and London: Duke University Press, 1989), 55.

3. Michel de Certeau, *The Writing of History*, trans. Tom Conley (New York: Columbia University Press, 1988), 231–232.

4. See, for instance, Stephen Greenblatt, *Shakespearean Negotiations: The Circulation of Social Energy in Renaissance England* (Berkeley and Los Angeles: University of California Press, 1988), particularly chapter 2, "Invisible Bullets," and chapter 5, "Martial Law in the Cockaigne." For the application of new historicist approaches to the later period, see Laura Brown and Felicity Nussbaum (eds.), *The New Eighteenth Century: Theory, Politics, English Literature* (New York and London: Methuen, 1987), especially 41–61.

5. *The Works of John Dryden*, ed. John Loftis, 20 vols. (Berkeley and Los Angeles: University of California Press, 1966), 9:25. Subsequent citations from this edition of *The Indian Emperour* are given in the text.

6. Ephraim Chambers, *Cyclopaedia; or, an Universal Dictionary of Arts and Sciences*, 5th ed. (London: W. Innys, 1741–1743), s.v. "Camera Obscura."

7. [Linnaeus], *An Universal System of Natural History, Including the Natural History of Man* (1735; London: Champant and Whitrow, 1794), 1:7.

8. George Lillo, *The London Merchant; or, The History of George Barnwell*, ed. William H. McBurney (1731; Lincoln: University of Nebraska Press, 1965), 40, 10.

9. Aphra Behn, *Oroonoko*, ed. Lore Metzger (1688; New York: Norton, 1973), 2.

10. Richard Altick, *The Shows of London* (Cambridge: Belknap Press, 1978), 42–46.

11. *The London Stage, 1600–1800,* 11 vols., part 2: *1700–1729,* ed. Emmett L. Avery (Carbondale: Southern Illinois University Press, 1960), 1:29, 34, 178, 220.

12. Richmond P. Bond, *Queen Anne's American Kings* (Oxford: Clarendon Press, 1952), 3–6.

The

Playhouse

and the

Committee

BARRY B. WITHAM

On 21 July 1948, Howard F. Smith, "rancher and hotel opera-
tor," testified under oath before the Canwell Committee on Un-American
Activities in Seattle, Washington, that the local Civic Theatre, the Repertory Playhouse, was a recruiting ground for communists and that he had
recruited there on several occasions while a member of the party. He remembered particularly well a time that he was invited backstage where
"they had it set up like a hootenanny. They had a bar, sold drinks and
there I saw all the actors and actresses . . . and this nigger, Mozee that got
knocked off . . . they had lots of colored folk there and lots of girls."[1]
Smith's lurid, misguided testimony in which "all of the actors and actresses" were guilty was typical of a lot of the sworn statements before the
Canwell Committee; its racial and sexual slandering was also typical of
the mudslinging, homophobia, and chauvinism that characterized similar
attacks on a national level.

There is no need here to belabor those familiar tales of Christopher
Marlowe and Hallie, the "Red Menace," but it is important to recall that
the innuendo and smear tactics that accompanied much of the red-hunting
were not limited to starstruck entrepreneurs like Howard F. Smith. Nearly
ten years earlier, during the congressional debate over the Federal Theatre

Project, the distinguished Everett Dirksen of Illinois reviewed a whole list of plays, none of which he had seen.

> I have one here—A NEW DEAL FOR MARY, which is a grand title. Also A NEW KIND OF LOVE. I wonder what that can be. It smacks somewhat of the Soviet. Then there is UP IN MABEL'S ROOM. There is an intriguing title for you . . . and BE SURE YOUR SEX WILL FIND YOU OUT. . . . Then there is CHEAT-ING HUSBANDS. That would do well for the front page of some Washington daily. Next we have COMPANIONATE MAGGIE, and this great rhetorical and intriguing question, DID ADAM SIN? Another one they have dished up is GO EASY, MABEL, and still another that would strike the fancy of anybody—JUST A LOVE NEST. . . . Now, if you want that kind of salacious tripe, very well, vote for it, but if anybody has any interest in decency on the stage, if anyone has an interest in real cultural values, you will not find it in this kind of junk.[2]

Dirksen's remarks were not fatal to the project, although they are indicative of much popular opinion of the time. The Federal Theatre expired for many reasons, including budget cutbacks, bureaucratic inefficiency, and the failure to develop a national rural audience. In the case of the Repertory Playhouse, however, the red-baiting was devastating. When combined with similar testimony, Smith's charges led directly to the death of a theater which had been a pioneer institution in the North-west for twenty years and had earned the respect and admiration of theater artists throughout the country. Caught on the uneasy landscape between art and politics, the theater had no defense against the brutal power of the Canwell Committee. In the words of historian Vern Countryman, its "loss of patronage is traceable primarily to the dubious testimony of such witnesses as George Hewitt, Howard Smith and Sarah Eldredge."[3]

Forty years later, the events of that era still resonate; the recent death of Florence James, a co-founder of the Playhouse, reminded many of battles lost and those left unresolved. At a memorial gathering in her honor, familiar tales circulated: the rumors associated with her Russian tour in 1934; her long-standing feud with Glenn Hughes, the powerful chair of the University of Washington Drama School; and the continued failure of the Seattle press and community to honor the achievements of Florence and her husband, Burton. How long, I wondered, would the shadows of those years persist and was it possible to pay some belated tribute to the Jameses' pioneering theater work?

Florence James's conviction for refusing to answer the questions of the Canwell Committee tarred her with a red brush as it did so many others who believed in the great "leftist" and socially relevant theater of the 1930s and 1940s. Clearly, her conviction for contempt was, for many, not only a proper indictment of her theater but an admission of her membership in the Communist party. Since the charge brought against the Jameses was for contempt of committee, however, the question of "communism" at the heart of the hearings was never an issue in their legal trials. Therefore, the focus in court was on the legal right of the committee to ask specific questions. As a result, the original charges were never rebutted or affirmed and the Jameses were never given the opportunity to respond directly to the questions raised by the Canwell Committee.

Had they been allowed the right of cross-examination or to respond to the charges, would they have been vindicated? Was it possible, I wondered, to reexamine the record of those turbulent years and help restore the reputation of a person as courageous and talented as Florence James? There was something provocative about the notion. The Jameses had pioneered a nationally respected, socially conscious theater in the Northwest and deserved to be remembered for that. And I, a middle-aged white historian, had recently been promoted to the position once held by their arch rival, Glenn Hughes.

The Seattle Repertory Playhouse was founded in 1928 by Florence and Burton James, who had moved to Seattle from New York City to teach in the prestigious Cornish School of the Arts. Their politics were liberal and their taste in drama reflected the "art theater" of the time. They had been active in the settlement house movement in New York and had vaguely articulated notions about the social mission of the theater which were not always compatible with the training mission of the Cornish School or the conservatism of its Board of Directors. When their proposed production of Pirandello's *Six Characters in Search of an Author* (1928) ran into trouble with the board—which believed that its subject matter was inappropriate—they resigned and founded their own theater.

The Repertory Playhouse, which was partially inspired by the Theatre Guild in New York and partially by a desire to involve the local community in the life of the theater, was at first enormously successful. In four years, they built their own theater and attracted a subscription audience of over 20,000 people. Located across the street from the University of Washington campus, the 340-seat proscenium house was quickly viewed as an alternative theater in the Seattle community. Concentrating on modern classics as well as plays that had a social concern, the Jameses developed a sophisticated and enthusiastic following. Their production of *Peer Gynt* (1932), for example, was widely hailed as one of the most imaginative and adventurous in the history of the city. Designed for, and heavily advertised in, a large Norwegian community, *Peer Gynt* sold out its entire run. And their 1933 production of *In Abraham's Bosom* featuring black performers as well as a black gospel choir had a similar impact. However, the Depression undermined their early success; as their audiences dwindled, they were forced to reassess both their theater and their political mission.

Like many other young artists of the day, the Jameses believed that the theater had to play a responsible social mission—that it had to be rooted firmly in contemporary times and deal with contemporary problems. Thus, by the mid-1930s, their "liberal" activity had increased dramatically. *Waiting for Lefty* (1936) had split both their board and their audiences into squabbling factions. Conservatives had been further disturbed by what they perceived as a decidedly leftist leaning in the philosophy and programs of the theater. Designed to appeal to a more proletarian audience, special performances were offered on Sunday evenings at reduced rates. The theater sought affiliation with the Marxist-oriented New Theatre League and produced a very controversial production of *The Hairy Ape* (1935) in which the alienation of the working class was described as central to the play and to contemporary life. The Jameses not only explored the emerging Stanislavski system of acting, but taught it in classes for their company within a context of Marxist ideology. What set them apart from a lot of other theaters, however, was not the boldness of their artistic vision but two specific incidents: Florence's trip to Russia in 1934 and Burton's active attempts to involve the black community in productions at the Playhouse.

In the late summer of 1934, Florence and a traveling companion, Marianne King (who had written two plays for the Repertory Playhouse), attended the Stratford Theatre Festival in England and then, along with several others, sailed to the Soviet Union to attend a theater festival in Moscow. It was an exhilarating experience. In her unpublished autobiography, "Fists upon a Star," Florence relates the excitement that they felt as they traveled to this new socialist world, anxious to see how the theater riches of the past, like the Moscow Art Theater (MAT), were flourishing alongside the new revolutionary stage.[4] She reports that many people cautioned her not to go and that she was told numerous horror stories about theft, sickness, political terror, and war.

What she found was, in nearly every respect, diametrically opposed to what she had been told, and her description of the revolutionary workers' state in those autumn days of 1934 would sustain her for many years. Women participated in the society equally with men, she recorded, working as sailors, streetsweepers, military sharpshooters, and bricklayers. There was no theft or shortage of food and everyone was courteous and eager to please. In addition, the theater was wonderful. She saw *Twelfth Night* at the MAT, *Prince Igor* at the Bolshoi, and many others. After seeing a production of *The Negro Boy and the Monkey* at the Moscow Art Theater children's branch, she was convinced that Russia had no race hatred. Moreover, theaters were central to the life of the society. They were being built, she wrote, in remote areas of the Urals and Siberia and amateur groups flourished in the factories and on the collective farms. In a personal interview with Vontsky, assistant commissar of the theater, she was told there was censorship, but only of "immorality, religion, counter-revolution and mysticism" (8). Her enthusiasm is clear, and her final comment on her visit invokes Lincoln Steffens: "I have seen the future and it works" (16). She was there for ten days.

Florence James's unbridled enthusiasm for the Soviet system and her perception of how artists were treated there confirmed her view that a theater could only be effective if it was contributing to social change. Thirteen years after her visit, she was still extolling the virtues of the USSR. "Unlike this country where talent development is dependent upon luck and accident, in the Soviet Union whenever a gifted person is detected the government immediately assumes all the costs of his education and living in order that the people may enjoy the fruit of his creation. . . . All the people indulge in artistic expression and their outstanding artists are their educators."[5] She also told her audience at a Labor Forum in 1947 that "the Soviets have no juvenile delinquency problem because their children are being trained in the artistic expression of their emotions."[6]

When not directly praising the Soviet system, she was embracing and fighting for the kind of liberal causes which would later become the cornerstone for so many "red" dossiers. She was active in antifascist refugee committees, campaigned for unions and labor groups, and lent her name to unpopular causes. She helped raise money to support the revolution in Spain and was active in the defense of labor leader Harry Bridges. In 1945, she was instrumental in leading the fight to get a fair inquest for a juvenile who had been killed while in custody in the King County jail in Seattle. Moreover, she and Burton produced benefit performances at their theater in order to raise money for leftist causes and events. In June 1946, for example, they did a benefit of the Owen Davis melodrama *Bertha the Sewing Machine Girl* for the Seattle Labor School. These benefits—and the receptions that sometimes followed them—would also come back to haunt them in the testimony of Howard F. Smith and others before the Canwell Committee.

The second major action that thrust the Jameses into the innuendo-charged testimony of the Canwell Committee was their attempt to involve the black community in the work at the Playhouse. In 1933, Burton James directed a production of *In Abraham's Bosom* in which he cast a number of black amateur performers from the local African Methodist Church. Although he had earlier used black actors in a production of *Uncle Tom's Cabin*, *Abraham* was a significantly larger venture. Only two of the cast members were white and the production included an onstage gospel chorus. The standing ovations and sold-out houses made the Jameses aware of the potential box office appeal of such ventures. (By 1933, they were having difficulty paying their bills as they sought to appeal to a more proletarian audience while also attempting to retain the middle class, who had initially supported them.) Inspired by the success of *In Abraham's Bosom* and buoyed by their social agenda of involving minority groups in the work of the Playhouse, Burton announced an "all Negro" cast for Andre Obey's *Noah*, which was produced in conjunction with the budding Federal Theatre Project.

The Jameses' proposal for a "Negro Company," housed at their theater and supported through federal monies, was heartily endorsed by national director Hallie Flanagan. She was devoted to this concept since she hoped that black units could be developed outside the major metropolitan areas. Her enthusiasm was rewarded. The work of the Seattle Negro Company was among the most vital contributions of the whole national project and included highly successful productions of *It Can't Happen Here* (1936), *Stevedore* (1936), and *Natural Man* (1937). It also included the controversial "Ethiopian" *Lysistrata* (1936) which was closed by the WPA after only one night for "lewdness." The company added national luster to the Jameses' reputation, although they were criticized by some for opportunism in gaining federal funds for the Playhouse and by others for permanently associating themselves with integration and civil rights, fundamental planks of the Communist party platform.

Burton's experiments with casting blacks also caused him to cross paths again with Glenn Hughes, director of the University of Washington School of Drama, which was their major theatrical rival in the city. Hughes, whose drama program operated two year-round student theaters, had been appointed by Hallie Flanagan to be director of the Federal Theatre in the Northwest region and thus had a great deal of money under his control. In the early days of the project, Burton had tried to outflank Hughes, for whom he had worked and whom he thoroughly disliked, but Hughes had gotten Hallie Flanagan's support and thus the power to approve any federally sponsored companies. Hughes, who was a visionary in the amateur theater movement, was also an autocrat, a Hoover supporter, and a boulevardier in his taste and was roundly disliked at the Playhouse. The *Logs*, which were kept by actor Al Ottenheimer, reflect the disdain they felt for Hughes: for his middlebrow taste in plays, his self-aggrandizement, and his dropping by their productions to "count the house."[7] Still, Hughes did support the Seattle Negro Company before the WPA and continued to employ Florence James as an acting teacher in his drama program until her dismissal in 1938. At the time of the Canwell hearings a decade later, the long-standing enmity between Hughes and the Jameses resurfaced with acrimony and vindictive charges.

The joint legislative committee to investigate un-American activity in the state of Washington was established in 1947 at the height of another national red scare. Chaired by Albert Canwell of Spokane, it leaned heavily on the tactics popularized by the Dies and Tunney committees and even imported professional anticommunist witnesses to provide an inside look at the way the Communist party operated in America. Its every action was reported in the headlines of the Seattle papers, and state troopers and national guardsmen were enlisted in order to keep order and crush any demonstrations. Those subpoenaed were allowed to have counsel but had no right to cross-examination and were constantly badgered about their personal associations and political beliefs. Canwell, like Joe McCarthy, constantly referred to secret information he had and to lists of names far beyond the number of people who were ever called to testify.

Florence James (along with Burton James and Albert Ottenheimer) was subpoenaed in June 1948 and charged to "go to the 146th. Field Artillery Armory and remain there until discharged by the committee."[8] They joined thirty-seven others—many associated with the University of Washington, which was one of the major targets of the investigation. There, in a highly emotional atmosphere, Canwell banged his gavel, roared his disapproval at any kind of demonstration or appeal, and conducted his inquiry by asking witness after witness what he termed the "64 dollar question": are you now or have you ever been a member of the Communist party?

Very quickly the case against Florence James came into focus. She was suspected of being a communist because, in addition to her known association with Russian issues and people and her numerous speeches on behalf of leftist causes, she had actually been named as a communist by three friendly witnesses. Moreover, the committee had repeated testimony that her Repertory Playhouse was a breeding ground for communism, where immorality was prominent and where teaching and party indoctrination took place.

The most damaging testimony came from black witness George Hewitt, who testified that he had seen Florence James in Moscow in 1932 and that she had been recruited by the party to be one of the cultural sparks to bring about revolution in the United States. Hewitt, who admitted his party membership, also testified that he had seen her at a variety of places, including the Comintern Building, and that she had admitted that she was a member of the American Communist party. He also testified that he had attended meetings at the Meyerhold theater, where Florence James had been discussed as one of the people party members could contact in the Northwest. His testimony was devastating. On 21 July 1948, Florence interrupted the proceedings and demanded to be allowed to cross-examine the witness. She was dragged from the armory by two state troopers. Two days later, while Hewitt was still testifying, Burton James called him a liar from the floor and was also evicted.

Florence was also accused in Howard F. Smith's testimony. He claimed to have been an executive secretary of one branch of the Communist party and recalled that it was widely known that the Seattle Repertory Playhouse was a recruiting ground for the party. He testified:

> Well, the Repertory Playhouse, a branch of the Communist Party, consisted of all the actors and actresses, and they were always at these main meetings of the Communist Party, and they were always selling tickets and if you didn't show up there you wasn't a very good communist, and they served coffee and showed you films of the Great Soviet Union. . . . I recruited a lot there. . . . That was where the Communists played and had their recreation and when the Communists go out and get gory-eyed they don't want any strangers asking them questions.[9]

Finally, Florence was named by Isabel H. Costigan, who admitted to being a member of the party for three years in the late 1930s and also testified as to the prominent place of the Repertory Playhouse as a recruiting ground:

> The Repertory Playhouse served a number of functions. It was a means of raising money at times for Communist activities. Also it served as a point of getting young people—ambitious young people into the Communist Party—likely young people who took English courses at the University, and who were told that they probably had dramatic talent, or dramatic ability, and they were sent to the Repertory Playhouse for trial, where they were given work in bit parts at first, and brought into the social activities of the Playhouse, which were largely Communist Party activities.
>
> QUESTION: In other words, it was a recruiting center then, for Communist Party activities?
>
> MRS. COSTIGAN: To my knowledge it still is.[10]

Since there was no means to confront witnesses, cross-examine, or even make them document their charges, and since the Jameses' lawyer was constantly threatened with expulsion, there was little that Florence could do to counteract the damning testimony. Notes she made during the hearings that were preserved by her bookkeeper, Bette Anderson, reveal how she and Burton struggled to decide what course they should take.[11] She was already on the public record opposing the Canwell Committee and she had been active in denouncing both its methods and its legitimacy. But since ignoring the subpoena seemed foolhardy, she decided that she would recognize the committee by appearing, but refuse to answer any questions and stand on her constitutional rights. Thus, on 22 July 1948, Florence James finally testified in her own defense. Her appearance was brief, outlining simple facts about her biography and then finally responding to counsel's request that she answer the "64 dollar question." She replied, "I resist with everything I have your right to ask that question, and I stand on my constitutional right to refuse to answer it."[12] Moments later, Burton followed her to the stand, was sworn "under duress," and also refused to answer questions about his political affiliations.

They were both indicted for contempt of the committee, charged with a gross misdemeanor for refusing to answer, and released on bail. Their case made the national headlines; with four others, they became known as the "Seattle Six" as they fought their way through the legal system trying to clear their names. When Florence was tried in October 1948, she and her lawyer took the offensive, attacking the legitimacy of the committee, the jury selection process, and the prejudices of the legal system. Even though the State Supreme Court had upheld the constitutionality of the Canwell Committee in March 1948, Florence nearly won. Her jury deliberated for twenty-nine hours and was unable to bring in a verdict. The judge declared it hung and ordered a new trial. In July, she was convicted, fined $125.00, and given a suspended jail sentence of one month. Her concluding remarks to the judge are worth preserving:

> I accuse the court of denying me my proper defense, refusing permission for my witnesses to appear for me—even my own daughter was refused an opportunity to appear as a witness in my defense on some flimsy legal pretext. . . . I accuse the prosecutor of defacing and destroying material evidence. Evidence so important that in the first of these trials it won acquittal. . . . Now, finally, and this is so terrible I find it difficult to phrase the words, I accuse this court, you, Your Honor, of being prejudiced against me, of

giving every assistance within the power of your high office to the prosecution, and of being more concerned with obtaining a guilty verdict than serving the ends of justice in this court.[13]

Burton was also convicted, but because of his increasingly failing health he was spared the jail term. Florence paid over twelve thousand dollars in court costs before the matter was closed.

The negative publicity surrounding the Canwell hearings and the subsequent James trials was catastrophic for the theater. At first, they counterattacked with a campaign called the Committee of 500 in which they appealed to supporters to send ten dollars each to finance the theater. But the effort was futile. Many people returned their letters with statements that echoed the prevailing climate: "If you are not Communists then what do you have to fear from a legislative committee? Why hide behind the fifth amendment?"[14] Subscriptions dropped; theater parties canceled. Their gross income dropped over $20,000 and their theater—which they had sold and were renting—was in turn sold out from under them and acquired by the University of Washington. Before his death, Burton accused Glenn Hughes of cultural vandalism. Angry patrons of the Playhouse wrote to the university protesting the acquisition of the theater, but the university insisted that it had been approached by the owner and that "Professor Hughes objected seriously at first and has never become reconciled to such an action. . . . It is hard to understand how you could have become so misled in the attitude of the university in this regard."[15] The records support this position. Hughes had been promised an additional theater, and the opportunity to gain a suitable space practically across the street was an option that the Board of Trustees could not pass up. Still, the perception lingered that the university had cannibalized the remains of its theatrical competition and capitalized on the "red" hunting that had driven the Jameses out of business.

In going through the records of the period, especially with regard to the accusations of communism, one thing is dramatically clear. There were several "reds" among the people subpoenaed. I can say this with certainty because they admitted it under oath. There was clearly a unit at the University of Washington and their dilemma was not one of admission—since they plainly believed they had done nothing wrong—but whether to name their compatriots. None of them named the Jameses as actual members of the party—not even Professor Winther, who was the "friendliest" of the witnesses and who provided an account of the way the party functioned at the university. Three people testified directly that the Jameses were very probably members of the party because they had been led to believe that by party officials in the Northwest. Two of them quoted Morris Rapport, who was district organizer, as assuring them that Florence and Burton were good comrades. Furthermore, three people testified that they believed the Playhouse also housed a unit of the party.

However, none of that constitutes evidence. As the Jameses' lawyer was fond of pointing out during their trials, American jurisprudence is based on individual guilt, not guilt by association. Moreover, the testimony which directly implicated the Jameses was largely ridiculous. George Hewitt was a pathetic anticommunist witness who was flown around the country as an authority. He perjured himself on several occasions and was under subpoena when he died in New York's Bellevue Hospital. In testifying that he saw Florence at various places in Moscow in 1932, he clearly committed perjury. In fact, Florence put together an elaborate record of her activities throughout 1932 which clearly demonstrates that she could not have been in Moscow when Hewitt swore that he saw her. She also obtained sworn affidavits from several people in Seattle who attested to her movements throughout the year.

Similarly, Howard F. Smith's testimony was bigoted, uninformed, and ignorant. He was so starstruck at being backstage at the theater and so chagrined by the actresses partying that he saw conspiracies at every turn. Isabel Costigan, who said the theater was a major recruiting ground, enrolled her daughter at classes there throughout the hearings. The other "evidence" against Florence was hearsay or guilt by association. As I reviewed the case, it seemed apparent that the accusations—like those against many others—were based upon prejudice, distortion, jealousy, and sour grapes.

I spoke to several people who had worked with Burton and Florence James. Some of them were reluctant to comment; the wounds had been too deep. One former leading man from the company summed it up philosophically: "They just got too political."[16] But most thought an injustice had been done in the harassment of the Playhouse, in the refusal of the *Seattle Times* to cover its activities following the production of *Waiting for Lefty*, and in the acquisition of their theater by the University of

Washington. I became convinced that if supporting Russians when they were American allies, advocating social justice, and using John Howard Lawson's playwriting text for their classes constituted being communists, then they probably were. If communism meant—as Canwell suggested—a covert attempt to overthrow the government of the United States, then the charges were unfounded.

Only one thing puzzled me. Why had Florence James never asked Marianne King, who had accompanied her to Moscow in 1934, to submit an affidavit about their travels? It seemed to be the most efficient way of proving George Hewitt a perjurer since Marianne could testify to what Florence did in the Soviet Union. In preparing for her contempt of court trial, Florence had gone to a number of people to testify about her movements in 1932. I pursued this puzzle back through the records of the Playhouse and the committee and ultimately found additional papers in the files of former Playhouse employee Bette Anderson, which had recently been opened to scholars after the death of Al Ottenheimer. Among these papers was a fascinating letter and response which Florence's conscientious bookkeeper saved, which further muddied the terrain of an already precarious landscape.

On 18 August 1948, Florence James—faced with a trial in superior court and not knowing what direction that investigation might take—wrote to Marianne King and asked for an affidavit about their Russian trip. Her letter reads in part:

> Now what I need, and I hope you will be willing to do this, is to give me an affidavit to this effect: First that you visited the Soviet Union with me in '34 between the dates of August 30th and September 9th. . . . Second that we went to the same places together and that at no time were we ever at the Profitern, Comintern, or Lenin Institute, and never were at a party given by a director or an actress of the Meyerhold Theatre.[17]

On 26 August, King replied from San Francisco. I quote at length here in order to provide a context:

> While I am opposed to certain methods of the Canwell Committee, I am equally opposed to the deceit and secrecy of the Communist Party. Since our very frank talk in San Francisco in 1941, this

can come to you as no surprise, and subsequent events have only strengthened my convictions. My personal affection for you and Burton is unchanged, but it would be impossible for us to meet this summer without political argument which would be painful to all of us and accomplish no good.

As far as an affidavit about our trip to Moscow in 1934 goes, I should be glad to testify to the correct dates and to the fact that as far as I know you did not attend the places mentioned by Mr. Hewitt. I remember that we saw a performance at the Meyerhold Theatre. There might have been a lobby reception or some such thing given by the company, I don't recall. Anyway it is a minor point.

But surely you must realize that if I am thus drawn into the affair, I shall be doubtless questioned further. In that event I should have no alternative but to tell the truth. Refusal to answer is a device that deceives no one. I should infinitely prefer not to be forced into a position where I could do you any injury.[18]

By itself King's letter means little, although it is tantalizing in its implications. Taken together with Florence James's uncritical admiration for the Soviet system, her commitment to social justice and a theater that was more than just mindless entertainment, and the numerous speeches and acting papers which extol the virtues of a dialectical point of view, it does seem clear that she was sympathetic to the Communist party as an alternative to the politics which had created an economic crisis in America. In this she was in fine theatrical company, perhaps even the mainstream of her day: Clifford Odets, Lillian Hellman, John Howard Lawson, and many others.

What shocked me about the letter, however, was that it revealed to me how I had been engaged in the same project as the Canwell Committee and that in my earnestness to "clear" the Jameses I had adapted the strategy of the "red" hunters themselves. In valorizing the question of membership in the Communist party, I had lost sight of the real issue: that the notion of "communism" was a construction intricately linked with issues of race, sex, and subversion. Not only is this clear in the testimony of the Canwell Committee—it is clear in a number of other committees that practiced the investigative techniques of the period. Take, for example, the following response to a petition from a number of Hollywood actors protesting the HUAC procedures in California as read into the official record by Congressman Rankin:

> They sent this petition to Congress, and I want to read you some of their names. One of the names is June Havoc. We found out that her real name is June Hovick. Another one was Danny Kaye, and we found out that his real name was David Daniel Kaminsky. Another one here is John Beal, whose real name is J. Alexander Bleidung. Another is Cy Bartlett, whose real name is Sacha Baraniev. Another one is Eddie Cantor, whose real name is Edward Iskowitz. There is one who calls himself Edward Robinson. His real name is Emanuel Goldenberg. There is another one here who calls himself Melvyn Douglas, whose real name is Melvyn Hesselberg. There are others too numerous to mention. They are attacking the Committee for doing its duty to protect this country and save the American people from the horrible fate the Communists have meted out to the unfortunate Christian people of Europe.[19]

The anti-Semitism in this construction of "communism" is as blatant as the subversive element that was a major factor in the Canwell hearings and helps to illuminate the vast gulf that existed between the committee and the Playhouse. For Canwell, communism meant a very distinct thing. Here is how it was expressed by University of Washington professor Herbert J. Phillips:

> At their first public hearing the Canwell Committee went to considerable expense to establish what their interpretation of the word "communist" was to be. According to them, a communist is one who advocates and works for the violent overthrow of the United States government and is an agent of a foreign power. I believe that force and violence as a means of social change is a fascist doctrine, that its advocacy constitutes treason and deserves the severest punishment.[20]

Indeed, for nearly all the witnesses, the party was most emphatically not violent subversion. It was idealism about a social order, uninformed in many respects, almost certainly ignorant of the Stalinist agenda, mixed with study groups, book reviewing, and endless meetings. It was passion about racial hatred, union organizing, and class inequities. When there were attempts to dictate from Moscow and to create the kind of network that was seriously subversive, most of those subpoenaed simply left the party. Thus, while many of those before the Canwell Committee admitted to being communists, none of them—including Florence James—were the kind of communists the committee was after. This was true in New York and Washington, D.C., as well as in Seattle. In Vern Countryman's rather astute appraisal, the committees that investigated theater projects, in their enthusiasm to root out the kind of political subversives who fit their definition of communism and in their denial of constitutional rights to hundreds of citizens, were ultimately more un-American than the people they accused.[21]

The Canwell Committee was not reappointed by the 1949 legislature and Canwell himself was subsequently defeated in his attempt to capture a U.S. Senate seat. Eventually, the secret files were opened; they contained virtually nothing. On 30 December 1950, *Pygmalion* closed as the last production of the Repertory Playhouse. Eleven months later, Burton James died and Florence James moved to Canada, where she continued to work in Banff and Regina. After she died in 1988, a tribute was held for her in her former theater in Seattle. It had been renamed in honor of Glenn Hughes and still bears his name.

NOTES

1. *Un-American Activities in Washington State*, Report of the Joint Legislative Fact-Finding Committee, Second Report (Olympia: Washington State Legislature, 1948), 225–227.

2. Everett Dirksen quoted in Walter Goodman, *The Committee* (New York: Farrar, Straus, and Giroux, 1968), 45–46.

3. Vern Countryman, *Un-American Activities in Washington State* (Ithaca: Cornell University Press, 1951), 354.

4. Florence James, "Fists upon a Star," unpublished autobiography, Florence James Papers, Box 2, Folder 7, Manuscript Division, University of Washington Libraries. Hereafter cited in the text.

5. Unidentified newspaper clipping, Florence James Papers, Manuscript Division, University of Washington Libraries.

6. Unidentified newspaper clipping.

7. See Playhouse *Logs*, Papers of the Seattle Repertory Playhouse, Manuscript Division, University of Washington Libraries.

8. "Fists," Box 2, Folder 9, 12.

9. *Un-American Activities*, 225–227.

10. *Un-American Activities*, 124.

11. Bette Anderson Papers, Canwell Committee, Manuscript Division, University of Washington Libraries.

12. *Un-American Activities*, 265.

13. James statement, 6 July 1949, quoted in Flyer, "She Spoke Up," Florence James Papers, Manuscript Division, University of Washington Libraries.

14. Papers of the Seattle Repertory Playhouse, Box 13, Manuscript Division, University of Washington Libraries.

15. Letter from Herbert T. Condon, secretary, Board of Regents, to Oren K. Sroufe, 27 September 1949, Papers of the Seattle Repertory Playhouse, Box 6, File: Wash. U.

16. Interview with Noel Schram, 4 May 1989, Seattle, Washington.

17. Letter from Florence James to Marianne King, 18 August 1948, Bette Anderson Papers, Manuscript Division, University of Washington Libraries.

18. James to King, 18 August 1948; King to James, 26 August 1948.

19. Quoted in Stefan Kanfer, *A Journal of the Plague Years* (New York: Atheneum, 1973), 73.

20. Quoted in Countryman, 75.

21. Countryman, 396.

Spectacle as Government

Dickens and the Working-Class Audience

JANICE CARLISLE

One Saturday night early in 1860, Charles Dickens attended a performance at the Britannia Theatre in a working-class East End neighborhood of London. Dickens was an observer particularly well suited to the task he set himself when he ventured into the alien territory of Hoxton to watch the audience watch the show. By 1860, he had many times over established his reputation as an enthusiastic, knowledgeable supporter of the theater and as a champion of working-class causes, one of those "right-thinking men" who, according to his own definition, "possess . . . sympathy with, or regard for, those whom fortune has placed beneath them."[1] Dickens was, as well, a great entertainer, the Inimitable Boz, the man who had built his fortune on his ability to satisfy the demands of a wide and diverse audience. In that capacity alone, he had every reason to think himself capable of judging the efforts of a comparable institution of popular entertainment.

Dickens liked what he saw at the Britannia, and he recorded his highly favorable evaluation in an article in his weekly magazine *All the Year Round*. This article, later entitled "Two Views of a Cheap Theatre," has become something of a staple in theater history: it is frequently reprinted and generally cited as reliable firsthand evidence in a field more than usually haunted by the ephemeral quality of human endeavors—although the second half of the essay, in which Dickens describes the Sunday evening worship service he returned to the Britannia to observe on the following night, has been studiously ignored.[2] The prominence that this account has been given since the 1860s evokes the comforting image of a great artist praising a working-class theater for the admirable job it was doing. That image is, I think, a construction of theater history that deserves to be challenged.

In fact, Dickens's report on the Britannia is valuable less as a disinterested account of a particular theater than as proof of the extent to which Victorian theater in general was seen to serve political functions conformable to middle-class goals. For the purposes of the modern theater historian who wants to reconstruct the performances or analyze the responses of the audience at the Britannia, Dickens's "Two Views" may, in fact, offer little help at all: in some ways, the essay is more remarkable for what it omits than for what it includes. The subject of the essay serves principally as a generalization, one that could be labeled "The Working-Class Theater." Although that generalization might have enlightened the largely middle-class audience of *All the Year Round*, the essay must inevitably frustrate the later historian interested in how Victorian popular culture affected its audience. If the question at hand, however, is how a highly responsive observer construed the effect of such entertainment on an audience with which he was not himself identified, Dickens's essay offers reliable and illuminating evidence.

What Dickens saw at the Britannia, what he wanted to see there, was a spectacle of working-class culture flattering to middle-class sensibilities. According to Dickens, the relation between the entertainment and those entertained in such a theater was nothing less than that between governor and governed: performance controls its audience by providing the standards of behavior, the moral and social laws, by which its members are expected to abide. Dickens's response to the Britannia, moreover, turns out to be highly representative of middle-class conceptions not only of a working-class institution like the Britannia, but also of the working-class audience who thronged the galleries of West End theaters. Dickens's essay therefore participates in the complex Victorian discourse dealing with "the people"—the "deserving" and the undeserving poor, the "lower orders"—and it defines the theater as the ally of such diverse institutions as the penal system, the emerging health professions, and the church.

In his responses to the Britannia Theatre, Dickens was paying tribute to the effects of the widespread attempts during the 1830s, 1840s, and 1850s to reform the ways in which the working classes passed their leisure hours by offering them "rational recreations." In *Alton Locke*, Charles Kingsley's novel of working-class life during the 1830s and 1840s, the poor tailor is corrupted as much by half-price seats in the gallery at the Victoria as he is by the gin he drinks and the foul air he breathes.[3] In 1833, Edward Bulwer Lytton recognized that the workers had available to them only amusements synonymous with "disorders" and debilitation. A decade later another commentator called for "innocent" pleasures that would function as "safety valves for the mind"—a way for the disenfranchised to let off a little mental steam to prevent them from having to resort to physical violence. For many reformers, such rational uses of leisure would also heal the ever more apparent divisions between classes, particularly between the working poor and their "betters."[4] This movement was part and parcel with the Victorian tendency to turn every activity, from courting to sightseeing, into a process of education. Just as John Stuart Mill hoped that participation in government would make the participants more capable of self-government, the reformers of the entertainment industry, Dickens among them, hoped that their enlightened and benevolent approach would educate, refine, and civilize those members of the working classes whom they were able to reach. The reformed theater was to be more school than carnival, more a source of social instruction than an invitation to escapism or misrule.

Dickens visited the site of the Britannia in 1850 when it was occupied by the Britannia Saloon and reported in *Household Words* on the "incongruous heap of nonsense" it dished up to its undiscerning audience.[5] Ten years later, what he saw at the new theater reflected the improved state of working-class culture, but, significantly, he offers his readers none of the information that would establish the unique character and reputation of the Britannia among other East End theaters. "The Brit," as it was affectionately called, was built in 1858 by the proprietor of the saloon, Sam Lane. Lane, himself a figure in the reform of the theater, had joined in the outcry that led to the 1843 Theatres Regulation Act, though there may be some elaboration in the stories of his two marches on Westminster with Chartist supporters carrying banners that demanded: "Workers Want

Theatres." Lane's theater produced original plays and adaptations, housed
its own resident company, and offered Shakespeare, along with the usual
fare of melodramas and pantomimes, to a loyal and enthusiastic neighborhood audience.[6] But Dickens ignores the individualizing features of
the Britannia, pointedly refusing to identify its proprietor by name, so
that he can emphasize the impersonal strategies of institutional management that this particular theater epitomizes. The enormous building,
capable of holding four thousand people, is in each of its appointments
"most commendable": in its provision of safe entrances and exits and
"refreshment and retiring rooms," it exhibits "a general air of consideration, decorum, and supervision, . . . an unquestionably humanising influence in all the social arrangements of the place." In this building, if not
elsewhere, the "motley" audience—which includes, besides its "prowlers
and idlers," "mechanics, dock-labourers, costermongers, petty trades-
men, small clerks, milliners, stay-makers, shoe-binders, slop workers,
poor workers in a hundred highways and byeways"—keeps "excellent
order." For all this, Dickens credits the "enterprise" of "one man," the
unnamed proprietor: "I must add that his sense of the responsibility upon
him to make the best of his audience, and to do his best for them, is a
highly agreeable sign of these times" (417–418).

Although Dickens describes the relation between the proprietor and his
audience as a reciprocal process in which the manager does his best and
the audience becomes its best, he actually wants to think of the audience as
the submissive and cooperative object of a process that makes it orderly.
Dickens praises the safety and comfort offered by the building, but he is
most impressed by its sanitation. He explores "every nook of this great
place" and discovers, to his pleased surprise, that there is no stench. This
theater, he explains, is the result of the modern architectural ingenuity
that has produced hospitals and railway stations. Asphalt, glazed brick,
and tile present polished surfaces to which none of the workers' characteristic dirt can adhere. The building is "ventilated to perfection." When
Dickens notes, "These various contrivances are as well considered . . . as
if it were a Fever Hospital" (417), he defines the impresario of the Britannia as a theatrical Florence Nightingale, transporting, as Florence Nightingale herself attempted to do, the sanitary technology of the Crimea to
the working-class neighborhoods of London. According to this analogy,

the audience is composed of patients. What they see on the stage is their medicine.

Dickens's description of the audience offers the most striking evidence of what Michel Foucault would have recognized as a panoptical perspective.[7] Dickens remarks that the excellent sight-lines throughout the theater are important less because they allow the audience to see the stage than because they reveal the audience so that it can be seen: "the appearance of the audience, as seen from the proscenium—with every face in it commanding the stage, and the whole so admirably raked and turned to that centre, that a hand can scarcely move in the great assemblage without the movement being seen from thence—is highly remarkable in its union of vastness with compactness" (417). The person on the stage is not the object of the audience's gaze, but the overseer of the audience as spectacle. What can be seen, as Foucault has pointed out, can be controlled or, more importantly, self-controlled. The moving hand of the pickpocket will not go unnoticed. Dickens explains that the audience polices itself, ejecting any disorderly "man or boy" with "great expedition" and keeping "excellent order" because its members see on the stage a performance that renders them "closely attentive." The Britannia does not need to put physical barriers between its clientele: because the members of the audience are watching the performance, they cease to be interesting to each other; they do not talk, quarrel, or fight; they become separate units isolated from each other, and such separation is a primary goal of modern disciplinary mechanisms.

The performance at the Britannia, moreover, encourages order on both a local and a national scale. The audience takes "unbounded delight" in a pantomime called "The Spirit of Liberty." In this entertainment, first performed as the traditional Christmas fare a week or so earlier on Boxing Night, the Spirit of Liberty discourses with the impersonated Four Quarters of the World and conquers the King of Rust in a kingdom of Needles and Pins. This dramatic action proves to the audience the "agreeable fact" that "there [is] no liberty anywhere but among ourselves," the English (418). In a patriotic establishment like the appropriately named Britannia, the members of the audience learn about the blessings that their country confers on them; doubtless in their day-to-day dealings out of doors, such lessons are more difficult to take to heart. According to

Dickens, "The Spirit of Liberty" plays to an enthusiastic crowd in a theatrical inspection house, and the illusion of freedom fosters the willing subjection of its inhabitants.

Dickens also emphasizes the touches of realism in an otherwise fanciful theatrical production, which allow the members of the audience to recognize the relevance of the pantomime to their own condition. In the pantomime, "I noticed that the people who kept the shops, and who represented the passengers in the thoroughfares and so forth, had no conventionality in them, but were unusually like the real thing—from which I infer that you may take that audience in (if you wish to) concerning Knights and Ladies, Fairies, Angels, or such like, but that they are not to be done as to anything in the streets." If the object is the "doing" of the audience, verisimilitude helps achieve that goal. There is even room for a little innocent rebellion as two youths enact the tripping up of the police before the melodrama proceeds to offer a moral version of the civics lesson inherent in the pantomime: Virtue triumphs, Vice and Villainy fail, all to prove unequivocally that "honesty is the best policy." Throughout this lengthy evening, the audience avails itself of the cheap and the substantial sandwiches for sale; sandwiches, like the theater, are one of England's "great institutions" (418). Both body and soul are nourished by the Britannia's fare.

Dickens highly approves of this reconstruction of individual members of the working class into a docile, well-ordered, well-fed, well-ventilated audience. In publishing his account in *All the Year Round*, he confirms the hopes for the theater that another middle-class journal entertained even as the theater was being built. On three occasions, a stuffily respectable architectural periodical, the *Builder*, commented on the theater under construction in Hoxton in 1858. On each of these occasions, the writer emphasized the moral and social mission that he idealistically envisioned for it. Calculating that the Britannia could hold 3,500 people a night, the *Builder* called the theater "a school for 500,000 or 600,000 persons annually." Because its "instruction . . . is conveyed in the manner which will leave the deepest impressions," such a school may "most powerfully operate on the moral and social conditions of society at large." The analogy to modern sanitary techniques was also evoked as strikingly by the *Builder* as by Dickens. Claiming that a lack of hygiene was "the chief cause of any prejudice against what are called the lower classes," the

The Britannia Theatre, Hoxton. *From the* Builder *(1858): 763.*
Newberry Library.

writer even imagined that the architecture of the place might "induce habits" of cleanliness in " 'the unwashed,' at 4d. and 3d. a head." A week later, the *Builder* was invoking the language of Jeremy Bentham to hail the Britannia as a reformatory machine: "Let us hope . . . that the engine, potent for good or evil, will hold its sway under what we have chosen to call the 'mollifying' action of art-dramatic."[8] As if to offer visual proof of this point, one of the drawings of the Britannia published in the *Builder* pictures a vast, sterile hall that might be construed as an architectural mechanism of intimidation. Not only the "art-dramatic," but also the building itself could work its " 'mollifying' action" on the spectators.

Dickens's account of the theater a year after its opening in 1859 goes on to emphasize the success with which the Britannia's theatrical offerings are fulfilling its mission by contrasting their effect on the audience to the relative failure of the religious services held there on the following night. Along with registering his disappointment that "the lowest part of the usual audience of the Britannia Theatre [has] decidedly and unquestionably stayed away," Dickens expresses his doubts about the trickledown theory of moral influence: such gatherings "will work lower and lower down in the social scale" only if their producers know how to attract and entertain a working-class audience (420). The minister on this particular evening knows how to do neither. He tells "remarkably unlike life" tales of a "supposititious working man" who doubts the validity of Christian faith, the deathbed conversion of an infidel philosopher, and the pious mouthings of a "model pauper." The preacher further alienates any workers among his listeners by addressing them as "fellow sinners," not "fellow creatures" (419). Dickens knows a bad con when he sees one. This inept performance could never begin to "mollify" a working-class audience as the tawdry but effective performance of the previous evening has done. The conclusion to be drawn from the explicit contrast between the Saturday show and the Sunday service is simple: according to Dickens, by mid-century a theater like the Britannia was performing the function of the church more effectively than the church itself.

Other sources confirm the extent to which a theater like the Britannia was seen to serve as an ally and adjunct of the church. Henry Morley, who regularly provided theatrical reviews for the *Examiner* and collected his diary notes in his *Journal of a London Playgoer* (1866), was particularly struck by the sacramental value of Shakespearean drama. When recording his attendance at a performance of *Twelfth Night* at Sadler's Wells, he expatiates on the pleasure offered him by its lower-class audience, "an audience mainly composed of hard-working men, who crowd a sixpenny gallery and shilling pit." Like Dickens, he watches the audience watch the show: "There sit our working-classes in a happy crowd, as orderly and reverent as if they were at church, and yet as unrestrained in their enjoyment as if listening to stories told them by their own firesides." Morley's collocation of the devout and the domestic identifies the firesides he has in mind as those of his middle-class equals, not the squalid, cold hearths of the poor workers. Shakespeare's verse, the "sweetest and noblest verse man ever wrote," has the power to cut across class distinctions as it heightens an awareness of them: "Shakespeare spoke home to the heart of the natural man, even in the same words that supply matter for nice judgment by the intellect." Morley concludes his comments on this subject by assuring his readers that the disadvantaged poor "must in their minds and characters be strengthened and refined" by the secular service of worship offered them by Shakespearean "entertainment."[9]

The records in the *Times* point to the factual basis for such a seemingly farfetched comparison of stage and altar. On one particular Saturday in January 1860, when Dickens's thoughts might well have turned to the theater because adaptations of two of his Christmas books were playing at the Princess's Theatre and the Adelphi, the usual theatrical notices in the *Times* appear three pages after the equally usual notices of the religious meetings on Sunday evenings in theaters such as the Britannia, Victoria, Garrick, and Sadler's Wells. As one ad proclaims, "Seats free. No collection at the doors." On this particular Saturday, however, there is also a notice paid for by the group that hired out the Britannia for such uplifting gatherings: the Special Services Committee for Promoting Religious Services for the Working Class and People of London. The announcement includes a boast surely intended to elicit contributions: the services at St. James's Hall and the Britannia "are attended [every Sunday] by upwards of 10,000 persons, of whom it is believed a very large proportion never attended other places of worship." The list of contributors that follows, some of whom have given as much as £50, proves that this boast was effective as an advertising ploy. One of the notices even suggests the parallel between such charitable goals and the Saturday performances at the Britannia. The Association for Promoting the Relief of Destitution in the Metropolis and for Improving the Condition of the Poor offers its services "by means of Parochial and District Visiting, under the superintendence and direction of the Bishop and Clergy." As Dickens sees it, the theatrical fare at the Britannia is a way of visiting middle-class values on its audiences without obtruding the bishop and the clergy or their minions into their homes. The rest of the announcements on this page of the *Times*—asking for donations for shipwrecked mariners and sailors' orphaned girls or "outcast females" (for whom a gift of £10 ensures the saving of a soul) [10]— point to the fact that the theater by mid-century had come to function as one cog in the charitable, paternalistic machine intended to control the poor.

Yet a look at the traditional *Times* reviews of the Christmas pantomimes staged on Boxing Day a little more than a week earlier, the day on which "The Spirit of Liberty" premiered at the Britannia, proves that this discourse of control and improvement extended not just to the Sunday uses of a conveniently large theater in the East End, but to the Saturday

George Cruikshank, Boxing-Night—A Picture in the National Gallery. *From the* Comic Almanack, *1845. Newberry Library.*

evening performances that took place in the West End. "If the test of a pudding is in its eating," the *Times* declares, "the test of a play is in its reception." The reception that seems to matter most to the observers sent out by the *Times* is the response of the "lower orders" in the galleries (27 December 1859, 7). More than half of these notices begin with comments that prove that the most unruly elements of the audience are tamed by the performances they see. At the Strand, for instance, the audience is "in the best of humours," an assertion proved by the fact that "the denizens of the gallery, though thronged to that point that it would have been difficult to have found place for another person, were more orderly than is general on such occasions." Only at the Princess's, where *Home Truths* is presented as "a sermon in three acts of dialogue," is there disorder: "in revenge" for the boredom, "the gallery whistled and stamped considerably between the acts, but on the whole the upper circle of society listened with much patience."

The Britannia's offering that night is not included in the theatrical survey conducted by the *Times*, but the account of its "transpontine" popular cousin, the Surrey, is most revealing in this respect. The reviewer conjures up the figure of a nineteenth-century Pepys—precisely the role that Dickens played when he visited Hoxton—and then asks how such a person could convey the "manners and customs" of the English on a "modern Boxing-day." The Surrey, he claims, is the best place for the recorder of social fact to find a "great crowd" of a "not very select" sort making "festival" of the "very worst weather of the whole year." Because this theater is not the Britannia, not all the seated members of the audience can see. "Stentorian shouts of 'Sit down!'" mar the evening, but even "such trifling occasional drawbacks" do not dampen the "highest good humour" of the audience. "None of those unpleasant *fracas*— a bloody nose drawn at sight in return for a black eye per bearer—disfigured the evening's entertainments." Even as the observer comments on the restraint of the audience, the possibility of incidental working-class violence shadows this event as if to point out the dangers that have been averted. Significantly, even a fistfight is presented as an economic transaction: a black eye is a check cashed in exchange for a bloody nose. Such a commentary again indicates how thoroughly a middle-class observer would identify the Christmas pantomimes as rituals of social order and control. Instead of church services, which many of the poor did not attend, theatrical events offered the entertainment that "humanized" those who saw it.

The plots of these pantomimes, offered with considerable condescension and mock seriousness by the *Times* reviewers, provide one explanation of this tranquilizing effect. The topicality and whimsical range of subjects in the pantomimes suggest that, within their encyclopedic purview, such Christmas entertainments erased all distinctions of race, class, and gender in order to emphasize the homogeneity of British patriarchal rule. At the Strand, the story of William Tell was enacted with the aid of a character called Liberty, "who by some freak of history, is boasting of the then freedom of his 'tight little island'" of Helvetia, clearly England in Swiss garb. At the Lyceum, a shrew who made life miserable for her father, the king Paterfamilias the Great, learned to respect and then to love her rightful lord, Hafiz, king of Persia, who disguised himself as a "begging minstrel." At the Haymarket, a woodsman and milkmaid overcame the barriers between them and found wedded bliss with the help of a bishop "in full canonicals." The *Times* description of the finale to this display deserves to be quoted entire: "The concluding scene . . . represents the Channel fleet off Eddystone Lighthouse during the great storm of last November, and this, with patriotic verses, the evolutions of admirably drilled volunteer riflewomen, a great show of union-jacks, and 'Rule Britannia,' brought the Christmas pantomime, at its first performance, to a most flourishing conclusion" (27 December 1859, 7). The audience at the Haymarket was being treated to a heady communal display of military might and patriotic self-congratulation. According to the *Times* reviewers, the power of the theater to control, reform, and subdue—the power that Dickens found so worthy of remark at the Britannia—was clearly not limited to theaters in the East End.

Yet this reconsideration of Dickens's "Two Views" raises, I think, more questions than it answers. Why, for instance, did Dickens choose to omit almost every detail of individualizing information about the Britannia? Would other, more specific material, particularly information about Sam Lane, grant to this working-class institution the kind of entrepreneurial energy and invention that might threaten a middle-class reader? Such a perspective would certainly have suggested that the working classes were a great deal less docile than Dickens and his readers generally assumed. (Less than a year after his visit to the Britannia, Dickens was ready to sue Sam Lane over an unauthorized stage version of one of his tales. Clearly, the good things being done at the theater were good only if they did not infringe on what Dickens took to be his own creative property.)[11] This question, in turn, suggests another, one that highlights the differing perspectives engendered by different class affiliations. The management of the Britannia was so pleased by Dickens's praise that it printed his account in full on the playbill.[12] Was this response merely a slavish capitulation to the advertising value and cachet of a famous name or would the working-class reader have seen in Dickens's report something other than an attempt to perpetuate the dominance of the middle classes by encouraging the consent and cooperation of the dominated?

These questions, focusing specifically on the Britannia and on the Victorian working-class theater, led to other, more general issues involving the relation between popular entertainment and the disenfranchised. According to Dickens's construction of the performances at the Britannia, the audience there was being constructed both by the space it sat in and by the plays it watched there. In Foucault's terms, its members were cogs in a machine that was grinding them into ever more efficient and functional shapes. Both Dickens and the reviewers for the *Times* clearly and repeatedly insisted that popular art in their society was a technique of supervisory discipline, although they certainly did not use such terminology. They, like so many observers after them, would have said instead that the theater, as a form of entertaining instruction, simply moved beyond social and political considerations into a transcendent realm of moral uplift. As Clement Scott puts it, the " 'dear old Brit' has . . . helped in a remarkable way to humanise the sad-hearted people 'down East.' " [13] Yet another look at the behavior of the "lower orders" as members of the Victorian theatrical audience suggests several rather different conclusions.

Less inclined to revolutionary violence than their counterparts on the Continent, the working classes in Victorian England were quite content to use the threat of violence as a way to achieve their political ends. During the 1820s and 1830s, the period of the first reform movement, a writer like James Mill openly elaborated upon the efficacy and feasibility of such threats. A little rowdiness from the cheap seats during a performance in the late 1850s and early 1860s, when a second reform movement was beginning to take shape,[14] might have reminded the "betters" in the more expensive seats that the self-restraint of the working classes was fundamental to the enjoyment, not only of a night at the theater, but also of the everyday comforts in which they normally indulged. The West End theater, more than the lecture hall or the exhibition room or the church, was the place in which members of various classes came together.[15] They might have entered by different doors, ascended or descended different staircases, and they certainly paid different prices for their seats—but, once seated, they did constitute a group defined by its embrace of various classes, occupations, ages, religions, and economic strata. Stamping feet and raised voices were one way for the "lower orders" to bear witness to their own presence and potential power.

Such considerations suggest why the reviewers for the *Times* were so obsessed with the behavior in the galleries and why Dickens was so impressed with the self-policing of the crowd at the Britannia.[16] The working-class members of an audience, once seated in the theater, did not have to be either quiet or attentive. They would be so only if they liked what they saw on the stage well enough to pay attention. A subdued and deferential lower-class audience was not only, as one reviewer put it, proof of the pudding or the play, but proof of the stability and success of middle-class dominance. George Cruikshank drew a memorable national portrait of rowdy and drunken disorder when he included in his *Comic Almanack* (1845) a punning view of "Boxing-Night—A Picture in the National Gallery." By 1859 and 1860, Dickens and the *Times* reviewers were redrawing that portrait along the orderly lines that flattered a middle-class self-image as thoroughly as it erased any evidence of an independent and vital working-class culture.

The Victorian theater was particularly well suited to do the work of social control that Dickens attributed to it. Whether it actually did such work, as I have emphasized, is another question. Unlike the law, the church, or politics—institutions that had, more or less, the power to enforce their dictates on the working classes—successful institutions of popular entertainment allowed at least the illusion of liberty. The working-class members of the audience could choose to go to a play or not, just as they could choose, once there, to pay attention or to cause a disturbance. The disposition to do one or the other may have been determined for such individuals by the pressures of the dominant culture, but attending the theater might seem a matter of genuine choice. Moreover, because the performances at the theater were not to be enjoyed free of charge like the seats offered at the Britannia on Sunday during the religious services there, one's ability to pay for those pleasures at however small a price was itself proof of one's membership in a society that defined itself, as many Victorians lamented, primarily in commercial terms. Even one of the scavengers whom Henry Mayhew interviewed was able to enjoy the Christmas pantomimes at the Victoria.[17] In a society in which the poor were continually subjected to self-satisfied and condescending displays of charity from their betters, the power to purchase admission to a theater might have encouraged the poor to see themselves less as the passive objects of a disciplinary process they could not escape than as consumers who could either accept or reject the commodity for which they had paid. The theater, therefore, might have served as a source of illusion, not only in the traditional sense that acting is deception, but also in the disciplinary sense that the institution offered the members of its audience the illusion of voluntary participation in a culture to which they were, in fact, subjected. Whether such an illusion was worth the price of admission—whether, indeed, the audience bought it at all—other voices than that of Dickens would have to say.

NOTES

1. "The Queen's Coronation," *Examiner*, 1 July 1838, 403; Paul Schlicke, *Dickens and the Popular Entertainment* (London: Allen and Unwin, 1985), 1. One theatrical journal called the *Thespian* even honored Dickens in one of its issues by offering his portrait in place of that of the actor or actress usually featured there because Dickens was so closely identified with the Victorian theater (8 July 1857, 6). Even the most cursory look at H. Philip Bolton's *Dickens Dramatized* (Boston: G. K. Hall, 1987) would prove why that was the case. By 1871, the *Saturday Review* was lamenting that the English stage was so thoroughly dependent on adaptations of Dickens that it would be without scripts once the flow of his novels ended (14 January 1871, 50–51, quoted in Allardyce Nicoll, *A History of Late Nineteenth Century Drama, 1850–1900* [Cambridge: Cambridge University Press, 1946], 1:2).

2. Dickens's untitled essay appeared as the fourth in his series of reportage, "The Uncommercial Traveller" (*All the Year Round*, 25 February 1860, 416–421), hereafter cited in the text. Dickens planned to attend the performance at the Britannia on Saturday, 28 January 1860, with Wilkie Collins and Edmund Yates; he had notified the management that he would be there on that date, but he kept to himself his plan to attend the religious service on Sunday (*The Letters of Charles Dickens*, ed. Walter Dexter, Nonesuch Dickens [Bloomsbury: Nonesuch Press, 1938], 3:148). Extracts from the essay were reprinted as "Charles Dickens on the People's Theatres," *Theatre Quarterly* 1 (1971): 12–14. For uncritical citations of this essay, see Clive Barker, "The Chartists, Theatre, Reform, and Research," *Theatre Quarterly* 1 (1971): 4; Michael R. Booth et al., *The Revels History of Drama in English* (London: Methuen, 1975), 4:26–27; Schlicke, 193. In a review of Schlicke's book, Michael R. Booth justly castigates both Schlicke and Dickens for their comments about the Britannia, which reveal "middle-class patronizing and Peckniffianism of the worst sort" (*Theatre Research International* 11 [1986]:257).

3. Charles Kingsley, *Alton Locke, Tailor and Poet*, ed. Elizabeth A. Cripps (1850; Oxford: Oxford University Press, 1983), 24. Chapter 10 includes a diatribe against the Victoria Theatre as typical of those "licensed pits of darkness" that cater to the "beggary and rascality of London" (108).

4. Peter Bailey, *Leisure and Class in Victorian England: Rational Recreation and the Contest for Control, 1830–1885*, rev. ed. (London: Methuen, 1987), 47–49. For the relation between issues of class and the reform of working-class amusements, see Hugh Cunningham, *Leisure in the Industrial Revolution, c. 1780–c. 1880* (London: Croom Helm, 1980), chapter 4.

5. "The Amusements of the Poor" (1850), rpt. in "Charles Dickens on the People's Theatres," *Theatre Quarterly* 1 (1971):12–13. The *Theatrical Journal* took exception to Dickens's comments on the Britannia Saloon, calling them a "spiteful and uncalled-for attack"; the journal also remarked jealously on Dickens's presumption: "*his* notices of theatrical affairs in general, cast by their intense brilliancy, those of every other person in the shade" (quoted in Charles Dickens, *Letters*, ed. Madeline House and Graham Storey, Pilgrim edition [Oxford: Clarendon Press, 1965–], 6:52n).

6. For information on Sam Lane and the Britannia, see Clive Barker, "A Theatre for the People," in *Nineteenth Century British Theatre*, ed. Kenneth Richards and Peter Thomson (London: Methuen, 1971), 3–24; Barker, 4–5; and Diana Howard, *London Theatres and Music Halls* (London: Library Association, 1970), 32–33. Howard's records prove, for instance, that Dickens exaggerated by a factor of two the amount of money that Lane had expended on the building of the Britannia. Errol Sherson claims that Sam Lane was "the most powerful influence" in Hoxton and that Sara Lane, his wife and an actress at the theater, was able to go unescorted where police did not dare to walk alone (*London's Lost Theatres of the Nineteenth Century* [London: John Lane, 1925], 363–364).

7. See Michel Foucault, *Discipline and Punish: The Birth of the Prison*, trans. Alan Sheridan (New York: Vintage, 1979), part 3, chapter 3. Foucault sees as the epitome of modern society Jeremy Bentham's plans for the panopticon, a prison in which the inmates would be segregated from each other and subjected to constant supervision. As the inmates became habituated to the surveillance that might or might not be trained upon them at all times, they would begin, so Bentham thought, to surveil themselves, and the disciplinary structure of the building would become a mechanism of self-discipline. Bentham saw this scheme as a societal cure-all: his inspection house, as he sometimes called it, would be universally useful as a model for factories, schools, hospitals, reformatories, and insane asylums, as well as prisons; it would serve the purpose of any institution whose goal is to train a number of people for the roles they need to play in a capitalist society. So trained, such individuals would never know, of course, that the discipline imposed upon them had not come from within.

Although Dickens despised anything that smacked of utilitarian cold reason— he wanted to encourage social change by promoting the ideals of charity, fellow-feeling, and common humanity—the Britannia Theatre was, for him, the perfect panopticon. Despite his rhetoric of charity and brotherly love, Dickens could display an unabashed authoritarianism: his 1850 essay on "The Amusements of the

People" proposed that the lord chamberlain's examiner of plays ought to use his office to improve the drama enjoyed by the poor (see Schlicke, 208).

8. The *Builder*, 13 November 1858, 762; 20 November 1858, 772. On 25 September 1858, the writer deplored the degraded taste of the audiences at East End theaters, then asked, "Cannot this taste be elevated, and made to serve to greater extent than the drama has yet served, the cause of social progress and good morality?" (644).

9. Henry Morley, *The Journal of a London Playgoer from 1851 to 1866* (1866; rpt., London: George Routledge, 1891), 137–138. Not surprisingly, Morley called in theater managers to "take for standard the people he would please as honest Englishmen of the educated middle-class" and labeled such people "akin to all that is human" (20). Michael R. Booth has called for a history of Victorian theater that would take into account the extent to which theater historians have seen that subject "through middle-class eyes" ("East End and West End: Class and Audience in Victorian London," *Theatre Research International* 2 [1977]: 102).

10. *Times*, 7 January 1860, 7, hereafter cited in the text.

11. Bolton, 45. See the *Times*, 8 January 1861 and 12 February 1861, for Dickens's outraged letters.

12. A. E. Wilson, *East End Entertainment* (London: Arthur Barker, 1954), 175.

13. Clement Scott, *The Drama of Yesterday and Today* (London: Macmillan, 1899), 1:57.

14. Harold Perkin, *Origins of Modern English Society* (1969; rpt. London: Routledge and Kegan Paul, 1986), chapter 9; Joseph Hamburger, *James Mill and the Art of Revolution* (New Haven: Yale University Press, 1963). A leader in the *Times* examined the possibilities for reform in the column adjoining the announcement of *The Christmas Carol* at the Adelphi (4 January 1860, 8).

15. Richard Altick in *The Shows of London* (Cambridge: Belknap Press, 1978, 102) establishes the fact that the shilling admission fee was a way of keeping the unwanted out of galleries and exhibition halls. In some cases, the barriers to admission were more obvious. From 1780 to 1863, a sergeant's guard was posted at the gate to the British Museum, even though that institution had been charted as one that would be open to all (26–27). By the end of the 1850s, the British Museum and the National Gallery were open without admission fees on a limited basis (415–419, 440–454, 500–502).

16. There is evidence that the audiences at the Britannia were not always as subdued as Dickens claimed. At a benefit performance of *The School for Scandal*, for instance, "the words were drowned by the choruses that gallery boys were singing" (Jim Davis, "Stage Managing the Brit: The Diaries of F. C. Wilton," *Theatre Notebook* 42 [1988]: 105). At the Victoria, the situation could be considerably more violent. Early in 1859, the management decided to go on with the

second show even though the bodies of sixteen dead killed in a fire during the first show had not been removed: the "brutal riot" that might have ensued if the crowds were denied their entertainment would have cost more lives than the fire had (*Illustrated London News*, 1 January 1859, 7, quoted in Altick, 472).

17. Henry Mayhew, *London Labour and the London Poor* (1861–1862; rpt., New York: Dover, 1968), 1 : 15. Mayhew also described the stench and crowded disorder of the gallery at the Victoria (1 : 18–20).

Constructing
Utopia

Victorian

Players and

Sages

NINA AUERBACH

It seemed natural for Victorian men to worship themselves; Wordsworth's sonorous self-reverence had shown them the way. His *Prelude* is unabashed in its admiration for its subject, his own mind:

> And here, O Friend! have I retraced my life
> Up to an eminence, and told a tale
> Of matters which not falsely may be called
> The glory of my youth. Of genius, power,
> Creation and divinity itself
> I have been speaking, for my theme has been
> What passed within me.[1]

The passage reverberates with aggrandizing nouns—eminence, glory, genius, power, creation, divinity—that come to rest in the short, drawn-out, deceptively humble syllable "me." Throughout *The Prelude*, Wordsworth skirts an abyss of Luciferian blasphemy: what saves the poet on his eminence, looking within himself with awe, from the flaming self-obsession of Milton's Satan, annexing heaven and hell as provinces of his mind? Satan's egomaniacal cry to the angel Ithuriel rings through all his speeches: "Know ye not mee? . . . Not to know of me argues your selves unknown, / The lowest of your throng."[2] Wordsworth, too, cries incessantly, "Know ye not mee?" but he reclaims himself from satanism by repeated invocations to nature as his shaping, saving spirit. Natural man will not displace whatever jealous God may glower down at humanity:

> Wisdom and spirit of the universe!
>
> .   .   .   .
>
>   not in vain
> By day or star-light thus from my first dawn
> Of childhood didst thou intertwine for me
> The passions that build up our human soul;
> Not with the mean and vulgar works of man,
> But with high objects, with enduring things—
> With life and Nature, purifying thus
> The elements of feeling and of thought,
> And sanctifying, by such discipline,
> Both pain and fear, until we recognize
> A grandeur in the beatings of the heart. (59)

Nature, not Wordsworth, is the vehicle of sanctity: the poet's heart beats grandly only in response to a grand endowment from without. As a receptacle for the discipline of a nature which is spirit, he can become, at strenuous moments, a hero, but he is too reverent to believe in himself alone.

Or so he hopes. Within his paean to the "Wisdom and spirit of the universe" that intertwines his soul with "high objects" and lifts him above contamination by the purely human condition, Wordsworth lays the shadow of a doubt: what if his soul takes its grandeur after all not from the "high objects" and "enduring things" toward which it yearns, but from "the mean and vulgar works of man" his prayer eschews? What if no shaping soul of nature exists to sanction his genius and power? If nature does not monitor our growth, then we make ourselves, raising images of a pageant too mad for sublimity to endure.

Wordsworth's terror of a purely human, and thus insanely theatrical, world infected a century of sages. Eighteenth-century moralists had denounced the playful chaos of the masquerade as (in Terry Castle's words) "a random, frighteningly irrational flight out of nature, a consorting with the unnatural";[3] its incessant transformations revoked not only the enduring order of external things, but recognizable human identity. In the nineteenth century, this transitory interlude of instability overwhelmed the sacred continuity of daily life. Theatricality became the bane of uniformity.

The Wordsworth of *The Prelude* cannot exist without nature; he evokes his agony of abandonment in the images of disjointed theatricality that torment him in the middle books, once he has left the anchor of nature and the lakes. Cambridge is for him no more than a mock world, a "pageant," a "spectacle," as is the London of book 7, delineated only in grotesque and unexamined images of theatergoing. Even the French Revolution becomes a human carnival, existing only for the poet as a retreat. He escapes its transformations by returning to his scarcely human home of mountains and mountainous shepherds, refusing to absorb the theatricality that pervades a denatured world, but leaving his nightmares to Victorians who longed to believe in nature by believing in Wordsworth.

But by the time Victorian descendants came to worship, belief in Wordsworth himself—along with other heroes who stood on eminences—had become dangerously tinged with the antinature of the theater. A vagabond community apart from respectable culture, whose existence canonical authors scarcely acknowledged, the Victorian theater evoked fears of theatrical specters invading daily life. If the impulses, the needs, and the development of the self were products of nature, despite the evolutionary vagaries and mysterious cruelty of nature's ways, that self could guide the growth of others; but theatricality, artificial, protean, teasing, and (in its disruptive associations) disturbingly female, made the self, that saving remnant "of genius, power, creation and divinity," a demonic antagonist of the soul that struggled toward immortality.

This struggle between the theater and a high-minded literary humanism, their conflicting claims to represent human nature, shaped both literary and theatrical history. Sages, poets, and novelists fought to prove their integrity against their implicit rival, the theater, which was officially beneath their notice; their works gained vitality and confusion from the competition. The theater itself, resisting the demonic role literary culture imposed on it, began to ape the codes of humanistic virtue. The result was a symbiotic antagonism that affected both media. For better or worse, the theater we now know would not exist had it not adopted certain strategies of assimilation to the antitheatricality of Victorian literary orthodoxy.

Jonas Barish's anatomy of antitheatricality in Western culture defines the ontological danger for audiences of identifying with others' performances, whether they are theatrical or heroic: "For when a player has given over his consciousness to some form of identification with a character, or when a spectator, identifying with that character, has done the same, what happens to his own self? Is it suspended somehow for the duration of performance? And if so, is this not a spiritually dangerous state of affairs? Does it not in fact resemble demonic possession?"[4] Transfigured by hero worship into vessels of salvation, but dangerously close to theatrical creations, performers—whether they are Wordsworthian bards, political dignitaries, lovable literary narrators like David Copperfield, or professional actors made up to recite words not their own—require only a shift of perspective to become devourers of the self they are supposed to heal.

The "own self," as Jonas Barish calls it, is as fragile an object of belief as the inspiring advice by Polonius ("to thine own self be true") from which it derives. Fidelity to one's "own self" mocks a *Hamlet* playacted from its murky, deceiving beginning. In the same spirit, Lionel Trilling's last, beleaguered book, *Sincerity and Authenticity*, plaintively invokes an "own self" pure of theatricality. For Trilling as for Wordsworth, who was one of his humanist heroes, theatricality subverts the writer's authority over his or her audience. Confronted with the spectacle of a playful, pervasive, multiplying psyche, Trilling responds: "The point is persuasively made but it doesn't, I think, silence the insistent claims of the own self."[5] But which self should we attend to, the self that stands aloof from transformations (as Wordsworth tries to do) or the responsive self that recreates itself freely *as* Wordsworth, or as Hamlet, Cleopatra, Jane Eyre? Which of these possible own selves do we "own"?

Fearing for the "own self," most Victorians justified its mutations as Wordsworth did: our growth emanates from nature's undeviating rhythms. Even when nature is "red in tooth and claw," devouring more than it gives—as it does in Tennyson's protracted lament, *In Memoriam A. H. H.*—its risings and settings save the poet, and "the voice of the human race, speaking through him,"[6] from vertigo:

> Risest thou thus, dim dawn, again,
> So loud with voices of the birds,

> So thick with lowings of the herds,
> Day when I lost the flower of men . . .[7]

The dawn brings no resurrection, but only a reminder of loss; it fulfills no desire. Nonetheless, it stabilizes the speaker's fluctuating emotions because it *does* rise on schedule, crowded with the continuity of other lives and life forms. With the dawn, the poet's spirits can rise. So can loftier, if vaguer, spiritual hopes. Like Wordsworth on his eminence, Tennyson steeps his affirmation in verbs that carry him above the intractable material of his poem:

> O living will that shalt endure
> When all that seems shall suffer shock,
> *Rise* in the spiritual rock,
> Flow thro' our deeds and make them pure,
>
> That we may *lift* from out of dust
> A voice as unto him that hears,
> A cry *above* the conquer'd years,
> To one that with us works, and trust,
>
> With faith that comes of self-control,
> The truths that never can be proved
> Until we close with all we loved,
> And all we flow from, soul in soul. (86; my italics)

Nature, its familiar noises, its seasonal cycles, makes no returns, but it does provide ballast to a poet with no inner impetus toward "self-control"; it hints, moreover, at a faith in the spirit's eternal life, though this faith rests on the slightest of foundations, "the truths that never can be proved." Like so many mid-Victorian characters, the speaker of *In Memoriam* identifies his being with a nature he can see, hear, and recognize, not because nature is infused with higher purpose, but simply because, if nature is so palpably, predictably *there*, then so must his selfhood be. The world of the spirit is always about to evaporate; men shine with heroes' radiance, but they die; only the night and the dawn, the sun and the rain, the animals and the birds, exude the reliability an "own self" requires.

Faced with the same cultural imperatives as men, Victorian women did their best to sanction their being by appeals to nature; though the taboos that hedged their lives were implemented by appeals to the natural—as they still are—women writers abandoned that ballast with as much despair as release. Even so seditious a culture heroine as Charlotte Brontë's Jane Eyre, whom it has become fashionable to segregate in a purely female tradition, authenticates as "natural" her highly unorthodox subjectivity, just as Wordsworth and Tennyson do. Jane Eyre is so imbued with the preternatural—she attracts ghosts, lives familiarly with visions and portents, and is repeatedly called a witch, fairy, or elf, appellations she never repudiates—that her stubborn equation of herself with nature seems inconsistent. Without this bond with nature, though, she might well have repelled believing readers. As a creature of nature, however bizarre she may be, she lives a sanctioned life; she can affirm, as she does so often in the novel, that her perceptions and her words are "truth."

Accordingly, as a child, she is possessed, like Wordsworth's and Tennyson's speakers, by landscapes. Extremities of nature are so embedded in her consciousness that her aunt's attack—"I abhor artifice, particularly in children"—can come only from a fool.[8] Mrs. Reed's imputation of artifice could not be more misplaced, for we have lived with a Jane consumed by nature. Jane's affinities with wild, scantly populated countries assure the reader that she is real; because she finds herself in landscapes, we may share her life without jeopardy.

In this spirit, most readers endorse without question a Jane Eyre who glowers, a stony and stormy truth-teller, at the same sort of charades they let delight them in *Vanity Fair*. In the name of nature, we accept Jane's most incredible godlike claims—just as we do Wordsworth's. When Rochester, now conveniently unmarried and mutilated, calls "Jane! Jane! Jane!" in a desperate prayer and Jane, many miles away, responds, she does not tell us the literal truth—that the laws of nature have been suspended on her behalf—but insists instead, as she has always done, on her oneness with nature: "'Down superstition!' I commented, as that spectre rose up black by the black yew at the gate. 'This is not thy deception, nor thy witchcraft: it is the work of nature. She was roused, and did—no miracle—but her best.' . . . It was *my* time to assume ascendancy. *My* powers were in play and in force" (445). To skeptical readers, Jane's sudden inspired ability to pierce the sound barrier does look suspiciously like witchcraft or a miracle, or in any case like something startlingly inimical to any nature we recognize. Jane Eyre's equation of her unique occult powers with that great Victorian talisman "nature" has little to do with her actual story, but it does give her a compelling identity—an "own self"—that has bewitched readers into forming an unquestioned alliance with her as a standard-bearer of their own humanity.

In *Villette* the bond is broken: finding nature an impossible guide, Charlotte Brontë regulates her heroine's self theatrically. Brontë's last novel is a great, murky achievement because it embraces rather than repudiating the theatrical specter that haunted its age. Its abrasive, alienated narrator Lucy Snowe has little affinity with landscapes; she concentrates instead on secrets she keeps even from the reader.

Victorian fiction's most intransigent heroine, Lucy Snowe withholds herself from the bonds that offer most Victorians final definition: "I shall share no man or woman's life in this world, as you understand sharing," she informs *Villette*'s sweet-natured ingenue.⁹ She includes her reader in her refusal to merge. Charlotte Brontë's story of a woman who will not share herself is, I suspect, a reaction against her strenuous efforts in *Jane Eyre* to universalize a heroine/narrator who was, in essence, eccentric and estranged. Lucy Snowe will not make Jane Eyre's wooing gestures. She has no naturally ordered self to bestow on her reader; instead, she erupts fitfully and multiply in a succession of disjointed performances.

Lucy's most consistent performance involves her refusal to give herself: we are spectators of her life, not sharers in it. Jane Eyre's tribulations with her foster family and at school instantly become our own, while Lucy Snowe writes only in cryptic metaphor of catastrophes that decimate her life. At the beginning of her story and its end, she describes in vivid detail shipwrecks that stand for devastating but unspecified upheavals, demanding that we "picture" events she will not recount. These shipwrecks take on the emblematic power of the spectacular shipwreck scenes that were the inevitable climax of the nautical melodramas that saturated the mid-Victorian theater.¹⁰ Rather than confessing, Lucy borrows a potent theatrical symbol of generic, charismatic catastrophe.

Performances are as central to her story as secrets. She finds her forbidden courage and imagination when she plays a man in a school play; in this cross-dressing carnival interlude, she vanquishes the pseudo-hero John Bretton she worships offstage. The incendiary actress Vashti becomes, for an evening, Lucy's type of the female artist. But beyond theaters, Lucy and the world she depicts are more incurably theatrical still. At work, the schoolroom is her stage. Her teaching, like her acting, is a mode of control, an attempt to capture and silence the refractory Belgian girls; she describes her examinations as flourishes of terrified, triumphant self-display. Knowledge and professional advancement matter less to her than does "the magian power or prophet-virtue" (251) she shares with the diva Vashti in the brief intervals when she unleashes suppressed selves.

Jane Eyre, according to her own account, receives her paramount illumination—Rochester's far-off call—as an uprising of the nature that sanctions her "powers." Lucy's parallel revelation is suffused in theatricality. It occurs in an unnatural, dreamlike night in which a local *fête* makes of Villette's park a haunt of theatrical tranformations:

> I see even scores of masks. It is a stage scene, stranger than dreams . . . where were they, and where was I?
>
> In a land of enchantment, a garden most gorgeous, a plain sprinkled with coloured meteors, a forest with sparks of purple and ruby and golden fire gemming the foliage; a region, not of trees and shadow, but of strangest architectural wealth—of altar and of temple, of pyramid, obelisk, and sphinx, incredible to say, the wonders and the symbols of Egypt teemed throughout the park of Villette. (440)

Stimulated by opium, her magical awareness of gorgeous chaos embodies all the confusions her age associated with theatricality. The transformed park recalls the extravaganzas that dominated the mid-Victorian theater. In 1849, J. R. Planché's *The Island of Jewels* concluded with a vast, gilded palm tree opening out onto a group of fairies supporting a coronet of jewels, while his *King Charming* in 1850 featured "a giant pie with four-and-twenty jeweled blackbirds perched on boughs of silver and precious stones."[11] Like Planché's surreal trees, *Villette* admits no semblance of nature to a landscape recomposed into exotic architecture and artifacts.

Lucy's illumination is as intoxicatingly illusory as the masque of nature and the wonder-generating drug. Spying on her beloved M. Paul, she realizes in a flash of revelation that he is betrothed to his young ward: "far from me such shifts and palliatives, far from me such temporary evasion of the actual, such coward fleeing from the dread, the swift-footed, the

all-overtaking Fact, such feeble suspense of submission to her soul sover-
eign, such paltering and faltering resistance of the Power whose errand is
to march conquering and to conquer, such traitor defection from the
TRUTH" (454).

The syntactic convolutions that announce Lucy's truth parody the
revelations of sages—Wordsworth and his followers Carlyle, Tennyson,
and Jane Eyre—but bereft of authorizing nature, it is as false as it can be:
plunging into a vortex of theatrical revelations, Lucy loses her grip both
on her own identity and on the plot of her novel. Buoyed by nature, Jane
Eyre acquired powers that transcended the laws of time, of space, of realistic fiction itself; discovering herself in an abyss of theatricality, Lucy
Snowe has little control over a narrative beset by disconnection and duplicity, a truth transformed incessantly into its opposite, like Planché's
trees. Jane's "own self" ascends in Rochester's incantation, "Jane! Jane!
Jane!"; Lucy's fragments of selves materialize only in Ginevra Fanshawe's
perplexed appeal, "Who *are* you, Miss Snowe?" (299), a question that
confronts only Lucy's multiplicity: "What contradictory attributes of
character we sometimes find ascribed to us, according to the eye with
which we are viewed!" (294). Flamboyantly stagy novelists like Dickens
and Thackeray never approach the radical theatricality of Charlotte
Brontë, in whose Lucy Snowe knowable character explodes into the di-
vergent creations of "the eye with which we are viewed."

Painfully, abrasively, *Villette* tears the Victorian novel away from the
sanction of sages. There are no Wordsworthian "high objects" or "enduring things" in Lucy Snowe's progress, but only a pageant of catastrophic
disclosures and self-revelations whose truth is ecstatic error and whose
protestations of sincerity mask secrets.

Lucy Snowe is so unforthcoming a narrator, so grim and shadowed a
heroine, that it sounds odd to define *Villette* as theatrical as opposed to
the naturalistic *Jane Eyre*. Jane, after all, is the magnetic presence; she
elicits powerful responses everywhere she goes, while Lucy obscures herself to all. Yet *Villette*, with its disjoined narrator who in her shrouded-
ness assumes many identities, its incessant, transitionless transformations, its secretiveness and illogic of development, is closer to the ethos of
the mid-Victorian theater than is the bravura expansiveness of *Jane Eyre*.

The theater in the 1850s inhabited a moral and social limbo, though it would shortly begin to ascend into the stately centrality of high culture. But at mid-century, when *Villette* appeared, the theater represented a genuinely popular, and thus by implication inherently seditious, culture of its own, according to theater historian Michael R. Booth: "The melodrama, farce, and pantomime of the nineteenth century, especially of the first fifty years, represented the last time that the English theatre was in touch with the mass of the population and popular sentiment, and the only time since the Middle Ages that it has been dominated by neither the aristocracy nor the middle class."[12] Shaping itself, like *Villette*, without any sanctioned authority, as free from definition by the higher classes as *Villette* is free from the shaping sanctity of nature, the theater was a protean, politically disruptive haunt of cross-dressing and disguise. Its spectacle relied on a shape-changing so incessant that it left ontological reality behind: "In the Regency harlequinade [whose form, as Booth defines it, lasted to the middle of the century] . . . things are not what they seem to be, or rather they are, but then they change frighteningly into something else. Nothing can be relied on; the very ground itself dissolves under the feet of the helpless characters" (155–156). Mid-Victorian theatricality does not denote flamboyant exhibitionism or self-display, but the elusive shifts of identities unanchored by the grand consistency of nature.

Jane Eyre's powers would wither in perplexity at such a world, for being always herself, she is always in control. Lucy Snowe can barely become herself, and so, like popular audiences at mid-century, she is at home in a world of transformations. But the unauthorized elusiveness of Lucy's theatricality would soon be banished from the actual Victorian theater, which was setting out to court middle-class novel readers who demanded, in themselves and in the characters they chose to applaud, Wordsworthian singleness of being.

In the 1860s, the "Robertsonian Revolution" was orchestrated by the Bancrofts' management of the Prince of Wales' Theatre, bringing Tom Robertson's muted domestic comedies into vogue. Robertson and the Bancrofts did not revolutionize the theater of the 1860s, but they did banish the mutable and exotic. Mistrustful middle-class families warmed to a pale blue theater with antimacassars over the chairs; the Prince of Wales' looked like home.

Onstage, Robertson's characters had the consistency the new audiences cultivated in themselves; their common virtue was predictability. Esther,

the heroine of Robertson's beloved play *Caste*, was an actress before falling virtuously in love, but she defines herself unequivocally at the climax
of her story: "I am a woman—I am a wife—a widow—a *mother!*"[13] Esther *is* the roles Victorian theatricality called into question; Robertson
accordingly rewards her integrity by returning her husband at the final
curtain. Like the Wordsworth of *The Prelude*, respectable middle-class
audiences shunned the dizzying tranformations of spectacle to cling to a
self immured against surprises. Their approval of the Bancrofts' cozy
pseudo-home purged from the Victorian theater its alluring, alienating
theatricality.

Newly respectable dramatists bestowed even on their liars and villains
the clarity and consistency of the upstanding bourgeoisie. Mary Elizabeth
Braddon's popular sensation novel *Lady Audley's Secret*, for example, is
a mesh of ambiguities, almost all of which C. H. Hazlewood's stage adaptation excises. The post-Robertsonian theater succeeded by leaving shadows and secrets to fiction, which, once the theater had absorbed some of
the lucidity of high culture, quietly began to experiment with variations
on the theatrically shrouded self.

Braddon's Lady Audley is a probable husband-murderer and a con-
summate actress; dimpled, clinging, childlike, she is defined by layers of
unknowability, simultaneously domestic angel and beautiful fiend: "She
defied him with her quiet smile—a smile of fatal beauty, full of lurking
significance and mysterious meaning—the smile which the artist had exaggerated [into an image of demonism] in his portrait of Sir Michael's
wife."[14] We have no access to her inner life; we see her only through the
eyes of the narrator and of her accuser, Robert Audley, to whom she is a
dangerous enchanting enigma. When revelations come at the end, two
mysteries seem to be solved, but, almost instantly, they return. Lady Audley has indeed pushed her husband down a well, but since he has crawled
out again, she is not technically a murderer; not knowing this, she offers
her sole self-revelation: "I killed him because I AM MAD!" (237). But
this theatrical truth is no more authoritative than Lucy Snowe's. A doctor
promptly denies Lady Audley the final definition of insanity: "there is no
evidence of madness in anything she has done. . . . She employed intelligent means, and she carried out a conspiracy which required coolness
and deliberation in its execution. There is no madness in that" (248). Her
unfeminine rage and rationality may isolate her as a madwoman or ex-

pose her as Everywoman. Guilty or not guilty, mad or sane, child-woman or brilliant fiend, reflection of the well-behaved female reader or awful antithesis of virtue, Lady Audley keeps the secret of the many Lady Audleys she plays.

The first melodrama to feature a stellar female villain, Hazlewood's adaptation makes Lady Audley one woman who is purely bad and mad. Instead of teasing the reader with inscrutable suggestiveness, she thoughtfully announces her wickedness in a series of soliloquies and asides. When her doting husband declares his faith in her—"if ever the face was an index of the mind, I believe yours to be that countenance"—she declares herself to the audience: "[*Aside.*] We may have two faces. [*Aloud.*] Bless you! bless you for your confidence! my kind—my good—my dearly loved old darling."[15] Having obligingly revealed her two faces (which are really only one), she pushes her first husband down a well by the end of the first act—a climactic wickedness not narrated until the end of Braddon's *Lady Audley*—flaunting smiling villainy until her penance in a concluding mad scene. This madness is not, like that of the novel's Lady Audley, the ambiguous confession of a perpetually unknowable self, but a conclusive stage turn: "Aye—aye! [*Laughs wildly.*] Mad, mad, that is the word. I feel it here—here! [*Places her hands on her temples.*]" (II, 5). She makes some more mad gestures, falls, and dies. The self-revealing extravagance of Lady Audley's performance assures the audience that she has no secrets. Stage madness asks no questions about character; it guarantees authenticity, rather than tantalizing us with unexpressed potential selves. The stage no longer makes us ask who, or if, we are: it reassures us that we own one self alone.

The newly respectable theater is beginning to change places with the stabilizing Victorian novel of mid-century. Hazlewood's Lady Audley is a paragon of knowability, while Braddon's, in her shifting, shadowy selfhood, is the more theatrical creation of the two. Braddon's character is an actress to the core; Hazlewood's only plays at acting while exposing her villainy with exemplary sincerity. "Let me again assume the mask," she soliloquizes, "which not only imposes on [Robert Audley], but on all the world" (II, i): devoid of mystery, deft at distinguishing mask from face, Hazlewood's she-devil nourishes her culture's rage for integrity. Melodrama had always featured broad, one-dimensional characters, but this stage Lady Audley exists only, it seems, to announce her intentions. The translucence of theatrical villains prepared for the coming of heroes.

The greatest stage hero was Henry Irving. Capturing London with his well-drilled Lyceum company at the height of England's imperial self-glorification, he specialized in villains even more single-souled than Lady Audley—Mathias in *The Bells*, Mephistopheles in *Faust*, Iachimo in *Cymbeline*—but as actor-manager of the Lyceum Theatre, in his majestic Shakespearean revivals in particular, he transformed himself into a hero of British culture.[16] The Lyceum over which he exerted absolute control realized the visions of all the sages that preceded it. At the end of *The Prelude*, Wordsworth had announced his own coming as an inaugurator of a new visionary priesthood: "Prophets of Nature, we to them will speak / A lasting inspiration, sanctified / By reason, blest by faith: what we have loved, / Others will love, and we will teach them how" (537). Oddly, obliquely, the stylized Irving turned himself into a Wordsworthian prophet of nature, shedding on all social classes who visited his Lyceum the consecration of high culture.

Even his eccentricities—the graceless, halting walk, the diction that suggested foreignness but derived from no particular country—assured audiences that he was Henry Irving always. He made himself appear heroically uncultivated by intensifying eccentricities of the sort more conventional actors labored to get rid of. In the 1880s and 1890s, having enlisted Shakespeare to consecrate him, Irving made himself the supreme absolute self that proclaimed itself nature's creation alone.

Long before Irving made theatricality a form of reverence, literary bardolaters had redeemed Shakespeare as an archetypal hero because a supreme emanation of nature. Matthew Arnold's sonnet "To Shakespeare" (1849) depicts this mercurial man of the theater as a mountain more mystically immobile than even Wordsworth could climb: "Others abide our question. Thou art free. / We ask and ask—thou smilest and art still, / Out-topping knowledge." Seventeen years earlier, Anna Jameson cried reverently in her *Shakespeare's Heroines*: "O Nature! O Shakespeare! which of ye drew from the other?"[17] Nursing their own stability too carefully to worship a man of the theater, Victorian acolytes transformed Shakespeare, as they did Irving after him, into a manifestation of the sense-giving nature that would soothe their own contradictions.

Shakespeare's characters became what he was: masterpieces of intricate unity, with no trace of the fragmented, improvisatory patchwork of theatrical production. Mary Cowden Clarke's bestselling *The Girlhood of Shakespeare's Heroines* (1850) bestows on such cryptic characters as Portia, Ophelia, and Desdemona dense childhood histories that make sense of all their behavior in the play: from pieces in a pageant, they become unified, dimensional selves. More majestically, A. C. Bradley's *Shakespearean Tragedy* celebrates the grand coherence of the heroes as proof of "that truth to nature" that makes Shakespeare worthy of worship.[18] Like the narrator of Tennyson's *In Memoriam*, who constructs a self modeled on nature's predictable rises and falls, ravages and returns—like Jane Eyre, whose most overweening act of control is authorized as nature's work—Shakespeare is integrated into a nature that may be cruel, but that has blessed powers of cohesion. Through Shakespeare, Irving borrowed for his Lyceum the sanction of nature that allowed Victorian heroes to forget their theatrical origins.

This search for a self to believe in ends with an actress's prayer, which is also a protest against the authoritarianism of a theater that had achieved respectability in literary terms by suppressing its mutable essence. Ellen Terry, Irving's partner at the Lyceum, had acted all her life. Irving's heroics demanded a subdued womanliness she never believed in, but she did believe in the Shakespeare whose productions were the splendor of the Lyceum. Writing to Charles Coleman toward the end of her career, she imagined herself dying into a heaven of Shakespearean characters where she would be a glorified self with many inhabitants: "I nowadays think that in 'another & a better world than this' (!) I <u>may</u> (?) open my eyes & say 'oh Bottom how art thou translated!!!' & find <u>no E.T. left</u>! but some creature begotten of Portia Beatrice Imogen Rosalind Volumnia Cordelia Hamlet Cesar <u>Silvius</u>!!!—& I'll say looking at some old Photograph (!!) 'that's <u>me</u>!!! <u>Was</u> me—Haven't I improved?!!'" (11 March 1902).[19]

This improved Ellen Terry retains, in her dream of heaven, the many selves Shakespeare allows her, though her age, and Shakespeare himself as that age understood him, mistrusted their multiplicity. Choosing as her heaven Wordsworth's hell, she dreamed the theatricality that hero worship had done its best to expel from her stage.

NOTES

1. William Wordsworth, *The Prelude*, ed. J. C. Maxwell (1850; rpt., Harmonds-worth: Penguin Books, 1971), 111. All quotations are from this edition, hereafter cited in the text.

2. John Milton, *Paradise Lost*, in *The Complete English Poetry of John Milton*, ed. John T. Shawcross (Garden City, N.Y.: Anchor Books, 1963), 308.

3. Terry Castle, *Masquerade and Civilization: The Carnivalesque in Eighteenth-Century English Culture and Fiction* (Stanford, Cal.: Stanford University Press, 1986), 72.

4. Jonas Barish, *The Antitheatrical Prejudice* (Berkeley and London: University of California Press, 1981), 76.

5. Lionel Trilling, *Sincerity and Authenticity* (Cambridge, Mass.: Harvard University Press, 1972), 10.

6. This is Tennyson's own immodest characterization of his poetic persona in *In Memoriam*. See Hallam Tennyson, *Alfred, Lord Tennyson, a Memoir by His Son*, 2 vols. (New York: Macmillan, 1897), 1:304–305.

7. Alfred, Lord Tennyson, *In Memoriam, A. H. H.*, ed. Robert H. Ross (1850; rpt., New York: W. W. Norton, 1973), 65. All quotations are from this edition, hereafter cited in the text.

8. Charlotte Brontë, *Jane Eyre* (1847; rpt., Harmondsworth: Penguin Books, 1966), 49. All quotations are from this edition, hereafter cited in the text.

9. Charlotte Brontë, *Villette* (1853; rpt., New York: Harper Colophon Books, 1972), 414. All quotations are from this edition, hereafter cited in the text.

10. For a detailed account of shipwreck as a compelling, catastrophic image in pictorial theater and popular painting, see Martin Meisel, *Realizations: Narrative, Pictorial, and Theatrical Arts in Nineteenth-Century England* (Princeton, N.J.: Princeton University Press, 1983), 189–200.

11. William W. Appleton, *Madame Vestris and the London Stage* (New York: Columbia University Press, 1974), 171, 178.

12. Michael R. Booth, *Prefaces to English Nineteenth-Century Theatre* (Manchester: Manchester University Press, 1969–1976), 28.

13. Tom Robertson, *Caste*, in *19th Century Plays*, ed. George Rowell, 2nd ed. (Oxford and New York: Oxford University Press, 1972), 384.

14. Mary Elizabeth Braddon, *Lady Audley's Secret* (1862; rpt., New York: Dover Books, 1974), 143. All quotations are from this edition, hereafter cited in the text.

15. C. H. Hazlewood, *Lady Audley's Secret* (New York and London: Samuel French, 1863), I, i. All quotations are from this edition, hereafter cited in the text.

16. For an overview of Irving's career in the context of late Victorian culture, see Nina Auerbach, *Ellen Terry, Player in Her Time* (New York: W. W. Norton, 1987), 175–250.

17. Anna Jameson, *Shakespeare's Heroines: Characteristics of Women, Moral, Poetical, and Historical* (1832; rpt., London: Dent, 1901), 25.

18. See A. C. Bradley, *Shakespearean Tragedy* (1904; rpt., New York: Meridian Books, 1955), 192–193.

19. Quoted in Auerbach, 222–223.

Charlie Chaplin,

Soviet Icon

SPENCER GOLUB

THE MASKING MACHINE

In 1917, Soviet power commandeered the mechanism of history, repro-gramming it with ideological meaning and content, generated by and in the revolutionary moment. The themes of lying and pretending, legiti-macy and illegitimacy, which played through Russian cultural history, as-sumed a greater urgency after a Bolshevik intellectual elite overthrew au-thoritarian rule with a tenuous claim to mass support. The Bolsheviks' primary constituency, the urban proletariat, represented a small percent-age of a population, which was marginalized by class, gender, education, and geography.

As the nominal producers of the revolution, the people legitimized the event and its real inventors, the Bolshevik leadership. Lenin and Stalin in turn controlled the people by instilling in them an inflated sense of their role in the revolution and a belief in the sanctity of the event. In the postrevolutionary years, iconography became the primary language of a faked reality designed to legitimize ideological closure and to shape the consciousness of a largely unformed and uninformed populace.

The postrevolutionary period coincided with what, in West European culture, was called the "first machine age" (1920s). An aura of industrial utopianism swept across Europe, the Soviet Union included. The Hun-garian Bauhaus artist Laszlo Moholy-Nagy enthused: "There is no tradi-tion in technology, no consciousness of class or standing." However, the machine advertised not only technical mastery over nature but freedom to become master of or slave to the technology created.[1] The dialogue in

Soviet culture of this period oscillated between the aestheticism and the social functionalism of the machine. The machine shared a heroic anonymity with the common person and defined the heroic dynamism of the future nominally captured and harnessed by the revolutionary masses.

Soviet power required an urbanist icon to help maintain the illusion of legitimate proletarian empowerment. The advantage of adopting a foreign icon was that, while it could be justified according to its usage, Soviet culture could disclaim responsibility for ideological flaws engendered by its parent culture. That the Soviets settled upon an American icon was not surprising, given the great enthusiasm of their artists and their public for American technology and popular culture, and for the medium which combined the two, the (silent) cinema.

Manifesting what Herbert Blau has called "the Taylorism of the Tramp," Charlie Chaplin celebrated the dynamism while condemning the depersonalization of the city which ran like a machine and of the machines which made it run.[2] In Chaplin's Tramp persona, the Soviets believed that they had found a generic social mask, adaptable for propaganda usage. This essay does not treat the Soviets' accommodation and cooptation of Chaplin's progressive humanist politics. It discusses how Chaplin became a symbol of universal humanity and of the theater-in-life reinvented by a revolutionary populace in search of a popular culture on which to inscribe its name.

The Soviet people saw in Chaplin a symbol of their concomitant glory and humiliation, their celebration and marginalization as postrevolutionary proletarians. The Little Tramp represented the common person as revolutionary and a suspect signifier, embodying the mechanical as a positive and a negative value.

While prerevolutionary symbolists, decadents, World of Art aesthetes, and even futurists fetishized then subverted subjectivity and reconstructed the spectator as idea and object, postrevolutionary artists sought to redesign the human body as icon. Kasimir Malevich designed the prototypes for the red square heart of El Lissitzky's "New Person" (*Novy chelovek*, 1923), the lithograph of an unrealized design for the futurist opera *Victory over the Sun*. The graceful, diminutive Charlie, who is linked with various marginalized female characters in his films, was, like these women, recast as gender-neutral and put to work in the factory as a human machine. Constructivists Varvara Stepanova and her husband

Aleksandr Rodchenko enthused over the spatial implications of Chaplin as "the geometricization of the human body." For the Russian formalists of the 1920s, influenced by their reading of Henri Bergson, Chaplin's movement manifested the throwing off of received rhythms and the deadly parodying of their mechanical nature. He made the mechanical seem *more* mechanical and thus *less* relevant. Chaplin's functionalism was consistent with the constructivists' and Vsevolod Meyerhold's antidecorative, pro-utilitarian approach to art in the 1920s. In his iconic image were conflated themes and elements devised and retrieved by the Russian avant-garde artists of the period: popular performance art, "supergraphics" (i.e., public art on a large scale), multimedia, folk art neoprimitivism, and the re-integration of art and life. Stepanova, who designed Meyerhold's circus and silent film–inspired production of Aleksandr Sukhovo-Kobylin's *Tarelkin's Death* (*Smert Tarelkina*, written 1869; staged 1922), completed in the same year a series of prints of Chaplin for the third issue of the Soviet film journal *Cinema-Photo* (*Kino-foto*, 1922), in which he performed somersaults and posed with such modern implements as an automobile, a tire, and a meat-grinder. Stepanova's meat-grinder set design for Meyerhold's production of *Tarelkin's Death* connected the ideas and images of food, the machine, and evil, much as did Chaplin in the factory sequences in *Modern Times* (1936). The labor-saving machine designed to feed workers, which almost succeeds in devouring Charlie, embodies an idea expressed in *Tarelkin's Death*: "The machinery will operate itself."[3]

Rasplyuev, Tarelkin's tormentor in the play, has devised a "mechanics" whereby a person may be broken down to the essential core, to the confession of guilty humanity.[4] This is essentially the task which the feeding machine performs upon Charlie, whose own physical mechanism cannot hope to match the machine's tempo or rhythm. The food, which falls out of Charlie's mouth at the moment it is forced in, constitutes an admission of guilt and serves as evidence toward Charlie's conviction on the charge of human instability. His on-the-job nervous breakdown, which follows shortly thereafter, closes the book on the question of his suitability as an assembly-line worker. His celebrated ballet through the gears of a giant machine reinforces, by way of juxtaposition of organic human form and inorganically assembled machine parts, how ridiculously unsuited he is to be a cog.[5]

However, Charlie's "sin" goes beyond his humanness. As a representative of capitalist mass culture rather than a true socialist proletarian, he can be assumed to harbor the anti-Marxist desire to become a consumer rather than a producer.[6] Those made or left hungry by the revolution were often the subjects of early Soviet drama. By casting this hunger, which was more often a desire for employment, enfranchisement, or a search for intellectual and moral truth, as greed, gluttony, and disloyalty, a new breed of postrevolutionary class enemy was defined. In Nikolay Erdman's tragic satire *The Suicide* (*Samoubiitsa*, 1928), it is not only the intelligentsia and the bourgeoisie but the proletariat which is ground up like liver sausage, in a conscious recycling of Meyerhold's commanding image for *Tarelkin's Death*.

In *Modern Times*, Charlie is set free of the machine and of the factory. The Marxists originally believed that the machine would be instrumental in retrieving labor for the common people and thereby in helping to create for them an image of the world and the self. When things did not work out as planned, they set out to restore human wholeness, lost in the division of labor into parts, which alienated the worker from the means of production. As Katerina Clark explains, "the guidelines for Socialist Realism [e.g., loyalty to the party and its leaders, the legitimacy and historical inevitability of the revolution, heroic struggle] were thought out during a wave of reaction *against* [my emphasis] machine-age values."[7] Thus, Chaplin's problematizing of the machine was only inhospitable to party thought during *particular* stages in its development.

Stepanova's 1926 image of Charlie as upended skater, inspired by his film *The Rink* (1916), shows us the machine-human out of order, much as does farce. Its antithesis appeared one year later in the celebrated and ideologically charged image of Dziga Vertov's brother and cameraman Mikhail Kaufman confidently grounded on the cover of *Soviet Cinema* (no. 1), with a camera at his eye—or, if you will, a cine-eye—and with roller skates for feet.[8] "The perfect electric man," embodying and expressing "the poetry of the machine," recalled Lenin's equation of December 1920: "socialism = Soviet power + electrification."[9]

The concerns and devices of the Russian and Soviet avant-garde, and in particular those of the Russian formalists of the 1920s—the viewing of art as technological craft and scientific process, the consideration of its virtuosity (individualism) and utility (collectivism), the application of a mechanistic metaphor to the discussion of the deautomatization of art and culture (via defamiliarization)—constituted the background upon which Chaplin's image in the Soviet Union was projected. There are two Russian literary-critical traditions. One, instituted by the nineteenth-century "social critics," Vissarion Belinsky, Nikolay Chernyshevsky, and Nikolay Dobrolyubov and culminating in socialist realism (1934–1953), ascribes to art the logical and consistent purpose of inscribing certain socially manufactured theoretical values upon life and culture. The other tradition, from Gogol to formalism, is alogical and does not attempt to transform its abstractions into rules or proofs. It is one of alienation and estrangement, a continuous dialogue, between clown masks and social masks, supermen and "superfluous men," the falsely empowered and the disempowered, on the theme of being/nonbeing and the overall masking of reality.

THE CHILD-CLOWN

The prerevolutionary Russian public was unprepared for Chaplin. Articles in the Russian press discussed American cinema, and the silent film comedies of Chaplin, Roscoe ("Fatty") Arbuckle, and others began to appear in 1916. American film comedies differed in style from traditional Russian comic fare, and they did not meet with immediate success. While Chaplin seemed like an amusing clown, there was nothing yet to distinguish him for a Russian viewer from his American colleagues. Prerevolutionary Russian and, for that matter, European critics found Chaplin's early style of acting to be coarse and inelegant (i.e., not very European). They were somewhat mystified by Chaplin's growing popularity in the United States. Much was later made of this prerevolutionary "critical blindness" by postrevolutionary Soviet critics, who, in retrospect, could appreciate Charlie's incipient proletarianism and acute deconstruction of familiar bourgeois types. On the battlefield of free will versus determinism which accompanied world war, revolution, and civil war (in Russia), the nineteenth century's romance with individualism expired and with it larger-than-life heroes. In its place was born collectivism and the (anti-)heroic little man, Charlie Chaplin and Jaroslav Hašek's *Good Soldier Schwejk*. Charlie's automatism could now be read as an absurd response to the crisis of modern times.[10]

Before the Russian critical establishment caught up with Chaplin's art, individual artists seem to have taken his creative measure. Meyerhold claimed in 1936 to have appreciated as early as 1916 Chaplin's "predilection for monumental subjects," which was manifest in his film *The Tramp*. Viktor Shklovsky recalled the conclusion of a 1918 film, entitled "Creation Can't Be Bought," written by the poet-dramatist Vladimir Mayakovsky (adapted from Edmond de Amicis's *The Worker's Teacher* and from Jack London's *Martin Eden*) and directed by Nikandr Turkin, in which the poet, rejected by his beloved and himself rejecting suicide after considering the option, "goes out on the road, homeless and free, like Chaplin. . . ."[11]

Chaplin became for a good many Soviet artists a talismanic presence, the image of freedom, in baggy pants and size fourteen shoes, warding off cooptation by the absolutist state and the mechanical age. Mayakovsky, the machine-age futurist, who ended as a suicide, fantasized consistently in his work about breaking free. Prisypkin, the antihero of Mayakovsky's play *The Bedbug* (*Klop*, 1928), is caged by a sanitized futurian society. His vulgar coarseness and sentimentalism undercut the false heroism of the new age, while his sloppy Romanticism struggles to break free of the play's futurist machine rhythms. Film director Lev Kuleshov spoke of Chaplin's ability to remain free, even of the burden of his own celebrity: "You have to be Chaplin to know how to carry the burden of real grandeur." With the appearance in the Soviet Union of *A Dog's Life* (American premiere 1918; Soviet premiere 1919), Charlie's image became more widely known. The Tramp figure directly influenced the Russian variety stage, theater, and film actor Arkady Boitler, who as an émigré performer in Germany in the 1920s gave his "mask" Arkasha a Chaplinesque mustache and cane, although not Charlie's penchant for social criticism. This tradition continued on the Soviet variety stage, most notably in the work of the late Arkady Raikin.[12]

"The subject and object of mechanical reproduction," Chaplin "*was* mass culture," J. Hoberman wrote in a critical appreciation, commemorating the centennial of Chaplin's birth. Wearing the face of collective desire, "the original parody automaton" was a proletarian who resisted not only authority but work. He was both the culmination of a long tradition in popular culture and the invention of a new form, an event signaled, said Viktor Shklovsky, by his parodic nature.[13] He simultaneously embodied the incursion of low into high culture and the attempt to extract more play—greater leisure time—out of work. He aimed, as did the Soviet Central Institute of Labor in the postrevolutionary period, to dismantle the artificial boundaries between work and leisure, production and culture. The Tramp as free man and agent provocateur lived an exemplary revolutionary life, with a ferocious grace bordering alternately on cruelty and heartbreak.

Chaplin considered his own work to be child's play, and the technology which had produced his cinematic work to be conducive to expanding people's horizons, along with filling their leisure time. Yet his consistent opposition to cultural and political fascism reflected not only his love of freedom but the war that he waged, with the mechanics of farce as his weapon, against machine-culture and machine-people. Soviet journalist and writer Ilya Ehrenburg wrote to Chaplin in 1942: "All your life on the screen you have defended the little man against the malevolent and soulless machine. We are glad to see you taking a stand against Nazism. It isn't humans who've fallen upon us but ersatz-men, brutal, repulsive automatons."[14]

According to his friend Sergey Eisenstein, Chaplin's fascination with the short-statured, terrifying child-clowns Napoleon and Hitler embodied the infantile dream of escape from reality (a popular theme in Russian/Soviet culture), the child's dream of "supreme egoism and absolute freedom from 'the fetters of morality.'" But this dream remains partnered by reality, "still taller, still more terrible, still stronger and still more ruthless," like the massive character actors Mack Swain, Eric Campbell, and Tom Murray, who pummel the diminutive Charlie in his films.[15]

In an eccentric pamphlet published in 1947, Parker Tyler conflated the images of Chaplin's two selves—the large adult and the small child—into one recognizable one: "Charlie is a little boy lost in the trousers of a huge man, the very man who is his classic enemy, the hoodlum from whom the little knight paradoxically flees." He is, said Tyler, "the daddy-envious presumptuous child who steals his father's pants." French aesthetician Elie Faure named this empowered child the "obstetrician to a new world."[16]

Chaplin performed "the two opposite poles of infantilism—the victor and the vanquished," its amoral cruelty and its appealing charm. Chaplin's child's way of seeing conformed to the formalists' definition of the function of art: "to restore . . . a fresh, childlike vision of the world." In his later films, this vision was partnered by the mature consciousness of a people's artist. Eisenstein argued that Chaplin's growing-up process was a typical rite of passage for the Western capitalist. Anxiety over the striving for material success and social standing breeds infantilism, which in turn engenders the dream of escaping from reality into fairy tale. Communism's classlessness and distribution of wealth commensurate with self-determined labor productivity frees people from this anxiety, thus transforming reality into a fairy tale.[17] This reality–as–fairy tale motif was espoused in the doctrine of socialist realism and was dutifully represented in a succession of drab plays with contrived, machinelike plots and heroes and with machines as central props. More interestingly, it recurs as a sad-ironic theme in plays of the same period by social satirists such as Mikhail Bulgakov, Mayakovsky, Yury Olesha, Nikolay Erdman, and Evgeny Shvarts, in which reality is measured against the fairy tale of revolutionary and futurian promises and dreams.

The doubleness of the child/adult Charlie was embodied in his impersonations of Napoleon and Hitler, the would-be conquerors of Russia and the Soviet Union, respectively. In Chaplin's unproduced idea for a screenplay, a "false Napoleon," the deposed emperor's double, dies on the island of St. Helena, just as the real Napoleon is secretly gathering his forces to reconquer France. When Napoleon hears of his double's demise, which robs him of his reality in the eyes of the world, he proclaims, "The news of my death has killed me." In much the same way, Chaplin contested Hitler for his identity. Journalists of their day were intrigued by the notion that these two men, born a mere four days apart in the same year into poverty and anonymity and eventually rising to become arguably the two greatest actors of their day, were somehow doubles. Chaplin accused Hitler of having stolen his mustache. It was a legitimate theft in that Chaplin had intended his mustache "to be a gibe at all pomposity." Chaplin's successful impersonation of a parodic Hitler, in The Great Dictator (1940), accomplished in part what the "false Napoleon" did at the expense of the real emperor—he made him seem simultaneously more threatening, less real, and more buffoonish, truer as a grotesque than as a man. "It is not too much to say," wrote a reviewer, "that no one but

Chaplin, not even Adolf Hitler, could have taken this part."[18] *The Great Dictator* bore out Shklovsky's 1923 prediction that "Chaplin is moving towards the heroic comic film, which means that he will use 'comic fear.'"[19]

Nineteenth-century Russian literature reveals the advent of the machine-person, the anonymous cipher and empty signifier best exemplified by Gogol's petty clerks, from Akaky Akakievich to Ivan Khlestakov. Meyerhold transformed the childish posturer Khlestakov (Gogol's own characterization of his creation) into an assembly-line bribery machine ten years prior to Chaplin's reassembly of the proletarian according to machine rhythms in *Modern Times*.[20]

The protagonists of postrevolutionary Soviet literature are alternately obsessed with the future and fearful that they cannot get out of its way. The hero of Mikhail Bulgakov's novella *Diaboliad* (1924), walled in by society's growing "fascination with elevators, skyscrapers and public transport," commits suicide by jumping off one of Moscow's highest buildings. Yury Olesha, an admirer of Chaplin's films and of the stories of H. G. Wells (also a Chaplin admirer), said that both present "little English clerks in bowlers and narrow ties who run every which way to escape the marvel of an emerging futuristic technology or on the contrary, who run to look at it and perish." Like Wells's little people, wrote Olesha, the bowler-hatted Chaplin "was frightened of technology; he too was unable because of the machine to find happiness." The opening title card to Chaplin's *Modern Times* reads: "A story of industry, of individual enterprise—humanity crusading in the pursuit of happiness." Chaplin's fairy tale sentimentalism counteracts somewhat the mechanical energy and impersonality of urban life.[21]

The heroine of Olesha's play *A List of Blessings* (*Spisok blagodeyanii*, 1931) may suggest the celebrated actor Michael Chekhov, whose anthroposophically based *Hamlet* (1924–1925) was vilified in the Soviet press and who emigrated to the West.[22] However, the real suspect signifier in Olesha's play is Chaplin, the self-proclaimed internationalist and alleged free man of the West, whose big-screen image lures Goncharova, a Soviet actress who longs to play Hamlet, into a Western world conceived as cinematic reality.

Olesha's heroine discovers her Charlie under a lamppost in Paris, eating his supper in his sleep, recalling in her mind, and just possibly in the mind of the sleeping character, the famous "inner dining" feast of boot and lace in *The Gold Rush* (1925). Goncharova is played upon as much by this fictional Charlie and the fictional idea he incarnates, a human definition of self, transcending class consciousness, as she is by the cabaret owner who recasts her Hamlet soliloquy as an obscene act performed with a wind instrument (a reference to the famous "recorder" scene in *Hamlet*). Goncharova's notebook, which she has divided into a list of crimes and a list of blessings bequeathed to the people by the revolution, recalls Chaplin's characterization of the modern era as "the age of crimes."[23]

Olesha's play slightly recasts the adage "If you want to grow up a communist, go to Paris. If you want to grow up an anticommunist, go to Russia." At play's end, the politically anomalous and personally conflicted Goncharova steps in front of a workers' demonstration and is martyred by a bullet meant for its leader. In *Modern Times* (1936), the Tramp found himself accidentally leading a workers' demonstration, waving the red flag that he was trying to return to the passing truck that had dropped it. This parody of the West's creation of Chaplin as communist fellow-traveler is another illustration of the individual swept up in the rush of modern times, "automatized" and blind-sided by "noncontinuous perception." The Tramp, who disorders bourgeois reality, making us all feel guiltily rich and empathetically poor, reminds us that fast-closing fate, now wearing the face of history, is the most infernal machine with which we do battle.

THE MAIN ATTRACTION

The formalist conception of the Tramp as a consistent "action-function," to borrow Vladimir Propp's term, rather than as a psychologically consistent character, was adopted by Meyerhold. Meyerhold shared with Chaplin the belief that only by working from within a popular tradition—circus, music hall (which Gorky said Lenin enjoyed in London), pantomime, *commedia dell'arte*, fairground booth—toward a mirroring of timeless popular reality could great art be achieved. The people may not embody the truth, but their cultural tradition performs the "action of actuality."[24]

While he at first rejected cinema as a viable new art form (1912), as of 1915, Meyerhold had reconsidered. He valued American silent film comedy, in particular, applying lessons he drew from its form and from its performers to his stage work. His theatrical productions and studio work, in turn, influenced the development of the Soviet cinema. He said that Harold Lloyd "cried with vaseline" and represented an even-tempered, underplayed, healthy image, unconflicted by pathology, as was the case with Chaplin's Tramp. Meyerhold's personal favorite was Buster Keaton, whose *Our Hospitality* (1923) was, he said, "the best American film comedy I have seen." What he admired in Keaton was his stylistic consistency and the precision of his play. Meyerhold stated that for him the essential problem of the actor's play was "the creation of the comic effects of the mechanism," and no actor-director, in his opinion, was more exact or more tactful than Keaton in getting results. Keaton's penchant for "frame tales" and sign systems has made him the darling of formalists, neoformalists, and semiologists, while these same theorists and critics have criticized Chaplin's work for being sentimental and self-involved.[25]

Still, Meyerhold considered Chaplin, along with Mikhail Chekhov, to be "the most genial" of contemporary actors and the one who best embodied the essence of contemporaneity. If he was less of a cool stylist than Keaton, he was more courageous and astute as a social critic and realist. "Through his caricature," said Meyerhold, "Chaplin seems to stress the monstrousness of the world he is unmasking," that being the world of bourgeois culture. Chaplin's naïve but tragic clowning was like that of the Kabuki actor, projected through a consistent mask. Chaplin's Tramp mask, Meyerhold was quick to point out, drew upon the example of the people and upon the strength of the individual artist. It was a respectful borrowing, not a coercive appropriation. Chaplin's *Modern Times* spoke directly to the role which Meyerhold envisioned for theater and cinema, "to decide the great contemporary problems."[26]

Meyerhold's linkage of Chaplin with social realism speaks not only to the naturalness of Charlie's clowning but to the unnaturalness of Meyerhold's position at that time. As a suspected "formalist," his statements were monitored by the watchdogs of government-sponsored socialist realism. Meyerhold saw tremendous relevance in Chaplin's work to Russian theatrical traditions and to his own work in the theater. He thought that Chaplin's brand of "laughter through tears" placed in the service of the oppressed compared favorably to Gogol's work (e.g., *The Overcoat*). Meyerhold's characterization of Chaplin as a citizen-poet and defender of the weak borrowed from nineteenth-century Russian Romanticism and social criticism. Chaplin's careful construction of "effects" reminded Meyerhold of Aleksandr Blok's *The Puppet Show* (*Balaganchik*, 1906) which he had already staged and now wished to restage as a "Chaplinade." Kh. Khersonsky, who worked with Meyerhold on his production of Fernand Crommelynck's *The Magnanimous Cuckold* (1922), saw stylistic similarities between it and Chaplin's film *A Woman of Paris* (1923). As a political artist, Meyerhold recognized Chaplin as a useful and evocative icon for proletarian culture. He saw in Chaplin's films an example of the revolutionary Romanticism necessary to preserve a lyrical element in realistic art. One found this lyricism, said Meyerhold, in Mayakovsky's art and in revolutionary artistic slogans. However, it was missing in socialist realist art.[27]

Chaplin's building of the stunt or gag, which Meyerhold so admired, reminded him of his own system of biomechanics, which has come to be overly identified with the fetishizing of machine culture in Soviet society of its day. In his constructivist manifesto (1922), Alexey Gan declared that "art is dead." Gan also attacked Chaplin, Meyerhold, Fernand Léger, who featured Chaplin's image in his *Ballet mécanique* (created with Dudley Murphy, 1923–1924), and music hall artists, which, in a sense, the foregoing all were in Gan's eyes, for compromising constructivist principles in art by, among other things, making it (too) subjective. In an article entitled "The Industrialization of Gesture" (1922), Soviet critic Ippolit Sokolov stated that "on stage the actor must become an automaton, a mechanism, a machine, a master of industrialized gesture, i.e., the gesture of labour, built on the principle of economy of effort . . . linear, a geometric order."[28] This gives some sense of the atmosphere in which biomechanics (1921) was invented. Meyerhold was interested in the scientific organization of material, and biomechanics was, in one sense, organized according to the principle espoused by Meyerhold's student, future wife, and lead actress, Zinaida Raikh: "The body is a machine operated by a machinist." However, Meyerhold's biomechanics, like Chaplin's plastique, aimed at achieving machinelike economy and mastery of expression and realistic human expressiveness, not at emulating dehumanized machine rhythms, or worse still, a machinelike mindset. In fact, the future film actors who were schooled in Meyerhold's system—N. I. Bogolyubov, E. P. Garin, N. P. Okhlopkov, and Igor Ilinsky—helped to develop Soviet film realism. The theater training which he offered in "the culture of movement" and in such specific techniques as "pre-acting" (which he observed as well in Chaplin's "momentary pauses for aim") and "self-mirroring" proved to be helpful to actors making the transition from stage to film. While the filmmaker Lev Kuleshov called Chaplin "our first teacher," Soviet film directors Sergey Yutkevich, N. P. Okhlopkov, A. M. Romm, and, of course, Eisenstein were first taught by Meyerhold.[29]

Chaplin and Meyerhold both problematized spoken language via the aesthetic of movement. Chaplin proclaimed that all of his film work was based on pantomime, and Meyerhold suggested that in this "crisis in the theatre" period, the "pantomime is a good antidote against excessive misuse of words." Chaplin claimed that he did not talk in pictures sooner because the sound equipment was too bulky to fit into his small studio. Once the equipment had been simplified (i.e., prior to the filming of *The Great Dictator*, 1939–1940), he said, he was able and willing to use it. Charlie's initial foray into speech was actually the French song which he coquettishly sang at the urging of the Gamin (Paulette Goddard). The foreignness of the song, which he performed in his workplace (a restaurant), and the marginalized status of his female ally further contributed to Charlie's Otherness. Mass culture, which Charlie represents, has, since Nietzsche, been inscribed with feminine characteristics.[30]

What Viktor Shklovsky referred to as Chaplin's "dotted" movement, broken up, mechanical, and ending in a pose, conforms to the episodic nature of film montage, its framing of noncontinuous perception, as well as to the new, episodic, "cinefied" stage which it and he helped to engender. Shklovsky called Chaplin the *first* film actor, in that he embodied fully and exclusively the medium's means and its aesthetic. Eisenstein stated that "the lyrical effect of a whole series of Chaplin scenes was inseparable from the attractional quality of the specific mechanics of his movements." Chaplin's films, said Shklovsky, make us aware of "the stunt as such," "a series of 'constant movements' repeated with varying motivations from film to film." Chaplin's prolonged resistance to the use of sound in his films defined an "aesthetic of laconism." This laconism, which Chaplin and his films had in common with the machine, achieved as well "maximum economy of the expressive means." It also assured maximum intelligibility of Charlie's cinematic image on the electrified world stage. As Meyerhold noted, "the Russian peasant refuses to understand Chaplin the Englishman. Chaplin was close to him and intelligible because he only mimed."[31] Another meaning can be extracted from a slight rephrasing of the end of this statement to read, "because he had no voice."

Chaplin presented an image of the machine "made strange," a mobile construction built from unequal parts—oversize shoes, undersized jacket and hat, slight cane, and truncated mustache. The mustache only became real in proximity to Hitler's, which it derealized. Charlie's gait was composed of a series of edits, which together demonstrated the destabilization of the mechanical by the human.

The protagonist of Chaplin's next film, *The Great Dictator*, returns to language as a neoprimitivist, rebuilding his memory and his semiotic reading of the world's social, moral, linguistic, and emblematic textual codes (e.g., the dictator Hynkel's "double cross" insignia) following a lengthy period of hospitalization after World War I. Language may be the weapon he uses to ascend to the heights of demagoguery and potential world domination, but it only works when he adopts the dress and gestural codes of the dictator. The assumption of the dictator's identity by the Jewish barber, his rise from the nonstatus of disempowered ghetto-dweller to the seat of unbridled power on a global scale, represents an inversion of status, in what may now be called the requisite "Bakhtinian carnivalesque" fashion. The Soviet proletariat could find in this a rough analogue to its transformation into a "dictatorship" by the revolution.

Both Meyerhold and Chaplin were influenced by the circus. Lenin, who quickly recognized the propaganda value of cinema, likewise saw the value of the circus, which satirized bourgeois reality. Mayakovsky wrote the satirical revue *Moscow in Flames* (1930) expressly for the circus to commemorate the twenty-fifth anniversary of the 1905 revolution. Gorky professed to enjoy the circus, because it resembled work more than play, and dreamed, as did Olesha, of becoming a circus performer.[32]

Yury Annenkov, in his "Merry Sanitorium" manifesto (1919) and his production of Lev Tolstoy's *The First Distiller*, Sergey Radlov at the Theater of Popular Comedy (1920), and the teenage stage and future film directors at Petrograd's Factory of the Eccentric Actor (FEKS, 1922) called for the "circusization of the theatre," privileging the machine and giving preference to "Charlie's ass [over] Eleonora Duse's hands!" Chaplin's work, for the Eccentrists, represented the "extension of the line of the music hall and circus." During his period, circus acts were frequently interpolated into the texts of plays for various special effects by Eisenstein, Meyerhold, Annenkov, and Radlov "to propel the action" and "generate tension." Meyerhold actually declared the circus to be "nobler than the theater." However, Shklovsky maintained that circus business was consciously employed in the theater to conceal the deficiencies of the text and so compromised the role of language in literary performance. Furthermore, he argued, circus acts and the then popular mass spectacles which incorporated them did not represent the real tradition of popular performance but were "merely condescending imitations of genuine folk art."[33]

The Soviet circus spawned many Chaplin imitators, the most famous of whom performed under the name "Karandash" (Pencil or Crayon, a.k.a. Mikhail Rumyantsev). In adopting the Chaplin persona, Karandash recognized that it had become a universal mask defined by its appearance and its function, not by the real personality of the wearer. The development of the Chaplin persona in the Soviet circus from mere pantomimic eccentric to an urbanite with a social conscience, "not drenched in flour, humane, real, truthful and no longer humiliated," paralleled Chaplin's own development of his persona in his later films. These films arrived belatedly in the Soviet Union due to a dispute over royalty payments, so the "mature" Chaplin was unknown to Soviet clowns in the early 1930s. By the time The Great Dictator arrived in the Soviet Union, Karandash had already quite naturally begun to perform Hitler parodies.[34]

THE HISTORICAL INEVITABILITY

The problematizing of the clown in Soviet society speaks directly to the difficulty in reconciling formalism and realistic social content in Soviet art. The Soviet attitude toward Chaplin parallels this. Chaplin was biographically attractive to the Soviets as a Gorky-like legendary tramp and autodidact, a self-made revolutionary populist, a former victim who now sought recompense not only for himself but for the poor, the ignorant, the inarticulate, and the oppressed. As regards self-education, Chaplin said, "I wanted to know not for the love of knowledge but as a defense against the world's contempt for the ignorant."[35] Chaplin was able to transform his unsentimental observations on life into sentimental art. The Soviets applauded both sides of this equation. He was a nonliterary type whose roots in popular entertainment made the Soviet people and especially the Bolsheviks (called "barbarians" by Lenin) feel themselves to be his equal. He showed himself in his films to be suppressed by bourgeois society and alienated from the meaningless jobs he was forced to take in order to survive. His rebellion was not so much against machines as against those who employed them to transform the worker into an object. This let machine-crazed early Soviet culture off the hook. He recouped his dignity as a human being by counter-objectifying the policemen and bosses who oppressed him. Chaplin boasted in 1941 that "ninety per cent of the public has often wondered just what the capitalist would do if he had his whiskers pulled, and now it is as plain as day." His image of "the bloated capitalist in dundering whiskers, light trousers, spats, frock coat, silk hat" recalled the straw figures targeted for extinction in the Soviet mass spectacles of the early 1920s.[36]

Chaplin's heroism was earned in the workplace, a cornerstone of the new Soviet order and the locale in which the new Soviet drama would be set. His environments were depicted realistically, while his characters contrasted sharply as social masks, as was also now the case in Soviet Theater. As he developed his social vision, the generic tramp became the unemployed proletarian, living in a specific sociopolitical context. The purely grotesque and mechanical elements were absorbed into a fuller, more realistic craft. His naïve internationalism intersected with Soviet utopianism. He had correctly identified the central theme of the modern era, this "time of crisis," as being the battle between capital and labor. He had even managed somewhat to overcome personal solipsism in his work. Like many Soviet orphans of the revolution, most notably Lenin (the revolutionary as common man) and Stalin, who lost their fathers at an early age, Charlie the fatherless child sought his identity in the "great human family" and in sociopolitical activism. His story, which tends to originate and conclude on the road, with no defined origin or destination, at least partially subscribes to what Katerina Clark has identified as the morphology of the socialist realist master plot (in the Soviet novel), with its questing, visionary orphans.[37]

The generally supportive American communist press sought to deromanticize Chaplin by criticizing his wealth, power, and limited understanding of Marxism-Leninism, historical process, and workers' movements. Under Stalin, the Soviet propaganda machine made a more virulent attempt to discredit Chaplin and his supporters. By 1949 the campaign against foreign influences in the arts had become a scarcely veiled form of anti-Semitism, under the slogan of "the struggle against cosmopolitanism." The cinema industry, with its high proportion of Jewish personnel, was especially vulnerable. On 4 March 1949 the minister of cinematography launched the attack by announcing in *Pravda* that the director L. Trauberg was the "ringleader of the cosmopolitans in the cinema." Attacks on other Jewish film writers and critics followed: one of the accusations made against some was that they had praised Charlie Chaplin (a non-Jew, "mistaken" for a Jew).[38]

Even those who admired Chaplin recast him in terms of personal or collective need. A Chaplin of the Soviet people's imagining was prescribed in a letter which Viktor Shklovsky wrote in 1931, under the disingenuous guise of a humble subject petitioning a distant king. The Soviet people, he indicated, did not wish to see a Chaplin who does honest hard work like themselves. They needed someone on whom to project their self-pity and desire for reciprocal empathic response. Western bourgeois society, said Shklovsky, had already lost the possibility of achieving true empathy.[39]

Much as the Soviet audience created its Chaplin, Shklovsky's letter created its audience, the Soviet people, and through them an imagined Chaplin. The open letter, like film, helped to distribute Charlie among "the masses," to dispel to some degree what Walter Benjamin characterized in another context as "aura."[40] Also, like film, it shortened the distance between "there" and "here," compressing space and time and manufacturing false intimacy. The open letter format achieves intimacy without having ascribed to it the stigma of covertness. In this way, it provides an alternative to and invokes the alternative specter of the "opened" letter, or its equivalent intercepted communiqués, which propel Russian fiction (*The Inspector General*, etc.) and Soviet reality.

To the Soviet people, it was as much the Chaplin persona's performance of the semantic and semiotic function of "named proletarian" as the quality of his work that counted. He was, like many Soviet workers, someone to whom work was of supreme value, but leisure the occupation of choice. The Soviets who valued Chaplin could draw upon a fairly orthodox example from the canon of proto-Bolshevik dramatic literature to make their case. Gorky's *The Lower Depths* (*Na dne*, 1902) opens with a scene in which the locksmith Kleshch, a self-proclaimed "working man," makes a futile attempt to get his fellow flophouse habitués interested in work. The most recalcitrant of the group is Satin, who by play's end will become Gorky's proletarian mouthpiece. "Fix it so I like working and maybe I'll go to work," Satin tells Kleshch. The implication that Satin is theoretically willing to work for a new order, in which labor will control the means of production and its own destiny, is undercut by all available evidence in the play. The author's treatment of Satin suggests that under any circumstances work to him is a fool's game. Satin shares the label that Shklovsky affixed to Charlie, another tramp, that of a "perpetual failure."[41] The two tramps wear it as a badge of distinction.

Charlie achieved what the Soviet worker could not: a critique of capital *and* labor, a defined morphology of comic subversion within the workplace, and a Romantic valorization of unemployment as the noblest profession of all. Charlie's heroic dwarfism, which was pitted against the heroic body of labor, the worker's physique, the massiveness of institution, and the force of institutional history, inverted the prescribed monolithic gigantism of Soviet culture (especially under Stalin), even as it subverted the hierarchically structured values of Western capitalism. Indeed, Chaplin partially revived the spindly figure of recalcitrant nineteenth-century Russian individualism, the little man engaged in a slippery, ambiguous revenge against the society that rendered him superfluous and little. While the Tramp could escape the burden of productivity, however, he could not and to this day cannot avoid being forged into a symbol of production.

Still, the value of Chaplin for the Soviet people, writ small, was largely positive, even if Charlie remained a somewhat problematical role model for the "Soviet People," which the engineers of Soviet culture had writ large. In a 1939 tribute to Chaplin, written on the occasion of his fiftieth birthday, FEKS co-founder Leonid Trauberg referred to Charlie's vast audience living "in remote districts [of the Soviet Union], which in the past hardly ever received a newspaper." Cinema and Chaplin's films in particular came to represent for these culturally disenfranchised people "the vividness of art made accessible at the cost of terrific struggles." Furthermore, as Trauberg had proclaimed in 1922, "Protest is inevitable, just like Charlie Chaplin's mustache."[42]

NOTES

1. Steven A. Mansbach, *Visions of Totality: Laszlo Moholy-Nagy, Theo Van Doesburg, and El Lissitzky* (Ann Arbor: UMI Research Press, 1980), 36.

2. Herbert Blau, *The Eye of Prey: Subversions of the Postmodern* (Bloomington and Indianapolis: Indiana University Press, 1987), 25.

3. James M. Curtis, "Bergson and Russian Formalism," *Comparative Literature* 28 (1976): 112; Professor Audrey Ushenko identified the themes and elements devised and retrieved by Russian avant-garde artists of the 1920s in her remarks for a panel discussion on "Russian Politics and Culture, 1900–1930," at Bellarmine College (Louisville, Kentucky), 26 September 1989; Alexander Lavrentiev, *Varvara Stepanova: The Complete Works*, ed. John E. Bowlt (Cambridge: MIT Press, 1988), 104 (quote); Aleksandr Sukhovo-Kobylin, *Tarelkin's Death*, in *Trilogy*, trans. Harold B. Segel (New York: Dutton, 1969), 253 (quote).

4. The notion of mechanical beings has a history in Russia constructed from native and imported sources. The traditional Russian puppet play was adapted for the legitimate stage and combined with the vampire tale (vampirism being another form of puppetry) by Nikolay Gogol and Aleksandr Sukhovo-Kobylin. They were influenced by the Romantic fables of E. T. A. Hoffmann, whose work featured automata and whose popularity reached its height in Russia circa 1822–1845. As Andreas Huyssen has pointed out, the aristocratic European cult of human automata was replaced by the more democratic fetishizing of the labor-saving machine which propelled the industrial revolution. Concurrently, the machine-person was transformed by the popular imagination from a symbol of human ingenuity into one of inhuman monstrosity. Tarelkin's "beautiful hair and marvelous teeth," all manufactured props, adorn a face that radiates the banality of evil incarnated by the new machine-person (Andreas Huyssen, *After the Great Divide: Modernism, Mass Culture, Postmodernism* [Bloomington and Indianapolis: Indiana University Press, 1986], 70, 163–164).

5. The human-cog comparison was made definitively by Stalin. Soviet director Yury Lyubimov has written of a visit by Stalin to a machine construction factory: "Brandishing a screw, he endeavored to explain to the workers that the new man, in communist society, would be as solid and as irreproachable as the most perfect screw they could produce" (*Le feu sacré: Souvenirs d'une vie de théâtre* [Paris: Fayard, 1985], 104).

6. Huyssen, 55.

7. Katerina Clark, *The Soviet Novel: History as Ritual* (Chicago and London: University of Chicago Press, 1985), 98–99.

8. Lavrentiev, 105, 129.

9. Dziga Vertov, "We: A Version of a Manifesto," in *The Film Factory: Russian and Soviet Cinema in Documents*, ed. Richard Taylor and Ian Christie (Cambridge: Harvard University Press, 1988), 71 (quote); "VII sezd partii, rech Lenina," *Pravda*, 24 December 1920, 2 (quote).

10. S. Ginzburg, *Kinematografiya dorevolyutsionnoi rossii* (Moscow: Iskusstvo, 1963), 260–265.

11. Vsevolod Meyerhold, "Chaplin and Chaplinism," in *Meyerhold on Theatre*, ed. Edward Braun (New York: Hill and Wang, 1969), 312; Jay Leyda, *Kino: A History of the Russian and Soviet Film* (New York: Collier Books, 1973), 129–130 (quote on 130).

12. Luda Schnitzer, Jean Schnitzer, and Marcel Martin (eds.), *Cinema in Revolution: The Heroic Era of the Soviet Film* (London: Secker and Warburg, 1973), 76 (quote); Ginzburg, 263–265.

13. J. Hoberman, "After the Gold Rush, Chaplin at 100: A Radical for Modern Times," *Village Voice*, 18 April 1989, 31–32; Viktor Shklovsky, *Literatura i kinematograf* (Berlin: n.p., 1923), quoted in Richard Robert Sheldon, "Viktor Borisovich Shklovsky: Literary Theory and Practice, 1914–1930" (Ph.D. diss., University of Michigan, 1966), 251.

14. Charles Chaplin, *My Autobiography* (New York: Simon and Schuster, 1964), 274; Charles J. Maland, *Chaplin and American Culture: The Evolution of a Star Image* (Princeton: Princeton University Press, 1989), 193 (quote); David Platt, "Chaplin, Master of Film Satire: His Genius Grew Out of Love for the Common Man," *Daily Worker*, 10 April 1941.

15. Sergey Eisenstein, "Charlie the Kid," in *Notes of a Film Director* (Moscow: Foreign Languages Publishing House, 1958), 183, 193; originally published in the collection *Charles Spencer Chaplin* (Moscow: n.p., 1945), 137–158.

16. Parker Tyler, *A Little Boy Lost: Marcel Proust and Charlie Chaplin* (New York: Prospero Pamphlets no. 2, 1947), 6–7. Elie Faure's remarks are quoted in John Willett, *Art and Politics in the Weimar Period: The New Sobriety 1907–1933* (New York: Pantheon Books, 1978), 65.

17. Eisenstein, "Charlie the Kid," 191, 195 (quote); Victor Erlich, *Russian Formalism*, 3rd ed. (New Haven: Yale University Press, 1981), 76 (quote); Robert Leach, *Vsevolod Meyerhold* (Cambridge: Cambridge University Press, 1989), 91.

18. Eisenstein, "Charlie the Kid," 194 (quote); Gerald McDonald, *The Picture History of Charlie Chaplin* (Franklin Square, N.Y.: Nostalgia Press, 1965), 47; "'Dictator' Box-Office Gross Passed GWTW," *Daily Worker*, 27 October 1940; Ella Winter, "Charlie Chaplin and 'The Great Dictator': He Lampoons Stuffed Shirts, Tyranny and Suppression," *FRIDAY MAGAZINE* (New York), 22 (quote); Daniel Todd, "Chaplin's Greatest Picture," *New Masses*, 29 October 1940, 30 (quote).

19. Viktor Shklovsky, quoted in Sheldon, 251.

20. Nikolay Gogol, "Advice to Those Who Would Play *The Government Inspector* as It Ought to Be Played" (written circa 1846; published posthumously), in *The Theater of Nikolay Gogol*, ed. Milton Ehre, trans. Milton Ehre and Fruma Gottschalk (Chicago and London: University of Chicago Press, 1980), 174.

21. Ellendea Proffer, *Bulgakov: Life and Work* (Ann Arbor: Ardis, 1984), 106–108 (quote on 106); Yuri Olesha, *No Day without a Line*, trans. and ed. Judson Rosengrant (Ann Arbor: Ardis, 1979), 235 (quotes); Elizabeth Klosty Beaujour, *The Invisible Land: A Study of the Artistic Imagination of Iurii Olesha* (New York: Columbia University Press, 1970), 42, 56–58, 84, 104, 159.

22. Yuri Olesha, *A List of Blessings*, in *Olesha: The Complete Plays*, ed. and trans. Michael Green and Jerome Katsell (Ann Arbor: Ardis, 1983), hereafter cited in the text.

23. Olesha, *No Day without a Line*, 217 (quote); Huyssen, 82.

24. Vladimir Propp, *Morphology of the Folktale*, trans. Laurence Scott, rev. and ed. Louis A. Wagner (Austin: University of Texas Press, 1986), 20–21. Vladimir Mayakovsky, a Chaplin admirer and early proponent of the cinema, saw the relationship between the dynamic actor and his changing background in film as representing "the action of actuality" (Vladimir Mayakovsky, "Theatre, Cinema, Futurism," trans. Helen Segall, *Russian Literature Triquarterly* 12 [Spring 1975]: 182 [quote]).

25. A. Fevralsky, *Puti k sintezy: Meierkhold i kino* (Moscow: Iskusstvo, 1978), 170–175. This source includes citations from books and articles by, among others, filmmakers Lev Kuleshov, Dziga Vertov, Vsevolod Pudovkin, and Grigory Kozintsev; Eccentrist Sergey Yutkevich; and Meyerhold, his actress wife, Zinaida Raikh, and his leading comic actor, Igor Ilinsky. Walter Benjamin's ill-considered dismissal of Ilinsky as "an unscrupulous, inept imitator of Chaplin" notwithstanding, Viktor Shklovsky wrote in 1962, "Given the right scenario, Ilinsky would certainly join Chaplin's ranks" (Walter Benjamin, *Moscow Diary*, ed. Gary Smith, trans. Richard Sieburth [Cambridge: Harvard University Press, 1986], 53–54; Viktor Shklovsky, "The Clown, Comedy and Tragedy," in *The Soviet Circus* [Moscow: Progress Publishers, 1967], 37–38; Meyerhold, "Chaplin and Chaplinism," in *Meyerhold on Theatre*, 319).

26. Fevralsky, 170–175.

27. Meyerhold, "Chaplin and Chaplinism," 323–324.

28. Alexey Gan, quoted in John E. Bowlt, "Modern Russian Stage Design," in *Russian Stage Design: Scenic Innovation, 1900–1930. From the Collection of Mr. and Mrs. Nikita D. Lobanov-Rostovsky* (Jackson: Mississippi Museum of Art, 1982), 34–35; Ippolit Sokolov, "The Industrialization of Gesture," originally published in *Ermitazh* 6 (1922): 9, quoted in Konstantin Rudnitsky, *Russian and Soviet Theater 1905–1932*, ed. Lesley Milne, trans. Roxane Permar (New York: Harry N. Abrams, 1988), 93.

29. Fevralsky, 170–175; Meyerhold, "The New Theatre Foreshadowed in

Literature" and "The Fairground Booth," in *Meyerhold on Theatre*, 37, 124, 142; Leach, 65; Huyssen, "Mass Culture as Woman," in *After the Great Divide*, 50–51.

30. Shklovsky, "Literature and Cinema (Extracts)," 98–99; Meyerhold, "The Fairground Booth," 124.

31. Shklovsky, "Literature and Cinema (Extracts)," 98–99 (quotes); Meyerhold, "The Fairground Booth" (Eisenstein quote, 124). See Adrian Piotrovsky, "The Cinefication of Theatre—Some General Points"; and Vsevolod Meyerhold, "The Cinefication of Theatre," in *The Film Factory*, 178–180, 271–275 (quote on 272).

32. A. Lebedeva, "Maxim Gorky's Impressions of the Circus" (1958), in *The Soviet Circus*, 205, 208–209.

33. Grigory Kozintsev, in *Ekstsentrizm: Sbornik statei* (Petrograd: n.p., 1922), cited in *The Film Factory*, 58 (quotes), 146; Viktor Shklovsky, "Kruzhevennoe varenie," in *Khod konya* (Moscow and Berlin: n.p., 1923), 50, quoted in Sheldon, 237–238; Schnitzer, Schnitzer, and Martin, 16 (quote).

34. Ilya Fink, "Karandash," in *The Soviet Circus*, 65–66, 68–69; "Karandash," *Nad chem smeetsya kloun* (Moscow: Iskusstvo, 1987), 22; Shklovsky, "The Clown, Comedy and Tragedy," 37 (quote).

35. Maland, 63.

36. David Platt, "Chaplin, Master of Film Satire," *Daily Worker*, 10 April 1941.

37. Clark, 134–135.

38. I. V. Sokolov, *Charli Chaplin: Zhizn i tvorchestvo, Ocherk po istorii amerikanskogo kino*, ed. N. P. Abramov (Moscow: Goskinoizdat, 1938), 99–102, 106–111; Robert van Gelder, "Chaplin Draws a Keen," *New York Times Magazine* (8 September 1940), 22; "Film" entry in *A Concise Encyclopedia of Russia*, ed. S. V. Utechin (London: E. P. Dutton, 1964), 110–111 (quotes); Sender Garlin, "Those Peculiar Reviews of Chaplin's Films," *Daily Worker*, 19 October 1940.

39. Viktor Shklovsky, "Pismo Charli Chaplinu" (1931), in *Za sorok let: Stati o kino* (Moscow: Iskusstvo, 1965), 119–121.

40. Walter Benjamin, "The Work of Art in the Age of Mechanical Reproduction," in *Illuminations*, ed. Hannah Arendt (New York: Schocken, 1969), 217–252.

41. Maxim Gorky, *The Lower Depths*, in *Twentieth-Century Russian Plays*, volume 2, *1890–1960*, ed. and trans. F. D. Reeve (New York: Vintage Books/Random House, 1963), 96; Viktor Shklovsky, "The Clown, Comedy and Tragedy," 37–38.

42. Trauberg quoted in the *Daily Worker*, 19 April 1939; Leonid Trauberg, "Cinema in the Role of Accuser," in *Ekstsentrizm*, cited in *The Film Factory*, 62.

Theorizing Utopia

Edward Bond's War Plays

JANELLE REINELT

> *May we not say then that imagination itself—through its utopian*
> *function—has a* constitutive *role in helping us* rethink *the nature of*
> *our social life? Is not utopia—this leap outside—the way in which*
> *we radically rethink what is family, what is consumption, what is*
> *authority, what is religion and so on? Does not the fantasy of the*
> *alternative society and its exteriorization "nowhere" work as one*
> *of the most formidable contestations of what is?*
> —Paul Ricoeur, Lectures on Ideology and Utopia

Socialism and feminism both entail a notion of utopia as the
horizon of possibility which critiques the present and suggests a future.
Paul Ricoeur's *Lectures on Ideology and Utopia* describes the function of
utopia as that which shatters the present order, counterbalancing a pejorative notion of utopia as escapist. According to Ricoeur, the decisive
trait of utopia is the preservation of opposition, because its destabilizing
function exposes the "credibility gap in all systems of legitimation, all authority. . . ."[1] Within the socialist tradition, attempts to theorize and live
out alternative arrangements of production, distribution, marriage, and
authority have taken various forms, from treatises to literature to the formation of communities.[2] Feminists, too, have participated in utopian discourse from a variety of vantage points. Science fiction and fantasy literature coexist with theoretical and actual projects of both a separatist and
nonseparatist design, all of which may be spiritual or materialist in their
underlying philosophic assumptions. The wide contrast between Susan
Griffin's notion of nature and Donna Haraway's, or Monique Wittig's

ideal community and Marge Piercy's, makes thematic grouping difficult, but functional grouping (as in Ricoeur) possible.[3] Feminist scholarship has discovered connections and affinities between feminism's early goals and nineteenth-century utopian experiments.[4] Recently, post-Marxist theory has reopened utopian discourse and explicitly linked it to feminism. This trend is particularly evident in Fredric Jameson's belief that the most urgent task facing Marxism today is theorizing utopia: "Historically, all forms of hierarchy have always been based ultimately on gender hierarchy and on the building block of the family unit, which makes it clear that this is the true juncture between a feminist problematic and a Marxist one—not an antagonistic juncture, but the moment at which the feminist project and the Marxist and socialist project meet and face the same dilemma: how to imagine Utopia."[5]

The theater, which seems a well-suited venue for conceiving imaginative or alternative worlds, has not experienced a contemporary outpouring of utopian plays. Britain, however, perhaps because of its well-developed socialist theater tradition, has produced several plays which might be considered at least functionally utopian. Women playwrights have, in general, been more preoccupied with histories than with futures, although Caryl Churchill has addressed utopian questions in Cloud Nine (for which, incidentally, she is generally criticized). Howard Brenton entitled three of his recent works "Plays for Utopia," and Howard Barker wrote about an alternative feminist community in The Castle.[6] However, to my mind, the combination of socialist and feminist issues raised in Edward Bond's trilogy The War Plays best approaches the imaginative task of conceiving and embodying an alternative reality. In the three plays, Bond examines the relationship between the family politics currently destroying human society and the possibilities for radical change. Red, Black and Ignorant represents the world at the moment of annihilation; The Tin Can People, the immediate aftermath; and Great Peace, the projected future of humankind.

From a socialist feminist perspective, these plays hold particular interest because of their speculations on the nature of family life and its social construction. The third play, Great Peace, deals almost exclusively with an examination of the bond between mother and child. While Edward Bond has not written feminist plays foregrounding gender construction, and while heterosexuality is the only form of sexuality represented, the

Alda Rodrigues as the Woman in The War Plays, *Teatro da Cornucópia, Lisbon, 1987.*

plays do address important issues concerning the socialization of family roles. They deconstruct the notion of "natural" mother, with its associations of an instinctual bond between mother and child based on birthing, and replace it with a notion of community nurturing, in which people play mothering roles to each other, apart from the criterion of biology.

In the remainder of this essay, I propose to do a kind of traditional text-based reading of the plays from a socialist-feminist position, acknowledging some implicit and perhaps not unproblematic assumptions from the beginning. First, both Bond's text and, occasionally, I as critic use a "hegemonic we" as a term of address. That "we" actually denotes a late-capitalist Anglo-American subset of the middle and working classes. Second, the childrearing practices of the bourgeois family locate this play in only one cultural context. Third, the issues of interest to me in the trilogy, specifically the feminist ones, might very well, I think, be received quite differently by an audience operating from patriarchal political assumptions. I have decided to write about these plays anyway because I share with Jameson and with Ricoeur a belief in the efficacy of utopian thinking at this moment in history and also because, as I have argued elsewhere, feminists need to have a critique of and approach to any major cultural objects which circulate widely, including plays written by men.[7] Indeed construing meanings in reading these texts is itself a political act. Bond's socialist commitments facilitate this (sometimes oppositional) "reading" project.

The three plays form a triptych, which is to say they form three separate, independent figurations of reality, and, taken together, also blend into one continuous whole. Thus, a diachronic approach to these plays emphasizes discontinuous meanings, what I call a "vertical" reading, while a synchronic approach emphasizes a single representation or figuration of the human condition which unfolds through the narrative—a "horizontal" reading. The combined impact of both aspects of the trilogy provides a critique of our time and a meditation on the future of human sociality.

Read vertically, the first play, *Red, Black and Ignorant*, represents the interpellation of dominant discourse in personal subjectivity. Bond shows how human beings are deformed in the innermost spaces of their personal lives—socialized through domestic codes and practices to become part of the ruling hegemony leading the society toward war. Scene vii, "The Army," provides a summary-image of the play as a whole. The parents dress the son in his army uniform, giving him his helmet and rifle, while he sings about his transformation into the army: "I am the army / My legs are made of tanks / My arms are made of guns / My trunk is made of nukes / My head is made of bombs / I am the army (*RBI*, 14)."[8] The son is under orders to kill one person on his street in an attempt to forestall food riots in the face of a famine caused by government spending on defense: "Even as they lay in their silos the rockets destroyed the societies they were said to protect." The son goes to the home of his elderly neighbors, intending to kill the old man, but finds he cannot. He comes home and kills his father instead.

This act, coming at the extremity of his transformation into "army," is a dramaturgical trope in the trilogy for the moment of refusal and change. Even though it involves self-destruction (through destroying kin), it is also the moment of resistance to ideological interpellation. However, when the only means of resisting domination involves self-destruction, it is perhaps too late for our time. Seen separately, this play is about the last moment of free personal choice, the last chance to turn back from destruction. "Praise him as you would the first wheel," says the dead father of his murderer son. "All that is needed is to define rightly what it is to be human / If we define it wrongly we die / If we define it and teach it rightly we shall live" (*RBI*, 18). This play is a figure for a world on the brink of destruction. The possibility for change exists, but is all but impossible, and the cost is very high. The hinge between this play and the other two lies in the question: how much change is necessary, and of what kind, before a new society can begin?

The Tin Can People presents an image of survival after nuclear destruction. This second play undercuts the public debates about whether or not anyone would survive a nuclear war by shifting the emphasis from survival to legacy—that is, the legacy of the past to those who might survive. The Tin Can People think they can build a paradise on the ruins of the old society, but they are trapped in the codes and practices of the dead social order and reenact those patterns. The tin cans which are stockpiled in warehouses ensure that this new society will not suffer the scarcity of the old, but they are also the visible sign of the previous culture with its emphasis on possession and greed. The survivors still think of themselves as continuing the old way of life and mistake the absence of scarcity for the presence of new values. When the "new man" appears, different it seems because of his long wanderings alone and lessons of self-survival, the community initially welcomes him, only to displace onto him and reenact the behavior of the dead culture toward difference. A mysterious disease strikes down the survivors, who project blame for the disease onto the newcomer. The play shows the gradual panic which overtakes the people, leading to the tin can riots, in which people stuff themselves with food in an effort to hold off the plague—the ultimate gest of life under capitalism: get as much for yourself as possible because of the constant fear that there won't be enough to live, the mistaken notion that more is always better. The people turn on themselves, fighting over a shirt, abusing the bodies of the dead.

Great Peace, the third play, is in large part a recapitulation of the first two. It combines a time just before the bombs were dropped with a time beginning seventeen years later when another attempt is made to colonize the "wilderness." In the first part, the trope of the ordered murder reappears as the command to choose and kill a child. As in *Red, Black and Ignorant*, the Soldier cannot kill the neighbor's child and instead kills one of his own family, this time his brother. Seventeen years later, his mother is wandering in the wilderness with a bundle she treats as her baby. She encounters a number of other survivors, including her son's old regiment—the living dead. In the course of her wandering, she helps another mother who is sick, whose daughter in turn offers to "mother" her. A man she mistakes for her son agrees to be a son to her if she will come back to the community which is struggling to start a settlement. She will not, however, judging it too late for her to rejoin human sociality. The third play's vertical reading reinforces the difficulty of change, the non-essentialized character of mothering, and the human cost of refusing radical change.

If the trilogy is viewed in its entirety, as a synchronic structure read horizontally, an Aeschylean motif appears most starkly: knowledge and wisdom only emerge through time, and each stage of development can only achieve the insights of its particular moment.[9] The primary figure for human change is the child, both its birth and its nurture. The first play thus presents the contradiction, which is not adequately resolved until the final play, that people go to extraordinary lengths to nurture children in their everyday lives, while simultaneously killing them.

The social roles inscribed in contemporary culture distort the parent/child relationship by creating a gap between a mythical world of unselfish care and generosity and a reality controlled by fear of scarcity, self-interest, and exploitation. Once these practices are acquired, they determine our reactions and responses to each other throughout life. While change is possible, these ways of behaving deform us, damage us like the baby in *Great Peace* who develops a permanent cough from nursing in the fire. So grave is the current situation, and so deeply embedded are these practices, that no utopian tomorrow can be posited without allowing for the huge struggle and cost of transformation. This is why Bond's trilogy is not strictly speaking utopian: a pessimism about our own generation's potential for change is inscribed in the narrative—most acutely in the behavior of the Tin Can People and the Woman at the end of *Great Peace*.

The present-time contemporary world participates in the constructed world of the trilogy, although only figuratively. *Red, Black and Ignorant* is placed just ahead of present-time. The scenes dramatized are both what *will eventually* bring the world to nuclear confrontation and yet also what is happening "as we speak." This strange time-status is immediately established. The main character is the Monster, an unborn baby ripped from the womb and thrown into the fire when the bombs fall. The Monster establishes that this event is contemporary: "Now we will show scenes from the life I did not live / If what happens seems such that human beings would not allow it to happen you have not read the histories of your times" (*RBI*, 6). The problematic use of the word "histories" and the insistence on conflating present and past suggest both the mimesis of contemporary reality and an apocalyptic retrospectivity, from the perspective of which "history" is already closed. The Monster's physical embodiment further represents the differing time strata.[10] He is a visible product, simultaneously, of the holocaust and of the conditions which are producing it. He is an image of what is being done to him within the play and also an image of the misfit and misplaced one who, because of his knowledge and still-existing sensitivity, is a monster in a world where the monstrous has become normalized. Bond's peculiar and equivocal time produces an urgency in the present as well as a projected future. The nuclear devastation of the play is not something which will come in some distant time—we are on the very brink of it. The continuum of social actions constituting our world and the Monster's includes the gradual escalation of nuclear menace into nuclear annihilation. The construction of the plays does not allow the audience to locate a precise moment at which "things went too far," or a single specific reason or event as the "cause" of conflagration. Bond insists, through this time-line, on the already-embarked-upon course of the represented events.

When the plays are viewed as one figure, several details emerge which reinforce this reading. Individual acts such as the Monster's son's refusal to kill the old man and the Son's refusal to kill the neighbor's baby, while admirable as first steps toward transformation, are not capable of preventing the conflagration. It would be bourgeois individualism to see those acts as the beginning of the revolution. The Tin Can People do not manage to start a new community which survives. The Woman and the First Man were able to start new life, but not to sustain it, and the other survivors all died (the original surviving men were sterile). This fact reinforces the difficulty of starting over, even when past ways of living are repudiated. Those who make up the settlement which is beginning to sustain itself in the third play are mostly young people who were children themselves instead of fully formed adults at the time of the war. This youth seems to be a requisite part of any possibility for building a future. Thus, the overall design of the trilogy emphasizes the time necessary for real human transformation to take hold.

The three plays approach the notion of utopia mostly through a negative technique reminiscent of Brecht's "fixing the not/but." What is wrong, what is missing, what might be otherwise—these aspects press forward as the trilogy unfolds. In response to Fredric Jameson's lament for the absence of utopian theory, I would reply that utopias tend to be ahistorical—a posited ultimate goal, which will be, perhaps, the end of history. The problem is that the vision itself is chimerical, constructed from the raw ideological materials of the present moment, which is another way of saying that all utopian visions are themselves historically bound.[11]

Relativizing the very notion of utopia, the plays foreground various limited conceptions which people develop in relation to their experience. Thus, the Tin Can People think they have built paradise "in the ruins of hell," but they are still in the grip of the fear of scarcity and their notions of prosperity still come from the previous destructive era: "We'll have the good life—our own swimming pools . . ." (TCP, 46). In the end, the unrevised emphasis on individual property and commodity fetishism destroys this fledgling society, because it is not yet able to think beyond the terms of the previous social system. Even in Great Peace, where Bond does portray the possibility of a new society which learns from the old and yet does not duplicate its values, the vision of the ideal life is not total. The people are slowly learning how to organize themselves into a just society. The Daughter tells the Woman that they are inexperienced, starting over: "Its like watchin babies: they babble and dont know that one day their noise'll be words" (GP, 53). The trilogy represents a path of inquiry and discovery, rather than a fully formed conception of an ideal world. At the end of The Tin Can People, the survivors start over without tins. "Now no tins—so we can only own what we make and wear and use ourselves" (TCP, 51). So, in part, a traditional socialist ideal is held out, but it is tempered with the implication that much of what has been done in the past cannot simply be undone in the present. The complete destruction of the previous system must precede the building of the new and the shape of a new society is an open question. "We can only tell you: you must create justice" (TCP, 50).

If the plays approach a representation of utopia at all, they do so by refiguring the nuclear family. Mother/child imagery dominates the trilogy and undergoes significant transformation. The opening moments of the first play show the mother/child dyad (the Monster and his mother). The plays move from a critique of a relationship between mother and child which is based on property rights and self-interest toward a definition of mothering which is relational, not limited by age or blood ties, and not restricted to one child, one mother.

Thus, the introduction to the first play sets up a contrast between the world we wish for our children—safe, healthy, welcoming—and the present world—"But now we kill them." The play then shows the contradictions in our present forms of nurture. Mothers who prefer their sons to kill the neighbors rather than their own family are perhaps not loving after all; in fact, they are contributing to a level of inhumanity which can only mean and lead to death.

That the Monster's wife is trying to carry out her mothering function is clear from the intertwining of concrete caretaking with the offer to help her son commit murder: "Go and do it / I'll help you with your jacket / There, I'll fasten the buttons / My boy I'll help you as I did when you were a child / I'll always be here to help you whenever you need me / I'll go with you to the corner house / Look: a loose button / that must be sewn on when you come back / There isn't time now" (*RBI*, 16). Thus, the scene alienates caretaking to raise the question: what does it mean to say, "I'll help you whenever you need me"? What constitutes real help in a situation like this?

The Tin Can People has no children in it, since it represents that time after the nuclear conflagration when a new life and social transformation are impossible. The sterility is a metaphor for the moral and political bankruptcy which, once "attained," cannot be easily overturned. The closing image of the play reintroduces the possibility of new life in the image of a wounded man who is nursed as a baby. From the hindsight of the third play, we learn the First Man and Mother 1 were able to conceive new life before their community died out.

The third play, *Great Peace*, returns to the issue of genuine mothering and extends the critique in a more radical way. In the first part, the Woman duplicates the actions of the Monster's Wife in reaction to the Son's order to kill. This time, the order is to kill a child, and the neighbor's baby is the physical equivalent to her own—the same sex, the same age. Again the concrete caretaking actions of mothering—going to the shop to buy the son cigarettes, washing his shirt—are interwoven with her efforts to obtain the death of the other woman's child. A good son wouldn't even tell his mother—he would simply do the deed. This desire to be ignorant of reality is part of the myth of "protecting" the mother, the counterpart to protecting the child.

The Woman is horrified when her son kills his brother in place of the neighbor's child. Years later, she still can't forgive him: "It's too close! It's out of nature!" (*GP*, 60). It is just this notion of the precedence of the natural which is questioned. This third play gradually offers several other models of mothering, as described earlier. The Woman is finally able to make a very important statement about her bundle: "The bundle wasnt my kid / It was the other kid / Or the kids in the ruins" (*GP*, 62). The Woman can now see the act of nurturing as having multiple recipients and no essential exclusivity based on biology.

The settlement community is represented in only one scene of seemingly traditional sex role behaviors. In fairness to Bond, it is not so clear that only the Daughter prepared the meal or that the men are only involved in laying the table and cleaning up. The interdependency of this new society *is* clear—they will all take care of a newly arrived sick woman, repairing her furniture or fixing up her room. The Man's children call the Daughter their "wilderness aunt," implying responsibility for nurture without linking the Daughter to the Man as a couple recreating a nuclear family. Thus, in the end, the direction of the new society struggling to establish itself is toward a redefinition of mother/child to mean the community members' caretaking for each other, beyond property, beyond blood, toward peace and justice.

The glimpse of "otherwise" provided by Bond's trilogy is perhaps so slim and tentative as to be unsatisfying for some socialist feminists thirsting after clear alternatives to an unacceptable and dangerous world. Yet the resistance of this vision to becoming prescriptive, what Ricoeur calls a "picture," is a substantial asset in theatrical representation. Better a suggestion than, as when mired in realism, a calcified mimetic model. More importantly, the plays provide a means to shatter the seemingly endless hegemony of the present power configurations, through their function as utopian:

The order which has been taken for granted suddenly appears queer and contingent. There is an experience of the contingency of order. This, I think, is the main value of utopias. At a time when everything is blocked by systems which have failed but which cannot be beaten—this is my pessimistic appreciation of our time—utopia is our resource. It may be an escape, but it is also the arm of critique. It may be that particular times call for utopias. I wonder whether our present period is not such a time. . . .[12]

NOTES

1. Paul Ricoeur, *Lectures on Ideology and Utopia* (New York: Columbia University Press, 1986), 17.

2. Ricoeur traces the relationship between the concept of ideology and that of utopia through a series of thinkers from Marx to Habermas, with special emphasis on the topic of utopia in chapters on Mannheim, Saint-Simon, and Fourier, providing a descriptive typography of Marxist and post-Marxist sociology on these two topics.

3. I cite, of course, "classic" texts displaying wide dissonance with each other: Susan Griffin, *Women and Nature: The Roaring inside Her* (New York: Harper and Row, 1978); Donna Haraway, "A Manifesto for Cyborgs: Science, Technology and Socialist Feminism in the 1980s," *Socialist Review* 15:21 (1985): 65–107; Monique Wittig, *Les guérillères* (New York: Viking Press, 1971); Marge Piercy, *Woman on the Edge of Time* (London: Women's Press, 1979).

4. Leslie F. Goldstein, "Early Feminist Themes in French Utopian Socialism: The St. Simonians and Fourier," *Journal of the History of Ideas* 43:1 (1982): 91–101. Compare Goldstein's analysis of the Saint-Simonians and of Fourier to Ricoeur's analysis in his special chapters on both. See also Nan Bowman Albinski, "Utopia Reconsidered: Women Novelists and Nineteenth-Century Utopian Visions," *Signs* 13:4 (1988):830–841.

5. Fredric Jameson, "Cognitive Mapping," in *Marxism and the Interpretation of Culture*, ed. Cary Nelson and Lawrence Grossberg (Urbana and Chicago: University of Illinois Press, 1988), 355.

6. Caryl Churchill, *Cloud Nine* (New York: Routledge, Chapman and Hall, 1984); Howard Brenton, *Greenland* (London: Methuen, 1988); Howard Barker, *The Castle*, in *Collected Plays*, vol. 1 (John Calder Ltd., 1990).

7. See "Gender and History in *Hurlyburly*: A Feminist Response," in *David Rabe: A Casebook*, ed. Toby Zinman, forthcoming from Greenwood Press.

8. All quotations are from the Methuen editions of Edward Bond, *The War Plays*, vol. 1: *Red, Black and Ignorant* and *The Tin Can People*; vol. 2: *Great Peace* (London, 1985), hereafter cited in the text.

9. Cf. "Zeus, who has guided men to think, who has laid it down that wisdom comes alone through suffering," Aeschylus, *Oresteia*, in *Aeschylus I*, 2 vols., trans. Richmond Lattimore (New York: Washington Square Press, 1967), 1:44.

10. "The Monster's skin, hair and clothes are charred and singed a uniform black so that he appears as if he might have been carved from a piece of coal. His hair sticks up in stiff spikes as straight as nails. (Alternately, the Monster may be a uniform red)" (*RBI*, 4).

11. Ricoeur provides some description of this problem in his chapter on Saint-Simon, opposing "fiction" to "picture," stating that when "utopia becomes a picture, time has stopped." His larger discussion of the relationship between ideology and utopia addresses precisely the problem of prescriptive, ahistorical tendencies in any model, including utopia (see especially 295 ff.).

12. Ricoeur, 300.

The

Academic Institution

and the Production

of Knowledge

Introduction

THOMAS POSTLEWAIT

In his satiric "romance," *Small World*, David Lodge tells the picaresque story of academics in search of the perfect conference, a quest for the grail of knowledge, prestige, and power. The novel gives the impression (surely false, of course) that scholars today do little else but go from meeting to meeting, attempting to outperform one another in the conference rooms. The academic conference, as Lodge well understands, provides far more than a symposium for scholarship in a field; it also serves as the nerve center and network for the intellectual and social politics of academic careers.

Quite appropriately, then, Case and Reinelt, in their introduction to this book, focus primarily on their own recent experiences at conferences in order to illustrate that these professional gatherings function as a forum for politics at various levels of engagement (and disengagement). For the theater scholar, the "performance of power" is to be discovered and charted not only in what is being studied—plays, performers, productions, audiences, administrators, institutions, ideas, and culture forces—but also, more immediately, in the act of scholarship itself, the procedures of writing, delivering, and publishing essays.

Accordingly, this collection, besides presenting a number of essays on theater and politics, offers in this last section a group of essays on the "state of the profession." As could be expected, these six papers, which are reports, proposals, or discussion papers rather than critical and historical essays, were all written for (or in conjunction with) past or future conferences. They present diverse—and sometimes contrasting—perspectives on the political and ideological nature of teaching, curricula, scholarship, administration, publishing, and professional organizations.

In the main, these essays take up issues that directly affect American theater scholars. Yet, despite this national focus, the basic concerns, if not the specific situations, are international. The theater scholars around the world, as the recent meeting of the World Congress of the International Federation for Theatre Research in Stockholm demonstrated, share many of the same political conditions, problems, and opportunities in their teaching and research.

Although each of these essayists identifies certain problems or crises in theater studies today, what strikes me most strongly is that all of them call for, if not always spell out, a program of integration. The key question, then, is whether the recommendations for integration are sufficient to meet the various problems. The list of concerns, challenges, frustrations, and complaints is substantial: the heavy teaching and production responsibilities, the burnout of overworked teachers, the conflicting demands of scholarship and production, the backwardness and lack of critical sophistication of many theater professors, the smallness of theater programs, the secondary status of theater studies in the university (and sometimes within theater departments themselves), the ethnic diversity of the students, the gaps in the curriculum, the shortsightedness and rigidity of administrators, the neglect of important fields of study, the confining arrangement of conferences, the financial limitations on salaries and travel, the lack of cooperation among scholars, the nostalgia for supposedly "commonsense" scholarship, the resistance to theory, and the pervasive disunity in the complex field of theater studies.

Faced with these problems, theater professors could easily throw up their hands in despair. But instead, if these essays on the state of the profession are any sign, they advocate a concerted effort to unify and advance the field of theater studies. Almost all of these essayists call upon theater scholars to respond to the ferment of ideas in other fields. As Margaret Wilkerson notes, "the path-breaking scholarship in these fields is revolutionizing the ways in which we see ourselves and the places where we look for knowledge." Also, the demographic and political changes in our societies surely should influence our teaching and research. The diversity of people, values, and ideas offers a formidable challenge to which we have not yet adequately responded.

The diversity of scholarly methods and ideas has unnerved some professors, but many others, as Marvin Carlson points out, have quite willingly wrestled with the new issues. Carlson reviews some of the key developments and reminds us that the study of culture is always ideological. The historical "context" for theater presents us with "a complex and not necessarily consistent interplay of ideological forces affecting both the production and the interpretation of any artifact or document being studied." In turn, the very discourse of the historian is always charged with ideological assumptions and values. This understanding underlies the argument of Bruce McConachie, who makes a strong case for the New Historicism, which offers a truly interdisciplinary basis for scholarship in American theater history. This expanded cultural-historical approach is necessary, he argues, "to open up the ideological assumptions, formal categories, and historical conventions that have dominated the writing of American theater history."

To meet these challenges we must have a sufficient number of well-trained faculty members. Clearly, as Simon Williams states, our theater departments need more than one to four scholars who are expected to cover all of theater history and culture. Both Jon Whitmore and Simon Williams, from different perspectives, call for increased faculty and an integrated curriculum. Whitmore focuses on internal methods of unification; Williams on interdepartmental needs and opportunities. Beyond the university, the professional conference should provide, as Gay Gibson Cima argues, a more diversified procedure for sharing ideas than the annual "blockbuster" convention, which is too often a show for scholarly stars and passive audiences. At present, there is insufficient opportunity for a community of scholars, drawn from interrelated specialties and disciplines, to share ideas on a continuing basis.

In all cases, as Case and Reinelt insist, these various issues and concerns cannot be separated from the politics of the university, the professional organizations, and the overall culture. These political conditions shape academic life and scholarship and thus underlie the state of the profession.

Demographics

and the

Academy

MARGARET B. WILKERSON

There are three discoveries external to the field of theater history research that are symbolic of certain factors which will affect what we think about, what we teach, and what we do in the next several decades.

First, scientists have traced the genetic origins of the human race back to *Australopithecus afarensis*, the scientific name for "Lucy," a black female who lived three million years ago in southern Africa, and who, based on genetic tracing, is essentially credited as the mother of the human race. In the signifying world of theater, the idea of a black African woman as our collective mother must give us pause and makes for interesting siblings and in-laws.

Second, a recent book by Martin Bernal, entitled *Black Athena*, not only documents the ancient Greeks' admitted indebtedness to ancient Africa for fundamental aspects of their civilization such as culture, language, and institutions, but documents a decision made in German universities in the late eighteenth century systematically to deny that history and black Africa's contribution to ancient Greece, the "foundation" of Western civilization. This well-documented work is built upon earlier studies by eminent African and African American scholars such as Cheikh Anta Diop, Chancellor Williams, William Leo Hansberry, Ivan Van Sertima, and J. A. Rogers, whose work was not published as widely as Bernal's.

Third, demographic projections indicate that, by the year 2024, 40% of U.S. 18- to 24-year-olds will be minority (black, Hispanic, Native American, and Asian American). Already my own campus, the University of California at Berkeley, is experiencing this demographic shift. Three years ago, Berkeley admitted its first freshman class in which white students were a numerical minority. This year blacks, Hispanics, Native Americans, and Asian Americans collectively comprise a majority of the Berkeley undergraduates. I am currently serving on a commission appointed by our chancellor to study the implications of this shift and to recommend to my university how it should respond to these changes. Among our many problems is linguistics—what do you call minorities when they become a majority?

These discoveries represent fundamental changes which confront this country. As "minorities" constitute higher and higher proportions of our youthful population, their access to higher education becomes ever more critical. A recent report by a Blue Ribbon Committee headed by presidents Carter and Ford, *One-Third of a Nation*, spoke to the urgency of the situation. If the lofty ideal of an educated populace does not excite you, then surely the necessity that these young people be able to contribute to the Social Security system will—since our retirement income will depend upon their productivity.

What are the implications of these demographic changes for our profession?

Theater provides an opportunity for a community to come together and reflect on itself. The liveliest of arts, it subsumes and utilizes the other arts and presents in the existential present of time and space an image of reality that has the potential to go beyond age and culture. It is not only the mirror through which a society can reflect upon itself—it also helps to shape the perceptions of that culture through the power of its imaging. We have viewed ourselves as inheritors of European cultural traditions and, in a colonialist posture, traced our roots to the ancient Greeks, ignoring the influence of ancient African civilizations on ancient Greek culture. That narrowing of our traditions not only defined out of existence the culture of whole groups of people, people of color and women (most of the world, I might add), but excluded with it alternative perspectives and ways of seeing and knowing.

Today, however, with the explosion of new scholarship by and about women and people of color both nationally and internationally, the customary view of our history and our culture is being challenged. The questions raised are so fundamental that they force us to reconsider our most sacrosanct notions—our canon, our period concepts, our curriculum, and our methods of structuring knowledge and ideas, to mention only a few.

We can no longer teach or even study theater as we have in the past. Those of us in theater production programs will find ourselves increasingly marginalized or isolated in our institutions if we do not include in very fundamental ways the new population (students of color and others) constituting our student bodies. Production choices, casting policies, and curriculum must be reexamined in terms of our culturally diverse society and the intellectual and pedagogical challenges which it poses.

These changes, of course, also have major implications for our own professional development. We are among the oldest group of Ph.D.s in higher education; the field of theater has been among the humanities fields with the slowest growth rates because of that fact. Thus, the responsibility for responding to these changes falls upon us. We are, I believe, obligated to expand our own frames of thinking so that we may better judge what is original and significant in theater research. In other words, faculty development (our own) must be a major part of our professional agenda.

I become very disturbed about the health of our field when I note its *lack* of ferment in contrast to the sister fields of modern literature, ancient literature, anthropology, and cultural studies. The path-breaking scholarship in these fields is revolutionizing the ways in which we see ourselves and the places where we look for knowledge. Although we have begun to open our field to the serious study of popular culture, we have not pushed our questions hard enough or far enough. Perhaps our conscious effort to establish ourselves apart as a profession has reinforced a form of specialization that is shortsighted and parochial.

The diversity of our own society, I hope, will open us to the richness of the world and the largely unexplored areas of research that exist beyond our national borders. Of course, that requires that knowledge of foreign languages be reemphasized, so that our students may have access to that world.

The challenge to us as educators is to bring more people of color and women into the academy and to prepare our students for change, for a world filled with technological developments that are likely to redefine theater or turn it into a relic or artifact of a bygone era.

We cannot predict how theater will evolve. So we must prepare our students to understand the complexities of being Lucy's children, to be creative and critical thinkers capable of questioning our most sacrosanct notions, to be inheritors of multiple cultural traditions, and to ferret out the best and most humane elements among them. They must be able to help others through their scholarship and teaching to create a theater that reflects while informing this new age and that can reach generations schooled on the electronic media without sacrificing theater's essentially human qualities. We will have to do more than clone ourselves, in order to prepare those who can go beyond our limitations—those who can be risk-taking, attuned to diverse audiences, tantalized by new ideas, and who can probe the deep, abiding questions and tensions of human existence.

I have tried to touch upon some of the issues of our profession posed by demographic shifts/changes in our population and in our intellectual framework. There are, of course, many other issues that I trust you will explore—for the challenges before Lucy's children on the verge of a new century are great.

The Challenge

to Professional

Training and

Development

SIMON WILLIAMS

The Williamsburg meeting of the American Society for Theatre Research seems to have been regarded by members who participated in it as representing, for good or ill, a watershed in the history of the society. Put simply, it confirmed a conviction widely held among theater scholars that the field of theater studies is finally being changed by the adoption of several new methodologies that have already transformed studies in the cognate areas of art history, musicology, and literary history and criticism. The change was clearly reflected in the papers offered to the membership at Williamsburg.

In one regard, the slowness of theater studies to adopt new methodology is not surprising. Theater history, arguably the central discipline of the field, is also the youngest discipline in the history of the arts and is, without doubt, the most difficult. In the absence of a primary source, a disadvantage that not even music shares to such an aggravated degree, theater historians have labored for years to determine precisely what the prime object of study, the play in performance, actually *is*. Understandably, for most scholars the best way to determine this has been to produce writings that are overwhelmingly descriptive and empirical in nature. No doubt, theater scholarship like this is not dead and will persist—indeed, all theater scholars will to a greater or lesser degree remain dependent on its findings. But now the field incorporates more varied approaches and wider interests.

In another regard, however, the slowness with which these approaches have been adopted by theater scholars is surprising. After all, one of the major tendencies of new theoretical studies in literature and the arts in general is to consider the works not in isolation, or solely in comparison with other works of the same genre, but as artifacts of institutions. The full meaning of a work can only be understood when the process through which it was produced, the context within which it was received, and the purpose for which it was created have been fully determined. Strangely enough, this has always been abundantly clear to theater historians, faced as they are with the complex apparatus of architecture, production, performance, and audience that goes to make up the multidimensionality of theater. No doubt several of them smile with understandable smugness as they see colleagues who teach drama in literature departments finally stumbling upon the fact that drama was written to be performed and that performance is where its ultimate meaning lies. Nevertheless, theater historians have been slow to pick up on the new techniques literary scholars have recently evolved in order to come to terms with the extraliterary dimensions of their studies.

There can be no doubt that methodology developed in cognate areas can aid the theater historian both in determining more accurately the object of study and in guiding her or him toward discovering greater resonance and complexity in the object, by placing it within the wider context of the development of theater or of society as a whole. But it is especially puzzling why certain methodologies have taken so long to be adopted by theater scholars. For example, reception-theory posits that we can best understand a work of literature as a transaction between the reader and the work. Such an approach would seem to be even more relevant to theater than to literature that is read—it can help determine the nature of the distinctly palpable transaction that takes place between actors and their audiences. Then again, New Historicism, in its capacity to lead us to detect previously unsuspected dynamics within society, allows the historian to account for the complexity of the theatrical transaction and to determine, to a greater extent than has so far been possible, the impact of theater upon society and vice versa. The future of theater history, as regards the interest of its own subject, its dynamics, and its standing among other academic disciplines, would seem to lie in this theoretical development. The ASTR membership seems now to have acknowledged it, and meetings are beginning to serve as a forum for the proverbial "cutting edge" of the discipline of theater studies.

But the Williamsburg conference was not entirely a success. Given the primary topic of the conference, "Theater and Politics," one might have expected a major theme of discussion to have been how the present political climate influences both the contemporary American theater and, even closer to home, the field of theater studies itself. The conference, however, seemed to be peculiarly lacking in self-awareness as far as these issues were concerned. One session was devoted to the impact of government upon theater (the nature of government subsidy and the withdrawal of subsidy), and other sessions touched upon issues relating to political control. But no one discussed the limitations that perhaps threaten the freedom of both contemporary theater and theater scholarship. At a time when the National Endowment for the Arts is under congressional pressure to withdraw funding from any artistic project that might bruise the sensitivities of certain interest groups, the absence of such concerns among the ASTR membership was surprising and, possibly, worrying.

Political and social factors bearing upon the profession of theater scholarship also received scant attention. For example, the implications of the disturbingly popular and yet restrictive ideas of Allan Bloom as to what does or does not constitute proper study of the arts within an academic setting have rarely been discussed in the context of theater studies. Nevertheless, these ideas, enshrined in *The Closing of the American Mind*, seem to have been endorsed not only by the general readership, but also by institutions that have a considerable impact upon the funding and therefore the future direction of humanistic studies in general—theater studies in particular. Especially distressing have been recent pronouncements by the chairperson of the National Endowment for the Humanities (NEH), who has rebuked the university professoriat at large for not teaching works of the imagination in a manner that awakens in their students a recognition of and love for the "eternal" values of "truth—and beauty and excellence."[1] Instead she complains that professors question these values, presenting them as the product of historic forces and therefore as subject to modification and change. In particular, she objects to professors who analyze the arts as "devices used by some groups to perpetuate 'hegemony' over others." In other words, if the Williamsburg conference is anything to go by, she would take exception to the majority of the work presently being conducted by theater historians. Clearly, such remarks are intended to disempower the humanist, reducing the function of humanistic studies to nothing more than the provision of passive support for the status quo.

To be quite fair, the bark of NEH is far worse than its bite. The most recent list of NEH awardees indicates clearly that projects which employ recently devised methodologies or adopt a historicist, ideological, or critically circumscribed approach—projects in particular that underscore the political function of the arts—do in fact receive a generous fair share of funding. Nevertheless, given the present propensity of Congress to exercise a direct influence over who and what projects receive funding, it would be well for humanistic scholars as a whole not to be lulled into too great a sense of security.

There are also factors within the profession that should disturb scholars of theater. In sessions at the Williamsburg conference unease was expressed at the ambition of the National Association of Schools of Theatre (NAST) to serve as an accrediting agency for doctoral programs in theater. For a start, it is questionable whether any meaningful process of accreditation can be devised for such programs. After all, the quality of doctoral instruction depends less on formal structures and more on the quality of personal exchange between faculty and students, so the most effective way to guarantee the high caliber of a program would seem to be through the normal university channels of promotion and tenure and the procedures by which departments recruit their graduate students.

It will be particularly disturbing if NAST's endeavors result in mandated performance components for all Ph.D. programs. It would be foolish to hold that performance should never be part of a doctoral student's training; many students require such experience both for professional reasons and because performance is integral to their scholarly work. Indeed, only a handful of the present thirty-odd doctoral programs in theater make no provision for their students to acquire experience onstage or in production. But to prescribe such experience is a different matter. First, the prime professional function of most doctoral programs is to train scholars in theater, so only those courses, seminars, and projects that guarantee the growth and training of the scholar should be intrinsic to the program. Second, as the Williamsburg conference so clearly demonstrated, the appropriation of a variety of new methodologies has endowed theater scholarship with a new vigor. Any attempt to use externally devised, "objective" standards to regulate the prime sources from which future scholars will be drawn runs the danger of encouraging uniformity among those sources and of discouraging the development of new and striking interpretations of the theater of the past and the present.

Developing standards for accreditation and insisting that all future graduands be scholar-artists rather than pure scholars will not serve the cause of theater scholarship well. Instead, the major challenge facing theater studies, and especially the doctoral programs where future theater scholars are trained, should be to ensure that the new energy, some might even say maturity, of the field should be used to elevate the importance of the discipline in the academy as a whole. It is not too much of an exaggeration to say that theater is one of the less privileged academic disciplines. In the recent Bloom-inspired public debate about the function of the arts and humanities in the university, theater is virtually never mentioned. Whenever it is, it is usually as an adjunct of literature. This, one might argue, is a sad measure of its relatively low ranking in academic priorities. Of course, talking among themselves, theater faculty members are often inclined to attribute the relatively low ranking of their discipline to an ingrained prejudice in the academic community as a whole toward performance, both the practice and the study of it. But whoever has had experience serving on committees in the wider academic community may well find reason to question this. The academic community, at least in those universities with resources sufficient to guarantee students a well-rounded and various education, is, despite the cavils of individual naysayers, usually well prepared to countenance the presence of theater as a fully operating academic unit on campus. If theater departments feel themselves to be underprivileged members of the university, this may well be because they perceive a weakness in their own programs, a perception that may be shared by the university community at large.

Essentially, the weakness of theater departments, perhaps in their general purpose, certainly in their capacity to train doctoral students, is that they attempt to do too much with too little. For example, all theater departments are responsible for offering instruction in performance and production as well as for mounting a full season of theater, so resources are greatly stretched. At the most recent NAST conference held to discuss Ph.D. programs in theater, it was suggested that four full-time faculty members in the area of theater studies was the minimum necessary to run an adequate doctoral program. But, in contrast to departments offering doctoral degrees in art history, musicology, and literary history and theory, this number is risibly small. It is quite possible that one of the main reasons for the slowness with which new methodologies have infiltrated theater studies has been the very small size of graduate faculties in theater. All teachers and scholars, whatever their accomplishment, have personal areas of backwardness and narrowness. In larger departments, these can be offset by the large number of other scholars available to students. But in a field as small as theater studies, the limitations of teachers can quickly be inherited by their students. There can be few graduate teachers of theater studies who have not had the experience of supervising dissertations and theses in areas in which they are distinctly unqualified. The lack of specific knowledge and expertise in the supervision of dissertations has justly been identified by a past journal editor as the cause of an unusually large amount of "slovenly research" that does not sufficiently take into account recent developments in the field.[2]

There is no instant panacea for these complaints, but the future does not seem entirely grim for theater studies or for doctoral programs in theater. The Williamsburg conference possibly suggested why. One of the most striking features of the papers in the conference, and, more generally, in much recently published theater scholarship,[3] has been the attention paid to the wider social, political, and cultural world that theater both reflects and helps to create. In other words, theater studies are not only being transformed by methodology, they are also becoming increasingly interdisciplinary in scope. Over the last ten years, the most distinctive trend in the study of the arts and humanities on university campuses has been the rise of interdisciplinary humanities centers that gather together faculty members from a variety of disciplines interested either in cooperating on a single enterprise or just in coming to understand each other's work. Through these centers and through the contacts with other departments they provide, theater departments should be able to expand their offerings and strengthen their programs. Indeed, it is perhaps in the environment of the humanities center rather than in the necessarily narrower confines of the theater department that doctoral students can best develop programs allowing them to explore fields contiguous to their chosen one of theater. This does not mean that the doctoral student will move entirely out of the theater department—it should be a *sine qua non* that all faculty members in theater studies participate in the activities of the center. Furthermore, the administration of the doctoral degree should properly remain under the auspices of the theater department. However, by working in the context of a humanities center, either through coursework or in research, the doctoral student will encounter a range of thought not available within the theater department alone or necessarily in the few courses that she or he can find time to take in departments other than theater. In short, instruction and research in the humanities center may well lead the student to develop a capacity to relate theater to other disciplines and arts in a way not possible in the theater department alone. I am not advocating that theater departments should abdicate responsibility for the doctoral degree, but in humanities centers broader perspectives can be found. Certainly, through them, theater scholars—both students and faculty—will be able to expand the horizons of their study, modify their old methodologies, acquire new perspectives on their subject, and thereby strengthen the field of theater as a discipline worthy of the respect of the larger academic community.

NOTES

1. Lynne V. Cheney, *Humanities in America* (Washington, D.C.: National Endowment for the Humanities, 1988), 7.

2. Roger Herzel, quoted in Rosemarie K. Bank, *The Status of Theatre Research* (New York and London: University Press of America, 1984), 19–20.

3. See, for example, *Interpreting the Theatrical Past: Essays in the Historiography of Performance*, ed. Thomas Postlewait and Bruce A. McConachie (Iowa City: University of Iowa Press, 1989).

Integrating

Instruction,

Production, and

Research

JON WHITMORE

On 23–25 September 1988, a task force, charged by the Association for Theatre in Higher Education Board and appointed by the Council of Theatre Chairs and Deans, met in Las Vegas, Nevada, to develop a position paper or set of guidelines on work assignments and workload distribution for theater faculty. The task force was reconvened because of its earlier recommendation in its "Guidelines for Evaluating Teacher/Artists for Promotion and Tenure" that sufficient time must be set aside for theater faculty to do the research and creative work required for promotion and tenure. The group believes that a pervasive problem facing our discipline is the overworking of many of our faculty and staff.

While attempting to identify possible solutions to the workload assignment problem, however, the task force began to realize that we were dealing with much larger and more fundamental issues. Overworked faculty and staff are only one symptom of a critical imbalance within the discipline. Other symptoms include the lack of quality of our productions, a decline in the number of competent majors, a tightening of budgets, the demand for more accountability and outcome assessment, a lack of employment opportunities for our graduates, and the difficulty in acquiring tenure or promotion to full professor for our faculty (particularly those with M.F.A. degrees).

The task force concluded that, before we could make a recommendation about how to address the workload issue, we (as a profession) need to deal with even more fundamental questions, such as the following.

1. Have we shifted the justifications for our production programs away from the education of our students and the advancement of research and development in our field toward such secondary concerns as box office income, gratification of artist egos, students' demands for performance, institutional public relations, or, simply, evolutionary habit (more is better)?

2. Has there been a proliferation of multiple degree programs (in many cases both graduate and undergraduate) on our campuses without an increase in faculty and staff?

3. Has the curriculum become more complex to meet what we see as the expanding knowledge base required for our students without increasing the faculty, or reeducating those trained in a simpler era?

If the answer to these questions is yes, and the task force believes it is, then a combination of these three circumstances has produced a fundamental imbalance in our discipline which has led to other workload crises, burnout of individual faculty, intrafaculty stress, lack of any true research and development to advance the field, and a diminution in the quality of our educational programs and productions.

WHAT SHOULD BE DONE?

1. Each department needs to state specifically and clearly the focus of its educational mission.

2. Each department needs to take a hard look at the number and kind of degree programs it offers in relation to its resource base (faculty, staff, facilities, equipment, and money), with an eye toward reducing the number of degree programs to a manageable level or increasing the base.

3. Each department needs to rethink the kind and scale of its production programs so that the primary missions of educating students and advancing the field through research and development become the focus of its work. Any other reasons for having a production program should be secondary and should be supported only if sufficient additional resources

are available beyond those needed to fulfill the educational and research and development missions.

4. Each department needs to assign equitable workloads to faculty based on the standard set at the individual institution. However, the nature of theater production work makes the assignment of workload a discipline-specific problem. For example, the following production responsibilities should be taken into account when calculating faculty workloads: playwriting, directing, acting, design (set, costumes, props, lighting, and sound), performance coaching (acting, voice, stage movement), technical direction, costume technology, and dramaturgy.

If we look at this issue from historical and evolutionary perspectives, it is easy to see why and how we arrived at our present crossroads. Years ago, theater production was an extracurricular activity. Fortunately, our predecessors were able to convince the academy that production experience was an essential part of our students' education. This led to the development of cocurricular production programs. But most of us also continued to teach our pre-cocurricular courses and simply added a production program. While we have improved this two-pronged system over the years, we have never fully integrated the curriculum and the production programs. With limited faculty, we are trying to do double-duty—a full schedule of regular classes, plus a full production program. This combination has resulted in the problem of overload we set out to address.

This task force believes that an extraordinary opportunity lies before us as a profession. It is time to reexamine the way we educate our students. We must attempt to strengthen and invigorate our discipline as we move toward the next century.

The following questions ought to form the basis for these discussions.

What do our production programs have to do with our educational mission?

How can we merge our curricula with our production programs so that we have a true symbiosis?

How should we give credit, equitably and meaningfully, to students and faculty for production work?

What are the real educational components of our production programs (and what is window dressing)?

Should we fundamentally restructure the way we schedule and do our work?

How can we distribute workloads equitably?[1]

This chair's report outlines a number of important problems facing the academic theater discipline, most of which are an outgrowth of the traditional way we carry out our instructional, research, performance, and service missions.

In most of our departments, the current model for theater education is based on a segmented learning structure. We offer skills and craft instruction in the classroom, while aesthetic development and practical experience take place in our production programs. Separately from both, faculty and students participate in research and development projects (finding new methods and materials for recording, studying, and producing theater). For the most part, these three activities function independently from one another. There may be an occasional crossover, but no true unification.

I propose a model for the future development of theater higher education, which brings classroom education (especially in performance training), production activities, and research and experimentation into a single integrated unit. To be certain, many theater departments already overlap bits and pieces of their curriculum, production program, and research activities in important and meaningful ways. What we as a profession should do is to seek out and identify such exciting integrated programs and set them out as models for future development.

This integration is more likely to happen now in some of our one-, two-, or three-faculty-member departments than it is in our larger ones. Out of necessity, the course work and production work become more closely aligned, because of a limited capacity to offer all of these activities as separate entities. Such was the case when I first began teaching in a two-person theater department at a community college. In one semester I found myself teaching advanced acting, stagecraft, lighting, and directing, while also directing Molière. Since I was only one person, it seemed to make sense to use the production as a major vehicle for learning lighting and stagecraft, and to make the advanced acting class a study in period comedy style, thereby bringing my work as director, and the production as a whole, into the core of the curriculum and classes for that semester. What I am describing, then, is a model where productions become one with the curriculum—not secondary to it. Productions are not extracurricular or cocurricular—they *are* the curriculum (especially for performance, design, and technical training).

MAJOR ADJUSTMENTS

If this model is implemented, several major adjustments must be made. We must

1. stop seeing our production programs as "commercial" enterprises or "community service";

2. provide significant lead time in selecting plays;

3. become more skillful at organizing complex interactive activities;

4. arrange for much longer rehearsal periods;

5. offer fewer formal classes;

6. provide more academic credit for participating in productions to *both* faculty and students (but insist that real educational objectives be reached);

7. find ways to be more cooperative and collegial;

8. be highly selective, limiting the number of students we allow into B.F.A. and M.F.A. programs;

9. think of ourselves as teachers during the production process, not just as artists;

10. put emphasis on the preparation, design, rehearsal, and construction *process* rather than on the performance outcome.

THE PAYOFF

If we do all of these things, there are some big payoffs.

1. By offering fewer formal courses, time could be freed to schedule rehearsals in the afternoon, thereby leaving evenings free for thinking, research, or perhaps a family life.

2. Students' lives might become more sane. Who knows—they might even have time to go to the library, participate in nontheater activities, or take challenging courses outside of theater.

3. Faculty members might become better teachers because of the need

to develop experiential learning activities as the core of their work as teachers.

4. Reintegration of research with instructional and production activities might take place.

The model I am proposing would place experimentation at the forefront of production activities. With more time allotted to the processes, we could explore methods of directing and acting; the design and construction of sets, costumes, sound, and lights; new techniques and materials for construction; the exploration and development of new performance spaces; and outreach to visual artists, musicians, composers, video artists, and film artists to develop new art forms, or to push the limits of the theater experience beyond current practice.

SCHEDULING

There is one major roadblock inherent in integrating instruction, production, and research: it is profoundly difficult to schedule all of these elements so that they happen simultaneously and sequentially. The solution rests in careful organization and multiple-year planning. The curriculum, teaching schedules, play selection, production staffing, and room assignments must all take place simultaneously—and well ahead of time. If we are actually *merging* courses with preparation, rehearsals, and production, so that we are doing fewer independent activities, the planning and scheduling can be done.

To summarize, then, what I am proposing is not new; we have always been attempting to integrate our teaching, production, and research programs. What may be new is the notion that we should merge (and therefore eliminate) some "normal" courses (especially performance and design training courses) into a much more extensive prerehearsal, rehearsal, construction, and performance program. Several classes would simply disappear in lieu of an instructional and research-based production program, where full credit is given to students, faculty, and staff. I contend that this approach will produce more dynamic learning, better productions, and more research and development. It also just might reduce the pressures on our overworked faculty and staff.

NOTE

1. This section of the chapter is a reprint of a report to the Association for Theatre in Higher Education president. Task force members included Donna Aronson, Beverly Byers-Pevitts, Larry Clark, Sherwood Collins, Mary Corrigan, Robert Hall, Wendall Josal, Lacy Nowell, Vera Roberts, Don Rosenberg, Jim Symon, and Jon Whitmore (chair). The report was published previously in *ATHE News* 3:3 (May 1989) and *ACA Bulletin* (August 1989).

Conferring

Power

in the

Theater

GAY GIBSON CIMA

At a time when new ideas materialize more quickly than we can disseminate them in books or even journals, conferences are emerging as an ever more crucial means for us to communicate with our colleagues. Books and journal articles take time to publish and frequently crystallize rather than generate new ideas. That has become the work of the conference. There, as scholars and practitioners, we share insights into the various ways in which changes in playwriting, producing, designing, directing, and acting alter the creation of meaning in the theater. We frequently read these changes as inscriptions of cultural attitudes, as encodings of sites of power. Increasingly, we discuss the ways in which ideas about class, gender, and race are constructed in the theater. We can profit in equal measure from analyzing our own performances, as directors and actors, on the conference circuit.

Conferences, in fact, provide a too-ready stage for the performance of established power in the academic theater world. They may be viewed as elaborate productions, imprints not only of dominant ideas but also of the authorized actors speaking those ideas. They enable institutions as well as individuals to display their faculties, through a complex process of selection and foregrounding. We act, at the conventional conference, as a massive stock company, with certain "lines of business" played by particular stock actors within the proscenium arch, with the same seamless drama unfolding onstage, hiding the ways in which power operates. New actors have joined the company; maturing actors have assumed appropriately larger roles in the ongoing drama; but the basic mode of production has seemed secure. Is it not time to rethink this collective performance on the conference stage?

Individual universities and professional organizations themselves resemble theatrical producers, deciding upon crucial matters such as funding and casting. Theater, speech, and English departments, responding to straitened budgets and proliferating travel requests, now customarily limit funding to only one conference trip per professor per year. That means, of course, that our ability to act depends directly upon our salaries: beginning assistant professors cannot generally audition for more than one conference presentation per year, precisely because of their constrained financial situations. Yet they need the experience onstage, not only to practice their skills, but also to prove their worth to the very institutions that refuse to pay for more than one performance per year. Tenure cases depend on conference papers as well as publications. Underemployed or unemployed newcomers to the field and graduate students face an even more difficult struggle. The American Society for Theatre Research has combated this problem, in part, by instituting conference travel grants for graduate students, a policy which challenges other organizations to follow suit. We can fight this funding dilemma on several fronts, lobbying within our organizations and universities, reminding chairpersons and deans about the integral relationship between conferences and research, uncovering new sources for financial support, distributing through our organizations information on agencies that handle travel grants. Even such a simple tactic as informing conference participants of low-cost room rentals at local universities would help. Voluntary contributions, sent in at the time of conference registration, could be used to establish a conference travel fund for retired, unemployed, or financially strapped colleagues, in the tradition of nineteenth-century actors' funds. The Modern Language Association now provides child care at its meetings, an important step toward acknowledging the real material conditions of many members' lives. Collective action may be needed if the conference is to remain, in the future, a viable means of communication among the members of our profession.

The current funding dilemma leads to the creation of a "blockbuster" mentality. Professional organizations such as the Association for Theatre in Higher Education (ATHE) and the American Society for Theatre Research, as well as the special interest organizations such as the American Drama Society, the Brecht Society, the Beckett Society, and so on, spend the better part of a year arranging for the major conference show of the season, devoting significant funding to that single production. (One of the common complaints about the now defunct American Theatre Association was that too much money was spent on conference trappings and not enough on newsletters and other means through which members might communicate on an ongoing basis.) Regional conferences do exist, of course, but frequently draw their audiences mainly from small colleges or other special constituencies. As they now operate, they do not often foster opportunities for local scholars from various kinds of institutions to convene.

There are several problems associated with this focus on one major collective production a year. We try to accommodate as many speakers as possible at the national conferences, to ensure funding for our colleagues, with the result that our postperformance discussions are too often rushed. Instead of facilitating the free exchange and testing of new ideas, we create scenes in which reports are given in rapid-fire fashion without sufficient time scheduled to evaluate or build on them. The more complex the argument embedded in the presentation, the more frustrating the process seems.

Furthermore, these "blockbuster" productions threaten to reproduce the same hierarchical features year after year, with the favored panels highlighting the work of the best-established scholars, lesser-known scholars on less prestigious panels, and so on, to the graduate student panels. Organizational apparatuses reinforce this class hierarchy in various ways: through requests for panels rather than calls for individual papers, for example. Only well-established scholars possess the information necessary to assemble an entire panel. We can, if we wish, try to subvert the class basis of the panel system. Within ATHE this would mean asking the division chairs to send out calls for papers, perhaps on specific topics, leaving them the responsibility for formulating panels. We can insist on "blind" submissions, proposals with the names hidden until the panels have been chosen, as is currently done for competitive panels at

ATHE. We can teach our graduate students how to write good conference proposals and establish a time, at conferences, when graduate students from across the country can meet each other, establishing their own network of power. They can be granted positions on executive committees. It might be useful for untenured assistant professors to meet each year at conference time, to address issues of common concern. Theater administrators now meet annually to discuss professional as well as scholarly issues; the rest of us in the profession can create similar opportunities to use our collective power to transform our work-related lives.

The single-production conference mentality also jeopardizes our ability to sustain truly interdisciplinary work. At ATHE meetings "academic" theater professors (who teach theater history, theory, or criticism) and theater practitioners (who teach design, acting, or directing) in fact attend virtually separate conferences. Historians who direct or directors who write history must constantly choose which conference to support. The process of structuring panels through the separate divisions within ATHE often subverts the productive energy that might ensue from a meshing of these two constituencies. The academic divisions often stage joint panels, but to my knowledge the Acting Division and the Women and Theatre Program, for instance, have never co-hosted a workshop, though there have been many WTP panels in recent years devoted to feminist performance. The need for crossdisciplinary discussion at the national level seems even more pressing for those who wish to consider ideas emerging from other professions. In the current national conference system, each discipline (linguistics, anthropology, folk life, sociology, psychology, etc.) meets separately, discouraging truly interdisciplinary conference work. We can respond, in part, to this challenge by staging symposia locally, inviting colleagues from neighboring institutions (those with similar interests but within different disciplines) to join us in thinking through issues of mutual concern.

At present, professional organizations perpetuate certain performance styles, circumscribing the way in which power is displayed. Each association promotes a certain kind of performance. Even theater scholars who are able to remain in the casts of several associations may find themselves internally monitoring their work, carefully selecting the appropriate performance code, determining which ideas will satisfy the desires of which audience, thereby preventing constructive debate rather than provoking it. Feminist theater presentations at the main ATHE conference, for example, tend to be much more formal, more traditional, than those at the Women and Theatre preconference. Another example of internal monitoring is the way in which as conference speakers we tend to assume the "voice of authority," constricting our natural voices in a way that must appall our voice colleagues. We have to find a way to speak with our own voices at conferences.

We have not changed our theatrical discourse as much as we think. We need to analyze the nature of our discourse as it is performed within its theatrical setting, to consider where and how we perform it. Let me give an example. At an American Society for Theatre Research Conference on the History of Popular Entertainment held in New York City in the mid-1970s, one of the panels featured a famous stripper from vaudeville days. She was scheduled to perform one of her original routines for the academic audience, which consisted primarily of white males. Just before her appointed curtain time, a speaker announced that she was "unfortunately" ill and that a member of the American Ballet Theatre would step in and perform the act that the aging stripper was unable to manage. Over a decade later, at the 1989 ASTR annual meeting, Tracy C. Davis delivered a very well received paper on the function of absent costume on the Victorian stage, analyzing in careful detail the fetishizing of women's bodies. Any voyeuristic pleasure the audience might have been tempted to steal from watching the slides was deflected by her unflinching professionalism and command of the material. The juxtaposition of these two scenes allows us to see how our discourse has changed over the past decade, particularly with regard to gender issues. In the current feminist climate, we would not think of reconstructing a stripper's performance, of fetishizing women's bodies in that way on the conference stage. But a glance at our neighbors may suggest how far we have yet to go to achieve a full awareness of the potential power of our conferences as performances.

At the 1989 Modern Language Association convention, the Shakespeare Division sponsored a session on "Shakespeare and Fetishism" in which the participants not only analyzed their chosen topics, but simultaneously performed parodies of them. Their playfulness and their use of the conference panel as theater marked their work. For example, one of the speakers, Julia Reinhard Lupton, spoke on "Object/Fetish/Thing:

Lear in Psychoanalysis," fingering a white silk scarf as she spoke. Another, Donald K. Hedrick, sported a woman's garter on his arm as he discussed "Shakespeare and Leather." (His fetish seemed somewhat superfluous, since in the front row sat a young man in full leather regalia.) I am not suggesting that theater scholars must employ stage props, or perform parodies, but I do think that we seem reluctant to use, in a conference setting, the skills, talent, and sheer intellectual rigor and inventiveness that we routinely exercise as directors and designers in the theater. Our reluctance may stem from a lingering need to legitimize theater study as a serious-minded, separate discipline, but, ironically, as long as we address that need, we cannot fully explore our own discourse.

Often we meet in rooms with elevated stages half-curtained off from the audience—stages that hinder interaction between the actors and the audience. This kind of setting duplicates the actor-audience relationship promoted in the realistic theater, where the actors' virtuosity is on display for the audience's pleasure: where the actors master the audience. Our new theatrical discourse requires a correspondingly new setting, if it is not to be subsumed by the conference apparatus itself. Within the constraints of hotel accommodations, we can try to rid ourselves of the "proscenium arch" setting at conferences, or at least ascertain whether or not it is an appropriate backdrop to the ideas being produced. We can even experiment with novel settings: for instance, what if we employed an environmental setting, interspersing speakers with auditors, all gathered at round tables, seating eight or ten each? Such a session might start with brief prepared statements by two or three speakers, to focus the topic, then proceed to simultaneous discussions at all of the tables. Real debate might then be encouraged.

In fact, we need to extend our examination of the theatrical settings for our discourse beyond even the conference room—to the site of the conference itself. The locale contributes to the production of meaning just as surely as the immediate conference room setting does; yet, given the present division of organizational power, the program committee generally has no part in the selection of the conference site or the setting for the meeting. As the program chair of the 1989 ASTR conference, I became painfully aware of the disjunction between the panels themselves and the colonial Williamsburg surroundings of the conference, including the Confederate trappings of the hotel itself. While the speakers analyzed how power operates with regard to race and gender, for example, the larger theater in which they performed celebrated colonial domination over African Americans and women, thereby subverting the panelists' power to move their audience. Of course, there is no neutral space. But we undercut the meaning we attempt to produce when we present a special award to a distinguished African American colleague, Professor Errol Hill in this instance, on such a stage. If we truly want to confer with one another at conferences, we have to set the stage so that such a process is possible: we have to have time for deliberation and a setting that promotes it.

Of all the conference production models currently in use, the Shakespeare Association paradigm, at least potentially, empowers the largest number of people. There are three main types of participation in this conference: the session, the workshop, and the seminar. The sessions provide the most traditional venue, with established scholars delivering prepared papers. The workshops and the seminars, however, are open to any serious scholar who applies. All participants receive formal letters of invitation and are listed on the program, so that they can request funding from their institutions. Frequently experts in one field use the workshops as a means of introduction to another field, so that the workshop participants represent various levels within the academic hierarchy. The workshop leader assigns essays in advance of the conference and conducts the actual discussion. While this format asks professors to perform the role of students, all ranks collectively stand to gain from the opportunity to study new approaches in a relatively safe environment. The seminars, in contrast, are composed of scholars who have gathered as experts to address a particular issue. Some months earlier, they have exchanged papers, abstracts, bibliographies, or notes about their work-in-progress. A seminar leader conducts their lengthy discussion-oriented meeting, which may have from six to twenty participants. One-page abstracts are available to audience members, who are invited to voice their ideas at the end of the meeting.

At the 1989 Shakespeare Association meeting, 351 speakers were listed on the program: there were 4 sessions, with 31 speakers; 3 workshops, with 49 participants; 19 seminars, with 269 participants, plus a keynote speaker and introducer. While ASTR might profitably try using this model wholesale (thereby potentially enabling every single scholar who attends to receive funding and a spot onstage), the divisions within ATHE would perhaps be a logical starting point for its adoption, on an experimental basis. I am not advocating that theater organizations meet in the same way year after year, however—just suggesting that we may be able to empower more of our ranks by experimenting, at least upon occasion, with alternative modes of operation.

The structure of our scripts, the papers that we deliver at conferences, also invites our reconsideration—especially within a theatrical discourse that purportedly embraces a multiplicity of approaches. Traditionally, the oration has served as the organizational model for conference presentations. Employing the argumentative mode with its standard thesis and several main points, we present at conferences what O. B. Hardison, Jr., calls "the literary equivalent of the foregone conclusion" ("Binding Proteus," in *Essays on the Essay: Redefining the Genre*, ed. Alexander J. Butrym [Athens: University of Georgia Press, 1989], 14). Within this mode of communication it is difficult to discover new ways of thinking, to acknowledge the actual moment of performance itself, or to build bridges between the public and the private spheres, between ideas and feelings, theory and practice. Feminists in particular have recently begun to experiment with various alternative kinds of critical writing, from Mary Ann Goldberg's "performance pieces for print" (for example, "Ballerinas and Ball Passing," *Women and Performance* 3 : 2 [1987/88]: 7–31) to Susan J. Leonardi's "Recipes for Reading: Summer Pasta, Lobster à la Riseholme, and Key Lime Pie" (*PMLA* 104 : 3 [May 1989]: 340–347). This experimentation is moving into the conference setting, too, in the form of dialogues, autobiographical narratives, and the like.

These attempts to find a new costume for academic speakers, one which enables them to ferret out new modes of thinking, to express passionate commitment as well as knowledge, strike at the heart of more traditional attitudes toward theatrical discourse. Standard scholarly presentations, with their customary references to the work of other academicians in the field, assume that together we are erecting a common edifice, that we can all cite the same experts, building on each other's work. But none of us can possibly master all the myriad approaches to the theater now, and we are, in fact, starting to build a varied assortment of theater structures, both literally and figuratively. At conferences we are currently constructing not one common monument or auditorium, but many smaller stages.

Many of us play on several of these stages, preferring to act as our own agents as we move from one scholarly company to another. While some feel nostalgic for a time when there was just one gathering place at conferences, others celebrate the new diversity in our theater community, the way in which power now seems to shift from stage to stage as we experiment with new ways to perform power.

New Historicism and American Theater History

Toward an Interdisciplinary Paradigm for Scholarship

BRUCE A. McCONACHIE

In the March 1989 issue of the *American Quarterly*, four scholars discuss academia's "malign neglect" of the field of American theater and drama. Despite finding that critics outside the United States continue to view American plays of the last forty years "as a major, probably *the* major world drama," C. W. E. Bigsby comments that departments of English, theater, and American studies in this country rarely treat our theater with a similar level of seriousness. As Susan Harris Smith notes, the "generic hegemony" of poetry and narrative fiction in literary studies excludes or marginalizes drama, particularly American drama. She traces this practice—evident in course syllabi, standard anthologies, and general literary histories—to several factors, among them: Puritan suspicions of theatrical representation, the tendency of the discipline to elevate English and continental plays at the expense of American drama, and academic dislike of authors who aspire to popularity or political influence. To this list, Joyce Flynn adds our cultural distrust of artistic forms that depend upon group rather than individual processes for production and reception. Flynn also cites the institutional shortcomings of most theater departments; oriented toward production rather than research, they are often inhospitable places for the pursuit of wide-ranging scholarship. Finally, Michael Cadden comments that many scholars foolishly view drama as "an unwholesomely compromised form of literature" since it must "traffic with commerce" to succeed. Smith concludes, and Bigsby, Flynn, and Cadden implicitly agree, that an examination of American dramatic theater "should not be limited to outdated, aesthetic proscriptions of canonical 'correctness,' but should enrich the literary [and historical] record by replacing American drama in its larger cultural context."[1]

Examining American theater in its cultural-historical context makes excellent sense. Few scholars working in the field today, however, grasp the potential theoretical approaches, the relevant social-historical scholarship, and the symbolic and rhetorical inducements of American drama for its historical contemporaries to handle the interdisciplinary demands of such a task. Most historians in theater programs know the relevant plays and their immediate theatrical context, but lack theoretical sophistication and knowledge of recent scholarship in social history. Critics of American drama in English departments are generally more up-to-date in theoretical issues as they apply to "major" plays, but have not needed to learn much theatrical or social history. Scholars in programs of American studies and similar interdisciplinary fields probably know more than their theater or English colleagues about social history and cultural theory, but few of them have studied American theater history or even read many plays. A glance at the published scholarship and the titles of papers delivered at major conferences over the last few years confirms these general observations.

The lack of an appropriate forum within which committed scholars might share their insights and concerns further hampers the integration of these disparate fields. Although several journals accept articles which fuse the scholarly interests of two of these three related fields, their essays rarely synthesize insights drawn from American theater history, dramatic criticism, and cultural studies. Likewise, many scholars of American theater and drama attend two of the conventions of major associations which serve these three fields (the American Society for Theatre Research, Modern Language Association, and American Studies Association), but few attend all three. The proliferation of publications and panels actually dissipates efforts to focus on the interdisciplinary promise of scholarship in the subject.

I believe that an interdisciplinary approach is necessary to open up the ideological assumptions, formal categories, and historiographical conventions that have dominated the writing of American theater history. The New Historicism offers scholars in English, theater, and American studies a general framework within which a new paradigm for the interdisciplinary study of the American theatrical past can emerge. Traditional American theater and drama scholars have tended to accept uncritically the notion that individualism, democracy, and progress characterized the "American way" and that the American theater has embodied and reflected these attributes. Assuming as well that theatrical art transcended politics and commerce, these scholars constructed histories that presumed and celebrated a single, unified tradition bereft of major internal contradictions, a natural "evolution" tending toward the realistic theater of the twentieth century. Although contemporary scholars have corrected some of the shortcomings of this point of view—especially its denial of the cultural plurality of the American theatrical past and of the disjunctures of postmodern theater—no thoroughgoing critique of this historical construction has emerged.

New Historicism suggests strategies for such a critique and mandates alternative foundations for the construction of new histories of American theater and drama. More theoretically and ideologically self-reflexive than traditional historians of artistic practice, the New Historicists recognize that they cannot employ value-free procedures for investigating historical subjects. Opposed to what Terry Eagleton has termed "the ideology of the aesthetic" (*The Ideology of the Aesthetic* [Oxford: Basil Blackwell, 1990]), New Historicists seek to understand the ways in which producing and enjoying works of art can both subjugate and liberate individuals and social groups. This leads them to examine closely the power relations implicit in historically generated concepts of difference regarding race, gender, ethnicity, and class and to question the ideological assumptions underlying such innocent-sounding terms as "entertainment," "style," "dramatic art," and "culture." Suspicious of univocal and teleological histories, New Historicists deconstruct the conventions which structure such narratives and urge the consideration of new contexts within which to understand the cultural experiences of the past. This is not to say that all New Historicists are in agreement about aesthetics, power, and deconstruction. In contrast to the positivist, progressive tradition of American historiography, however, of which conventional American theater history is a part, the orientations of the New Historicists occupy significant common ground.[2]

New Historicists committed to rethinking American theater history can draw inspiration and guidance from the work of Sacvan Bercovitch and his collaborators in *Reconstructing American Literary History*. Bercovitch's summary of their approach includes the notions

> that race, class and gender are formal principles of art, and therefore integral to textual analysis; that language has the capacity to break free of social restrictions and through its own dynamics to undermine the power structures it seems to reflect; that political norms are inscribed in aesthetic judgment and therefore inherent in the process of interpretation; that aesthetic structures shape the way we understand history, so that tropes and narrative devices may be said to use historians to enforce certain views of the past; that the task of literary historians is not just to show how art transcends culture, but also to identify and explore the ideological limits of their time, and then to bring these to bear upon literary analysis in such a way as to make use of the categories of culture, rather than being used by them.[3]

Specifically, I recommend that historians of American theater and drama focus the lens of New Historicism on three topics: historical erasures and representations of race, ethnicity, class, and gender in the American theater; context, narrativity, and explanation in constructions of the theatrical past; and the ideological limitations of the major movements of theatrical realism in America. Under the interdisciplinary gaze of New Historicism, these three topics will generate significant tensions that any new history of the field must either contain or resolve.

The tensions in the first topic result from historicizing definitions of race, gender, and ethnicity. If, as many scholars now contend, these terms of cultural difference are the products of historical rather than biological determination, the traditional ways of recognizing and celebrating the pluralism of American theater history may no longer be adequate. In particular, denaturalizing these concepts challenges the process of pluralizing the canon (e.g., making room for *M. Butterfly* alongside *Raisin in the*

Sun and *Long Day's Journey Into Night*) since this practice rests upon differences in authorship that are historically contingent. Indeed, New Historicism questions the legitimacy of any process which judges the aesthetic worth of plays or performances on the basis of ahistorical criteria. Rather, the New Historicists emphasize the changing means by which the theater has helped to construct and maintain images of the "Other" through containments and erasures of race, gender, class, and ethnicity.

On the other hand, there are political risks to historicizing terms of difference and decoupling the process of canonization from the writing of theater history. If the achievements of oppressed groups can no longer be celebrated in the old way, what strategies might historians use to recognize these accomplishments and to locate them as a part of the usable past for Americans whose own experiences differ from those of the historical groups in question?

The problem of constructing shifting categories of difference impinges on the second topic: context, narrativity, and explanation. New Historicists question the validity and the assumptions of histories structured to tell the story of the triumph of cultural pluralism and democracy in the United States. Part of this problem has to do with narrativity itself, a nexus of difficulties exacerbated by the destabilization of the notion of context. In the "good old days" historians could confidently separate aesthetic experiences from the context of politics and economics. If historians accept the view that the aesthetic and the practical are not isolable realms, that both involve operations which create and mediate the flow of power, then a stable notion of context within which theatrical production and reception occurs is no longer possible.

This does not mean, of course, that American theater historians can retreat from the need to contextualize. Indeed, New Historicists in American literary studies are currently explaining historical formations of reading and writing within such contexts as the dynamics of consumer capitalism and the developments of postmodern culture. Clearly, any interpretation of the popularity of the Ziegfeld Follies, for example, that did not account for the racial and gendered values of its elite audience would be inadequate. Assuming theater historians proceed self-reflexively to work within narrative discourse, how might they use its conventions to explain significant periods and changes in the American theatrical past within destabilized contexts? Put another way, how can scholars write American theater histories that go beyond localized interpretation yet avoid the pitfalls of totalized explanation?

Any reconstruction of American theater history must question the dominance of stage realism in the United States during the present century. The relative success of New Historicists in containing or resolving the tensions implicit in the first two topics can be measured, to a significant degree, by their ability to distinguish among types of American realistic theater and to probe the ideological limitations shared by the producers and spectators of these performances. Interdisciplinary understandings of cultural difference, context, and narrativity, in other words, will facilitate rewriting the histories of American realistic theaters. While Roland Barthes's insight that bourgeois realistic fiction seeks to reduce its construction of signs and affects to "naturality" may be applicable to Belasco's turn-of-the-century stage realism,[4] do later realisms in the theater continue to mask the social construction of race, gender, class, and ethnicity in the same way, for example? And what are the appropriate contexts and possible narrative strategies for explaining the ideological transition from the modern, psychological realism of O'Neill, Williams, and Miller to the postmodern, ironic realism of Shepard, Gurney, and Mamet? If ideology is the "interested" construction of the real, whose "interests" do late Victorian, modern, and postmodern realisms serve?

The questions and tensions posited above are only a few of the directions a New Historicist American theater history might take. Given the mix of disciplines and methods such scholarship must involve and deploy, I applaud the ongoing interdisciplinary conversation on American theater and drama and urge the formation of societies, programs, and other institutional sites to further the dialogue.[5]

NOTES

1. C. W. E. Bigsby, "A View from East Anglia" (128); Susan Harris Smith, "Generic Hegemony: American Drama and the Canon" (120); Joyce Flynn, "A Complex Causality of Neglect"; Michael Cadden, "Rewriting Literary History" (135); Smith, "Response"—all in *American Quarterly* 41 (March 1989): 112–140.

2. For an overview (and several critiques) of New Historicism, see *The New Historicism*, ed. H. Aram Veeser (London: Routledge, 1989).

3. *Reconstructing American Literary History*, Harvard English Studies, no. 13 (Cambridge, Mass.: Harvard University Press, 1986). The essays in this collection by Walter Benn Michaels and Werner Sollors are especially useful.

4. See *Mythologies*, trans. Annette Lavers (London: Granada, 1973).

5. This essay is mostly excerpted from a prospectus I wrote for the American Theatre and Drama Society to enable ATDS to secure an NEH conference grant for "Reconstructing American Theater History." Tentatively scheduled for the spring of 1992, this conference will bring together major scholars from theater programs, English departments, and American studies programs at the CUNY Graduate Center.

The

Theory of

History

MARVIN CARLSON

During the past decade or so, a considerable intellectual up-heaval has taken place in the study of the humanities and social sciences in Europe and America, and in those areas of the arts such as art history, musicology, and theater history most closely allied to these disciplines. Both the rapidity with which this change has occurred and the range of disciplines affected by it have been astonishing, but perhaps no less surprising has been the similarity of the struggles between old ideas and new in a wide variety of fields, despite enormous differences in material being studied and the wide diversity in the methods, assumptions, and even the vocabulary of the new approaches themselves.

Theater history, a small and recently emergent field, has not experienced these changes in so severe a form as disciplines such as literary criticism, anthropology, or intellectual history, but the developments, if muted, have been clearly felt here as well. Our experience has been perhaps more similar to that of the closely related discipline of art history. Recently, I was struck by how applicable to theater studies were the remarks of Michael Ann Holly, an art historian at the University of Rochester, on recent developments in the study of art:

> About ten years ago, scholars began to speak of a "crisis" in the discipline. No longer secure with the idea of empirical research, an insecurity sparked in large part by post-structuralist critiques in lit-

erary criticism, historians of art began to speak of "theory" as that something which was ideologically opposed to "history." At stake seemed to be the conception of art as such. . . . those scholars who long had an investment in positivistic pursuits proudly reasserted their role as "historians" and became outspoken in their dismissal of extra-artistic analyses, particularly those that paraded their origins in psychoanalysis, feminism, semiotics, and Marxism. On the other hand, the self-proclaimed "new" art historians (read "theoreticians") descried the politically invested, what they called the conservatively capitalist, motives of academically entrenched art historians, particularly in England and the United States. . . . Voices have become a little less strident in the past couple of years, and it now seems possible to map the historical evolution of the disciplinary changes. . . .[1]

Clearly theater studies have felt many of these same forces in recent years and certain theater historians also may have felt that theory, once a quiet, minor part of the discipline accommodated by the occasional survey course working its way through Barrett Clark's respectably dull anthology, had suddenly become a serious matter, not merely a rival area attracting the interests of Ph.D. students who in the past had preferred history or dramatic literature, but even more serious, a kind of alien growth within the discipline that threatened to convert everything into theory.

Certain anxieties doubtless remain, but on the whole the accommodation to the new theoretically oriented forces in theater history seems to be progressing with much less tension than has been the case in other disciplines. A whole series of recent panels, papers, conferences, and publications testifies to that. Perhaps the most obvious result of the recent challenges to traditional procedures has been the growing realization that our traditional separation of history and theory was both mistaken and misleading. Historians have been involved in theoretical strategies all along though, like M. Jourdain, speaking prose, they may only recently have become aware of it.

What does it mean to realize a relationship between theory and history? After all, the term "theory" has long been encountered in theater

history, as historians spoke of rival theories of the origin of Greek tragedy, for example, or of the shape of the Elizabethan stage. Theory in this
sense has long been at the heart of historical research. On the basis of
certain known data, a hypothesis or theory was advanced by a researcher
to "explain" the known data or to predict the discovery or appearance of
further data. The model was the empirical scientific method, with each
new theory advanced in the hope that, after sufficient corroborative evidence, it would take its place in the body of accepted fact and form the
bedrock for further theoretical speculation. All of this procedure was
similar to a game played with generally recognized and accepted rules—
rules for the formulation of theories, rules for the testing of these theories, rules for the starting point, for the evidence acceptable, and for the
sort of conclusions to be drawn.

The contemporary confluence of theory and history operates on a more
fundamental level, insisting that the traditional rules, indeed the whole
system which generates such rules, is itself a theoretical construct, suitable for organizing the raw data of existence in certain ways, but by
no means the only or necessarily the best way of doing so. It is hardly
surprising that this view has proved enormously stimulating and productive for some, but dangerous and threatening for others. Kant suggested
that his system involved a kind of Copernican revolution in philosophic
thought, not just a new approach but in many ways a reversal of the previous intellectual structure.

A similar observation might be made of the intellectual revolution in
Western thought of the past twenty years, as may be seen in Hayden
White's perceptive remarks on the modern conflict between ideology and
science. In the course of the nineteenth century, White suggests (although
I would argue that Enlightenment thought clearly prepared the ground
for this), science "conceived as *some kind* of objective view of reality,"
and ideology, "conceived as a distorted, fragmentary, or otherwise deformed view, produced to serve the interest of a specific social group or
class," were seen as locked in a "manichaean struggle that could end only
with the extirpation of ideology and its replacement by a scientific view
of reality."[2] The historian, allied to the cause of science, contributed to
this noble work by producing objective and reliable reconstructions of
past reality, shorn of any ideological distortions which might be present

in the material being analyzed, usually by reference to an original historical context similarly purified of ideological distortion by the historian. In
this system, scientific methodology grounds and authenticates theory, as
in the development and testing of the theories concerning the shape of the
Shakespeare stage.

All of this presupposes a neutrality or potential neutrality of language
or discourse and of at least certain types of physical records. This, however, is challenged by the new approaches which argue that all cultural
material is ideologically charged—the texts themselves, the contexts built
upon these texts, and the mental world of the researcher who selects and
relates these texts and contexts to each other and to his or her own concerns. Thus, we begin a consideration of the work of the modern historian not with science but with ideology, and thus inevitably with theory.

This does not mean that it is no longer possible to engage in traditional
theater history, but it does mean that historians can no longer assume
that the values and strategies of the traditional empirical contextualist approach are self-evidently superior to others, that one can continue simply
"doing" theater history, under the assumption that a common audience
exists for such work with a common theory of what history is or should
be and a common methodological procedure. Like Schiller's sentimental
poet, today's historian must wrestle more directly with issues of reflex-
ivity and justification, seeking a voice and a meaningful discourse in a
world of many voices and discourses, and none of transparent authenticity.

Deprived of a common authenticating discourse, today's historian
must begin with theoretical questions, which White suggests may be ethical and political questions as well. What is the purpose of this historical
writing, what is its relationship to its historical subject and to its assumed
public, and, perhaps most important, in White's terms, "to what is the
historian responsible, or rather, to what *should* one be responsible?"[3]
Such questions now should be faced at every step of the historical process. First, what is the historian's hoped-for relationship with the past?
Again drawing upon White's distinctions, is one attempting to "reconstruct" it, in the manner of classical philological hermeneutics, to "explain" it in the manner of Marx or Hegel, or to "interpret" it according to
the strategies of many contemporary theoretical voices?

Next one might consider the choice of what is to be examined, a concern deeply involved with ideology. Traditional theater history developed in the shadow of European high culture of the late nineteenth century and almost universally accepted the values of that culture. Theater history was by no means considered a study of the phenomenon of theater in all periods and cultures, but a study of the production conditions of the already acknowledged major periods and accepted canon of the European literary drama. The Greek and the Shakespearean theater were thus considered favored topics for historical investigation (as they still are), while the rich tradition of popular and/or spectacle theater, even in Europe, was ignored as undistinguished, decadent, or generally unworthy of critical attention. The growing interest in popular culture in recent years and, even more recently, an attention to the traditionally excluded theater of women, nonwhites, and various culturally marginalized groups have alerted the discipline to the ideological biases hidden in the traditional topics considered proper for scholarly investigation.

The selection of topic and the orientation of the research thus involve the historical researcher in ideological concerns even before an investigation begins, and parallel concerns are encountered at every subsequent step of the study. Traditional distinctions between reliable, neutral, or "objective" documents and "biased" or ideologically distorted texts are no longer generally accepted. Ideology is seen as affecting all texts, in their creation, in their preservation, in the interpretative tradition that has preserved them for us, and in our own selection and reading of them. Nor is the situation necessarily to be deplored. The researcher influenced by New Historicism or by various versions of the history of mentalities in France may welcome precisely those texts that seem most clearly to reveal ideological presuppositions, since the attempted reconstruction of the mental processes of another era is the goal sought. The historian involved in cultural studies or ethnohistory, seemingly closer to the traditional goal of interpreting theater in its cultural "context," now sees that context as a complex and not necessarily consistent interplay of ideological forces affecting both the production and the interpretation of any artifact or document being studied.

Finally, of course, the researcher must organize and present his or her own discourse, reporting to others the results of this particular encounter with the ideas and artifacts of other time. Since this presentation, like the majority of the material studied, is involved in language, the theoretical must be dealt with yet again—here concerning the relationship not between historian and subject, but between historian and audience.

Of course, one choice, and still the most popular one, is to follow the traditionally accepted rules of historical presentation. Dominick LaCapra, with a certain ironic distance but still fairly accurately, describes this process:

> one attempts to understand the past in its own terms and for its own sake, as if the past simply had its own terms and was there for its own sake. . . . each proposition in an account [must] state a fact that may be footnoted, preferably with a reference to an archival source. . . . a premium is set on straightforward prose (the no-jargon rule) and on assumptions and assertions that illuminate or extend commonsense without contradicting or disorienting it. The commonsense in question is of course that of a relatively restricted elite of middle-class individuals with a general education. . . . [and] the voice or perspective of the historian . . . [should] be that of an invisible or transcendental spectator who looks down upon his or her account from a detached and at times safely ironic distance and attempts to eliminate all problematic traces of production from his or her own work.[4]

For an audience trained in and comfortable with this approach, it may indeed be transparent and thus offer no difficulties, but in today's intellectual world, where a text may encounter other publics with other expectations, such an approach may seem at best naïve and old-fashioned, and perhaps smug and oppressive. At the same time, a historian writing for an audience different from this traditional one (and there are now many) necessarily makes, at least for the purposes of that project, a commitment to an alternative theoretical position, and one which very well may prove as unacceptable to traditional readers as an approach framed for them will prove to others.

Hans Kellner, a theorist of historiography, has suggested that the writing of modern European intellectual history is pulled in three directions by the competing theoretical fields of Marxism, psychoanalysis, and structuralism.[5] The pull and power of this triangulation is rather recent, though its varied concerns have much in common with a long-standing variation of emphasis among those scholars who attempt to explain a cultural event or artifact in terms of its social context, those interested in its intent, and those interested in its internal organization and relationship with other similarly organized phenomena. Not only does each look to different organizing principles for all cultural phenomena, but each has by now developed a rich tradition of writing and a distinctive critical vocabulary—so much so that a reader with some sensitivity to the modern critical scene can normally pick up a contemporary historical study and place it within the proper theoretical tradition after reading a paragraph or so. Moreover, these orientations, already internally varied a decade ago, have not only continued to develop in complexity, but have witnessed radical elaborations or reactions, such as Lacanian psychoanalytic theory and French and American deconstruction, so different in assumptions as to be essentially new fields. The complexity of the field of contemporary theory has also been increased by the recent developments in questions of race, class, and gender, concerns which may become allied with other theoretical orientations already established. Thus, for example, one may clearly distinguish in the rapidly developing field of feminist theater studies orientations corresponding to each aspect of Kellner's triangulation—Marxist, psychoanalytic, and structuralist.

One can understand a certain nostalgia for the simple days of the past, when, with the possible exception of a few odd Marxists, historians shared a common and thus essentially transparent theory of the subjects and procedures proper to their discipline, but for good or ill that situation no longer exists. The blending of some elements and insights from different parts of this cluttered field is not uncommon in contemporary continental thought, but the principles behind the many critical approaches being pursued today are so various in type that some future "total" theory, uniting the insights of all, seems a hopeless project. The task of today's historian, then, would seem to be to recognize the new multiplicity of the discipline created by the challenge of modern theory and to utilize this freedom for the positive expansion of the discipline. Many more questions can now be asked in many more ways, and many more tools are available for the analysis of both new questions and old. The convergence of theory and history obviously presents us with major new challenges, but the change need not be threatening—it may be profoundly liberating.

NOTES

1. Michael Ann Holly, "Art Theory," in the forthcoming *Johns Hopkins Guide to Literary Theory and Criticism*, ed. Michael Groden and Martin Kreiswirth.

2. Hayden White, "Method and Ideology in Intellectual History: The Case of Henry Adams," in *Modern European Intellectual History: Reappraisals and New Perspectives*, ed. Dominick LaCapra and Steven Kaplan (Ithaca: Cornell University Press, 1982), 286.

3. White, 283.

4. Dominick LaCapra, "Intellectual History and Critical Theory," in *Soundings in Critical Theory* (Ithaca: Cornell University Press, 1989), 196.

5. Hans Kellner, "Triangular Anxieties," in *Modern European Intellectual History*, 111–136.

Notes on Contributors

Nina Auerbach is Morton Kornreich Professor of English at the University of Pennsylvania. Among her books are *Women and the Demon, Ellen Terry, Player in Her Time,* and *Private Theatricals: The Lives of the Victorians.* She has lectured and written widely on Victorian literature and the theater in Victorian England.

Gregory W. Bredbeck is assistant professor of English at the University of California, Riverside. This essay is extracted from a forthcoming book entitled *Sodomy and Interpretation: Marlowe to Milton.*

Sarah Bryant-Bertail is assistant professor in the School of Drama, University of Washington. She has published widely on epic theater and semiotics. She is currently completing a book on spatiotemporality in the epic theater.

Janice Carlisle, Tulane University, has published *The Sense of an Audience: Dickens, Thackeray, and George Eliot at Mid-Century* (University of Georgia Press, 1981) as well as numerous essays on Charlotte Brontë, Eliot, Trollope, Dickens, and Mill in such journals as *ELH, Victorian Studies, Studies in the Novel,* and *Virginia Quarterly Review.* Her book *John Stuart Mill and the Writing of Character* is forthcoming from the University of Georgia Press.

Marvin Carlson is the Sidney E. Cohn Distinguished Professor of Theatre and Comparative Literature at the Graduate Center of the City University of New York. He is the author of many articles and books on theater history and theater, the most recent being *Places of Performance* and *Theatre Semiotics: Signs of Life* (both 1989).

Sue-Ellen Case is professor of English, University of California, Riverside. A past editor of *Theatre Journal,* she has published widely on feminist and German theater. Her books are *Feminism and Theatre* and the anthology *Performing Feminisms: Feminist Critical Theory and Theatre*. She is currently completing a book on feminist theory, lesbian theory, and performance.

Gay Gibson Cima is associate professor at Georgetown University. She has published articles on modern and contemporary drama in performance and on feminist theater history. She has just completed a book manuscript entitled "Authorizing Action: The Playwright and Performance from Ibsen to Beckett."

J. Ellen Gainor is assistant professor in the Department of Theatre Arts at Cornell University. She has published articles and reviews in *Theatre Journal*, the *Journal of American Drama and Theatre*, the *New England Theatre Journal*, and *Paideuma*. Her book *Shaw's Daughters: Discourses of Gender and Female Identity in the Work of George Bernard Shaw* is forthcoming from the University of Michigan Press.

Spencer Golub, associate professor of theatre and comparative literature at Brown University, has published widely on the subject of Russian theater and drama. He is the author of *Evreinov: The Theatre of Paradox and Transformation* and is presently at work on a study of Soviet theatrical iconography.

Kim F. Hall is assistant professor of English at Georgetown University. She is currently working on a book tentatively titled *Acknowledging Things of Darkness: Race, Gender and Power in Early Modern England*, which explores the ways "aesthetic" tropes of blackness are informed and altered by changing conceptions of race, gender, and empire in the Renaissance.

Bruce A. McConachie teaches courses in theater and American studies at the College of William and Mary. He is the co-editor of *Theatre for Working-Class Audiences in the United States, 1830–1980* and *Interpreting the Theatrical Past: Essays in the Historiography of Performance*. He has also published essays on theater historiography and American theater history in several interdisciplinary journals and anthologies.

Jeffrey D. Mason teaches performance and theater studies at California State University, Bakersfield. He is writing a study of myth and ideology in nineteenth-century American melodrama.

Thomas Postlewait is associate professor of theater and drama at Indiana University. He is the author of *Prophet of the New Drama: William Archer and the Ibsen Campaign* and co-editor of *Interpreting the Theatrical Past*.

Janelle Reinelt is professor of theater arts at California State University, Sacramento, and is the former book review editor of *Theatre Journal*. *Critical Theory and Performance*, edited with Joseph Roach, is forthcoming from the University of Michigan Press. She is currently writing a book on Brecht and the contemporary British theater.

Joseph Roach, Tulane University, has published *The Player's Passion: Studies in the Science of Acting* as well as articles on the history of the theater for *Theatre Survey* and *Theatre Journal*. With Janelle Reinelt he is editing *Critical Theory and Performance*, forthcoming from the University of Michigan Press.

David Savran teaches English at Brown University. He is the author of *Breaking the Rules: The Wooster Group* and *In Their Own Words: Contemporary American Playwrights*.

Jon Whitmore is dean of the College of Fine Arts at the University of Texas at Austin, where he holds the Effie Marie Cain Regents Chair in Fine Arts. He is the editor of the *Handbook for Theatre Department Chairs* and the author of numerous articles. He was the founding chair of the Council of Theatre Chairs and Deans, a program of the Association for Theatre in Higher Education.

Margaret B. Wilkerson is professor of Afro-American studies at the University of California, Berkeley, and is Berkeley's former director of the Center for the Study, Education and Advancement of Women. A former vice-president of the American Theater Association, she served for four years as chair of the Black Theater Program. She is the editor of *Nine Plays by Black Women* and is writing a literary biography of Lorraine Hansberry.

Simon Williams is professor of dramatic art at the University of California, Santa Barbara. He is the author of *German Actors of the 18th and 19th Centuries: Idealism, Romanticism, Realism* and *Shakespeare on the German Stage 1587–1914*. He has published on Continental drama and theater history in several leading journals. He is on the executive committee of ASTR and recently acted the role of Mephistopheles.

Barry B. Witham is executive director of the School of Drama at the University of Washington. He has published widely in American theater history and contemporary English drama. This piece grew out of his current research in the Federal Theatre Project in the Northwest.